THE

MARCHING

ANT

Inspired by True Events

THE
MARCHING
ANT

ALLYSON CHAPA

Dedicated to the sacrifices

we make to achieve our dreams;

the dreams that will inspire

our families for generations

thereafter.

PROLOGUE

"Take a second and close your eyes. As you sit here, I want you to think of something you want to be in this world: a teacher, a bus driver, a lawyer, an artist … anything." Dressed in their finest Petite Plume pajamas, the three children closed their eyes with glee as they sat cross-legged on the floor of the imagination room. They couldn't help but fidget as they attempted to preserve focus. "Remember," their mother said delicately, "anything you dream to become in this world, you can make happen. Now open your eyes slowly. Who would like to share first?"

"Me! Me! Me!" The eldest of the three jumped up excitedly, her tiny feet rocketing off the exquisite white rug, her little curls bouncing. "I know, I know," she shouted. "I want to be a firefighter and save people from big fires. Rawrrrrr!" As she roared, she ran around the room with her hands by her face, emulating a mighty lion. Their mother smiled and nodded her head in approval.

"That's awesome, sweetie. I think you're going to be an amazing firefighter one day. Okay, who wants to share next? How about you, bug?"

"Mommy, I want to ride my bike when I grow up," said her son. His thin eyebrows furrowed to demonstrate how committed he was to his dream. It's hard not to crack a smile at the earnest aspirations of a four-year-old boy. His answers during imagination time always made her nod her head with conviction: he was certainly her son.

"And I know you'll be the best bike rider there ever was, won't you?" Their mother looked around the room to gauge their attention. The kids' smiles were wide, but their eyelids were getting heavier as their bedtime approached—moving around like little zombies, moaning and groaning at everything and everyone.

"All right, anyone else want to share before bed?" Their mother subtly made eye contact with her shyest, who often didn't like to be the center of attention. "How about you, sweetie? Do you have anything you want to become when you grow up?"

"I want to be like you, Mommy." Her young face blushed and she immediately ran into the mini teepee in the corner. She hid her face between all the stuffed animals that were arranged in two perfect lines by the au pair.

Her mother's heart fluttered with warmth and a tear rolled down her face. She crawled into the teepee to be closer to her daughter. "Thank you, boo bear. When I was little, I wanted to be like my mommy too. And you know what? When we decide what our dreams are, anything is possible." She gently wiped the tears away and took a deep breath. Her children's responses hit deeper than she had expected.

The kids brushed their teeth in their individual bathrooms and lay in bed, waiting for a goodnight kiss and prayer from their mom and dad. Each room was perfectly decorated, as if from a photo spread in the Pottery Barn Kids catalog. As their parents tucked each child in like a tiny taco, they puckered up their lips and hugged the kids tight to make sure they'd doled out every ounce of love before bedtime.

As the evening quieted, the couple held hands and silently made their way up to the third floor of their mansion to enjoy one another without distraction on the terrace. The view overlooking the city beneath them was never anything less than spectacular. But as breathtaking as it was, the romance was ignited by a tall glass of Château Musar. Bergamot candles surrounded the iron railings, creating an atmosphere of both sensuality and warmth. A gray knitted wool blanket covered them both as they relaxed into the luscious sofa.

She laid her head on her husband's shoulder and started to analyze the day with great precision, as she always did. "You know how we're always asking the kids to dream big and be whatever they want to be in this world."

"Yes, of course," he said, listening closely. He could tell his partner had something heavy to share. The shakiness in her voice was uncommon from such a confident and strong woman. His large hands gently tucked her long hair behind her ear, a silent action that confirmed she had his undivided attention.

"Boo bear told me she wanted to be like me today." Tears interrupted her train of thought. After a long pause she took a sip of wine and continued, "It scared the shit out of me. My skin crawled and I felt like, I mean, I feel like a fraud and a phony. What if we're doing too much for them?"

"Love, I don't understand what you're saying. We wanted all of this for them. We planned, we worked hard, and we've made the right decisions to provide the life we never had growing up."

"Exactly. We've worked so hard to live here, in this house, with these things, to build this life. We've always kept a smiling face so that our children never have to experience the struggle. What if we're doing them a disservice? Life isn't easy, and I hope they can learn to appreciate our life and know that it wasn't easy to get here." Her breathing increased as her thoughts raced.

"Look at me." He pressed his forehead against hers. Her eyes closed in subtle disobedience. "Look at me, please," he continued softly. She opened her eyes slowly and swallowed the emotion caught up in her throat. "You are incredible, and everything we've done for them is more than enough. They will learn that whatever their contribution to the world, it will be an amazing one. Our dreams and our journey don't have to look like theirs."

"Thanks, babe. I just worry that we've given them too much and they won't ever learn how we had to. I'm so proud of what we have, but also so scared." She wiped her eyes and took another big sip of her cabernet sauvignon. "I think of my parents and all they sacrificed for me, to give us a better life. I want to make my mom proud of what we've built. I want her to look down and know that everything she did was worth it, and because of her, we are sitting here today."

He held her hands tight and looked her in the eyes with conviction. "We can't all write books, or be award-winning scientists, or even love our jobs, but what we're teaching our kids—is to be true to themselves, to stay humble, and follow their dreams. That's all we can ask for. We want to be able to give them the opportunity to succeed at whatever they want."

Nodding her head, she reached for her mother's book, which lay neatly on the outdoor coffee table. She lifted it to her mouth and kissed the cover, then held it tight to her chest, over her heart. She closed her eyes and drifted away to a place where she was with her mother again, laughing and crying, struggling and succeeding. It was all enveloped in this book, and she knew that a piece of her mother's soul was placed on every page, within every word.

PART I

1954
EIGHT YEARS OLD

At first glance, Big Spring was an all-around simple Texas town. During this time of day, there was no commotion, no traffic, just the sound of the gravel crunching as Antonia walked down County Road 34. On her right were miles of cotton fields as far as the eye could see, and to her left was a forest of tall pine trees that ran adjacent to the old train track. It smelled pure outside, exactly how God intended. Take a deep breath and you inhale freshly cut grass and warm country air.

The heat was particularly intense this time of year. A heat unique to Texas, where the wind burned your skin and sweat dripped down your face before 6 a.m.; by noon, the temperature was so high it could make a strong man feel weak in the body, mind, and soul.

Within Big Spring's simple town was the not-so-simple life of

Antonia Rivas. Antonia was particularly small for an eight-year-old. She was thin, short, and had a several gaps in her smile from missing baby teeth. Truth was, the biggest part of her was her hair: big brown curls that were untamed and frizzy. Opposite of her stature, Antonia was uniquely mature for her age. The way she observed others, she was like a sponge, soaking in everything about the people around her in order to emulate them.

Her route to work was mindless and she knew it like the back of her hand: *From the house, go straight and then turn right at the end of the road. Walk to the other end until you see the broken street sign, then turn left, cross the street, and keep going until you reach Mr. Brown's farmhouse.*

Before she had even reached the end of the road, clusters of short curls began to stick with sweat to the top of her forehead. She tilted up her freckled face, squinting her deep green eyes to watch the sun's game of peekaboo with the clouds. Despite the heat, she always enjoyed the morning's quiet time.

As part of the work uniform, Mr. Williams (Mr. Brown's right-hand man) had instructed Antonia to wear boots that covered her toes and loose-fitting clothing to ensure her movements remain unconstrained. She made do with what she had: black cowboy boots three sizes too big, blue cotton pants, and a stained white T-shirt. She looked like she was playing dress-up in her mother's old clothes, which was not far off from the truth.

3

Antonia dressed herself every morning, making sure she was prepared for a long day of work. She carried her lunch in an old T-shirt she used as a sack, filling it with just enough food to get her through the day: a container of rice and beans and a small can of StarKist. For most of the walk, her lunch sack stayed in her left hand; she deliberately gave her right arm a break because that was the arm that usually held the cotton basket, and she tried to balance out the strain.

Her gait was bouncy, full of energy, as if you could see the joy radiating off her—a natural joy that young children are innately born with until the hardships of life drain it away. Her mind traveled to different places during the thirty-minute walk to Mr. Brown's. *What if all the cotton on the farm just changed into snow?* she thought. *Oh boy, I bet Mama Jo and all the others would be shocked.* She giggled, then pictured herself running around and embracing the world of snow. She tilted her head up with confidence. *I'd run around in the snow until it all melted away and I wouldn't even work that day.*

As Antonia walked past the rusty old mailbox and piles of barbed wire, she was brought back to her reality, the visions of snow melting behind her. She knew the mailbox meant that she was almost at work, where it would be another long day: eleven hours, to be exact. A big sigh came out of her little body. Then she looked down and listened keenly to the sound of the gravel as it hit her boots, inhaling slowly, taking in her last moments of rest. Walking closer to the farmhouse, Antonia involuntarily strutted a big gapped smile on her beautiful young face and headed toward the giant oak tree for the morning check-in with Mr. Williams.

Mr. Williams was a short, round man and what was left of his hair was strawberry blond. His breathing reminded Antonia of someone suffocating, which made her extremely uncomfortable in his presence. His thick silver glasses shrank his brown eyes, and the black suspenders accentuated his potbelly. He was generally mild-tempered, except for when he had to move from his post; he was awfully pale and tried to stay under the oak tree as much as possible, so he didn't get fried by the sun. If for any reason his duties caused him to move anywhere outside of that perimeter, you could bet your bottom dollar he was going to be one mad motherfucker, as she'd heard him say.

As Antonia approached Mr. Williams, he glanced at his clipboard, breathing heavily, and wrote down the time next to her name. "Morning, miss." He greeted her with an insincere nod and handed her a wicker basket from the stack on his right-hand side.

Carrying her lunch in her left hand and the basket in her right hand, Antonia headed over to the side of the farmhouse to drop off her lunch in the shade. She looked at the map taped on the blue door and saw large red pen marks circled around the section of land that the workers were expected to focus on for the day.

Burr by burr, Antonia began picking cotton: grab, twist, and toss. The cotton went into the old basket until it was full. Then she would head over to the mill to dump her hard work into her bin and repeat it all over again. It was the kind of work that wasn't difficult at first glance, but as the day went on the heat beat you down and sometimes your body started to fatigue without cause. Sweat got into your eyes and it burned. Many of the workers complained of back problems and had calloused hands from all their years of picking. Antonia was far too young for those problems, but she knew what her future would entail: the others reminded her nearly every day. However, to pass the time, and make lemonade out of lemons, or so they say, the workers often sang songs together and relived old stories. But not Antonia; she passed the time with her imagination and memories:

It's late at night and she's sleeping on the old brown sofa. Her father comes in half drunk and awakens her angrily.

"Antonia, no puedo hacer esto. I can't do this anymore." *He pulls his black hair in frustration and his face reddens with anger.* *"You can only stay here if you work. I found you a job and you'll start tomorrow morning. Otherwise, I want you out of here."*

Antonia's small eyes are adjusting to the light and all the yelling. She's wearing her mother's T-shirt as a nightgown and looks at her father, expressionless, "Apá, what do you mean it starts tomorrow? No entiendo."

"You don't have to leave, understand? You can stay here, but you will help. I've talked to Mr. Brown and you're going to work for him and make money. You'll start picking cotton tomorrow and every day after that. And when there's no cotton to pick, you'll be cleaning the farmhouse and making sure the animals are fed and cared for."

"I'll be good, I'll do whatever you want, Apá. I don't want to leave."

"Bueno. Be ready. Five a.m."

Antonia often relived that night as if it was yesterday. Sometimes she closed her eyes while her fingers continued to meticulously pick cotton and she pretended the conversation never happened. She'd imagine a life where her apá was loving and kind. *Where would I be then?*

Fortunately, in the year and a bit on Mr. Brown's staff, Antonia had built a strong routine for herself. She would get up at four a.m. before the rooster's crow and head to the bathroom, her eyes still closed, to take a quick tinkle in the comfort of her own home. Once her eyes were finally opened with the help of a splash of water, she would go into the kitchen to quietly pack a lunch in the dark—especially in the dark, so she didn't wake Apá. She had memorized the kitchen with her eyes closed so she didn't need to turn a light on to find anything she needed. Once her lunch was packed, she would take her pants and shirt off the clothesline, slip on her boots, and begin her trek.

The days were long, and the work was draining, but the routine was soothing. She always knew what to expect, and there was a sense of harmony that filled her soul out in the field that she didn't have anywhere else. It was as if everything had a perfect place in the world, and she was a piece of the puzzle that belonged in the field with her peers.

Yesterday was June 25, 1954, and it had been the best day in Antonia's life. Every week, Mr. Brown, the head honcho on the farm and for most of Big Spring, gave out an award to the worker who had picked the most cotton. Before each one of them dumped their bin into the mill, Mr. Williams weighed it and documented it on his clipboard, tallying up the totals at the end of the week so Mr. Brown could award the bonus. It almost always went to Mr. Gerry: he'd been picking on this field for nearly forty long hard years. Gerry had the best technique out there and was angry enough not to let anything get in his way of picking cotton faster than anyone else.

Yesterday, as all the workers were wrapping up their day, they had gathered by the water hose, waiting for Mr. Gerry to get his weekly award. But when Mr. Williams announced this week's winner, you could've heard a pin drop a mile away.

He cleared his throat for what felt like an exceptionally long time before making his announcement. "Well, this is a mighty fine surprise. Antonia is this week's highest contributor for the most cotton picked. Come on up, Antonia, and get your bonus." Mr. Williams couldn't have sounded less excited for Antonia, and Mr. Brown checked the clipboard three times, making sure it was correct; indeed, it was. When Antonia awkwardly ran up to the front of everyone, one person clapped, and then another person clapped, and then a roaring cheer came from thirty workers— everyone except for Gerry, who was still in shock and mighty pissed.

Mr. Brown personally thanked Antonia with an extra dollar for her hard work. In all her life, Antonia had never been the recipient of any sort of recognition. She felt like she could scream on the top of a mountain—*I DID IT!* The feeling of accomplishment was the best feeling she'd ever experienced. After all those days when she had walked home, tears streaming down her face, feeling like a foreigner with her Spanish accent—here she was now, earning a loud and cheerful celebration from every single worker. She had earned herself the respect and acceptance she never knew she'd wanted.

During Antonia's first month of picking cotton, she felt like she was knocking on death's door. Every minute in the field had seemed like hours of excruciating pain. Her hands had bled, her feet had been covered in open sores and friction blisters, and the heat had been unbearable. She had peeling skin and sun blisters all over her neck and shoulders. But what almost took her consciousness was the dehydration. There were moments when her fingers were picking cotton, but she couldn't see or stand up straight. She'd blink slowly to try to regain control, but the power of dehydration had overtaken her body. Not only that, but as her health had started to deteriorate, none of the other pickers stepped up to help her; it was like Antonia was some sort of disease everyone wanted to stay away from. With no real family at home to support and guide her, Antonia's hair would sometimes fall out from stress, and she would get tiny sores in her mouth from biting her lip due to nervousness.

You see, being the only Mexican on the field *and* being the youngest, the others (the colored people, as Antonia knew to call them) treated her as an outcast. It was as if they each had their own battles to fight and getting involved with Antonia was going to be too overwhelming for them.

Many of the workers had been picking together for decades and they had a bond that no one could penetrate. Over the years, they had become very particular about who was allowed into their family, and there wasn't any way in hell a *little fair-skinned girl* was going to be welcomed as part of *them.* Their triumphs as hardworking African Americans were not commonly spoken about. Truthfully, this was also something Antonia knew very little about, especially at her age. All she could understand was that there were different water fountains for different colors, and black people were always separated. Crossing those cultural barriers wasn't going to be easy, which led to a very lonely and isolated start on the cotton field.

After about six months of showing up and working hard from sunup to sundown, an olive branch had been extended, and she timidly accepted.

"Hey, little honey," hollered an old lady with a small face and long limbs. "Whatcha name?" Antonia thought her accent was a bit funny, but she didn't mind.

"Antonia," she said under her breath while she continued picking anxiously, hoping they weren't bothered by her Spanish accent.

"Awn-what?" the woman responded with a smile and a wink. Without wasting a second, she continued, "I'll call ya Annie. It's easier. Folks around here call me Mama Jo." She wore olive-green overalls and a brown shirt underneath. Her small head was overshadowed by a large straw hat that had big holes on the top from years of wear and tear.

Mama Jo's short figure was bent over like she was suffering from a terrible stomachache, and she looked uncomfortable when she walked. Mama Jo slowly lifted her straw hat and then turned around and shouted to the others, "Hey y'all, the name's Annie."

At that moment, "Annie" felt little tingles rise up her body. Could it be from the excitement that she'd finally met someone she'd worked next to? Certainly.

The two continued picking cotton side by side with big smiles on their faces. Annie couldn't help but feel the eyes of the other pickers staring her down, but slowly, one by one, they all welcomed her and greeted her with a nod or a smirk. Antonia's heart was fluttering, and her smile wouldn't dare fade. She even loved the name Annie. This endearment was such a revelation compared to the way they had treated her for months.

It's fascinating how life can go from crawling the bottom of the trenches to feeling like your heart is going to explode from delight. Annie was grateful for this experience and the friendships she was starting to build. Maybe one day they'd even consider her part of the family?

That day came sooner than she could have ever imagined, and now it was topped with a cherry from winning yesterday's bonus.

"Well, good morning, Miss Annie," welcomed Mama Jo as she walked up with her basket and plopped it down next to Annie. "Don't ya look chipper this fine day?"

"Buenos dias, Mama Jo. I'm very excited! Ayer … yesterday was the best day ever. And, and," she stuttered, "everyone was cheering for me. It was incredible. I felt like queen of the world!"

"I'm so proud of ya, Miss Annie. Did ya get ta tell anyone at home about it?"

"No, I didn't have anyone to tell." Annie's head tilted forward in shame as her fingers kept picking quickly. "But that's okay. I'm happy to be here today, happy to be here with all of you."

"Child, that's just fine. We are all so proud of ya and we love ya ta pieces. Remember that."

"Yes, ma'am," Annie said, smiling. Today, the extra recognition Mama Jo paid Annie was exactly the validation she'd yearned for through the unbearable heat.

Across the field you could hear Grumpy Gerry getting all riled up as he heard others snickering about Annie's bonus. Gerry had white curly hair on top of his head, and he was thin and frail-looking. He was probably sixty-five years old and worked to the bone. He wore raggedy clothes and a small ballcap he'd bought from a local thrift shop. Annie liked to call him Grumpy Gerry because, well, he was always so damn grumpy. And sometimes he yelled and cussed when he got angry at the plants for not cooperating with him. You heard that right, he would yell at the plants. That crazy Gerry, he's a wild one, all right.

"Don't get yourself a big head over there, little girl," Gerry yelled across the field. "I see you over there hustling and I'm coming back. Yesterday I done had a bad back, but today I'm coming for ya and the rest of these assholes out here. Ain't none of y'all deserve that extra bonus."

"Oh Gerry, if yo hands picked as fast as yo mouff moved, den ya wouldn't be all grouchy ass today, would ya? No, you'd be

13

enjoying yo bonus," chimed in Ruth with a loud laugh. Ruth was a big-boned lady, unlike Mama Jo, and didn't speak much. She was one of the angrier women, so when she did speak, everyone listened. "Now, Annie, don't give into old Gerry. He's just an ass who needed to get whooped. But nobody thought you'd be the one to do it, so he's feeling a little sore from the whooping you gave him yesterday."

Annie blushed, keeping her eyes and fingers focused on the cotton as Ruth and the others laugh hysterically. This was a rare way to start the day: lots of laughter and poking fun. She could always tune out the negativity from the others and channel all her energy into the sequences of cotton picking. Her fingers could move faster than she could think. It was as if thinking actually inhibited her hands from doing what they knew how to do.

It wasn't long before Annie became the best cotton picker on Mr. Brown's farm. Gerry never again took home the extra money for the most cotton picked, and Annie never went a week without it.

There wasn't a whole lot of excitement in Annie's life. She worked hard in the field and loved the family she had cultivated. She began to identify as Annie, realizing that Annie was loved and cherished by everyone in the field even if she sometimes pissed off Grumpy Gerry or annoyed one of the workers for asking too many questions about the world. But what mattered most was that *she was one of them.*

She had found that her purpose in life was to work hard and enjoy the work she did. She was a piece of the puzzle that completed the staff in a way they never knew was possible. She was always bringing such joy to the fields, contributing an intangible lightness that would be greatly missed one day.

Johnson's Tavern lay smack in the middle of Big Spring, on the corner of Maple Way and Goldsmith Avenue. Built in the late 1930s, JT's stood out like a sore thumb in a town full of commonplace buildings. Black shutters and red stucco complemented the seven-foot-tall wooden oak door.

During any night of the week, you could find the town's biggest hotshots sitting amid low lighting and cigar smoke, along with regular folk wheeling and dealing over drinks and a game of pool, often behaving like monkeys in a zoo. Tonight was no different: Elvis's biggest hits were radiating from the jukebox in the corner of the bar as an influx of loyal customers made their way into JT's to enjoy a drink after a hard day of work. As small as Big Spring was, there always seemed to be some sort of drama creeping into JT's.

JT's bartender, Marco, had been running the place for the

past fifteen years, since it opened. His jet-black hair was always oiled back and meticulously parted on the left. Occasionally his curls would loosen up at the end of a long night; and though unintentional, it was undeniably sexy. Marco was in his early thirties, his deep brown eyes paired with a perfect amount of soft wrinkles complementing his mysterious smile. He never moved quickly—every action was methodical and intentional, a demeanor that so many men envied and even more women desired.

Being the bartender at the town's most popping tavern meant that Marco didn't have to speak much. In fact, he just had to appear interested, kind, and make others feel comfortable as they shared their intimate details on the good and the bad days. Every good bartender knows that the key to a successful night and a lucrative career is to maintain face and keep your customers talking.

Marco didn't have a lot of authentic companions, as he opted for a life of seclusion. He simply didn't desire to share his feelings, heart, or mind with anyone. The truth was, he felt his soul leave years ago and there wasn't much of him left inside. He was a hollow man, and a bitter one at that.

It's as if he was beautiful to look at but was rotting from the inside, so he did everything possible to cover it up. It wasn't like others didn't try to connect with him; they did. And every now and then he'd find himself in bed with a woman who was passing through from one town to the next. But it always ended the same way: with him sneaking out in the middle of the night and never seeing her again.

There was a woman, once. The mere mention of her name, Isabelle, could cause his body to hurl over in pure grief. Sometimes when he thought of her, as he closed his eyes, he could smell her hair and feel her touch his chest. Isabelle was the love of his life, the most beautiful woman he'd ever seen, his wife. When she died eight years ago during childbirth, his life was never the same. Instead of grieving, he built up a wall of anger and pain, disguising it behind his work.

To an outsider, it would appear that Marco lived a simple life behind the bar, a bachelor who could do close to anything he wanted—a liberating life of women, booze, and no limitations. To say Marco was well known in small-town Big Spring was an understatement. Here, everyone knew a little bit about everybody. They would describe him as a "kind man," a "great bartender," and that "he kept to himself." But his element of mystery kept folks at a distance. Everybody thought they knew him, but nobody really knew Marco to his core. Nobody but Don.

As the large clock above the entryway approached 7:30 p.m., Marco anticipated the arrival of his most loyal patron, Mr. Donald Brown. He set aside a clear six-ounce glass filled with exactly one lime, two fingers of whiskey, and a splash of club soda: Mr. Brown's usual. Like clockwork, Don Brown walked in at 7:31 and took his spot at the bar.

Without skipping a beat, Marco slid the cocktail across the marble countertop and shot him a confident head nod. Don, as most knew him, kept most of the town employed and had an ego bigger than God himself. His family had left him a trust fund, which he'd used to build an empire in Big Spring. He was a smart businessman and had a knack for knowing what to invest in. At this stage in his life, Don owned a majority of the local cotton farms as well as the town's grocery stores and a profitable butcher shop. Big Spring was a chessboard and Don was the master behind every move.

The relationship between Don and Marco was interesting, to say the least. Marco had everything that Don didn't: good looks and desirability. Women held on to every word Marco said, whereas Don was like a stinky fish that women wanted to get rid of, but the smell just lingered.

Eight years ago, when Marco's beautiful wife passed away tragically, he didn't have the funds for a proper burial. During his desperate time of need, Marco went to Mr. Brown for a loan, which he had every intention of paying back. However, this was no simple funeral. Marco was burying the love of his life and wanted everything to be as spectacular as he felt Isabelle deserved. The flowers alone were close to $1,000. Being business-savvy, Mr. Brown knew he would never get that money back. It's not that he needed the money: he had no wife and kids to go home to; however, he did see an opportunity. Don wanted to gain everything Marco had, and now he had a way to demonstrate power over someone he so desperately wanted to be like.

This loan would be Mr. Brown's main connection to Marco. It certainly wasn't a real friendship. With the amount of power Don had, Marco knew to never disagree with a man that influential. Nonetheless, they had good conversations and Don tipped well—even though they both knew it went back into Don's pocket at the end of the week. Over time, their relationship had more negative impacts on Marco than he could have ever predicted. Marco wanted to be more and more like Don but couldn't afford the lifestyle. He started borrowing and buying, borrowing and spending. Each man wanted what the other had and was unable to appreciate the life they were given, whether it be the money and power or the looks and desirability—they were both miserably jealous of the other. And jealousy had permeated itself into their veins, into the thoughts and decisions they both made.

"You're lucky you don't have to deal with fucking idiots all day," Don said as he took a swig of his strong drink. "I give people a great job and pay them so they can keep feeding their families. I even help them keep a roof over their heads. And you want to know what I get? Un-fucking-gratefulness. They all want more more more more. More money, more days off, more breaks." He

19

chugged the remainder, then slammed the glass down against the marble, nodding at Marco for an immediate refill.

Without losing eye contact, Marco fulfilled the request and Don continued on his tangent. "It's like, ain't nobody in this town fucking know how to say thank you anymore? Everybody wants handouts, and I sure as hell am not giving any damn donations."

"Si, señor," Marco said. "No saben. They don't know how lucky they are to have a boss like you." Pause, swallow. "You commit your life to giving us all jobs. Sounds like those workers feel like they deserve more just for the hell of it. Si, a ellos no les gusta … if they don't like it—"

"Leave." Don became impatient with Marco, cutting him off. "That's exactly what I think. If they don't like it, they need to leave. Quit. Then they'll realize how good they have it here. It's all of them idiots up north putting thoughts in my workers' heads to feel like they don't have enough. What more could they want?" He finished his second drink and sighed loudly, tired of the conversation and looking for a change of subject. "So, how are you holding up, Marco?"

Marco analyzed Don's manicured hands, the purple and blue veins coloring the top of them, a silver ring squeezing around his left pinky finger. This was the first time in years that Don had asked him anything personal. He was taken back but articulated his response slowly to ensure that his English was accurate, and he maintained his cool with a man he so deeply despised. "Soy bueno. I stay busy here in the evenings, I go home and—"

"The kid's doing good, real hard worker you got there," Don said as he took another mouthful of alcohol and wiped his lips with a black bar napkin.

Almost losing his composure, Marco's eyes quickly grew wide. He looked deep into Don's eyes and in a firm whisper said, "Mr. Brown, I made it very, very clear that I want nothing to do with her. Nada. I don't want the extra responsabilidad. Sabes, I'm paying you back as quick as I can, and I can't have any more stress."

"Now, now, settle the fuck down. I was just letting you know she's a hard worker." Don wasn't ever intimidated by anyone, and Marco sure as hell wasn't going to be the first. He brushed him off and started talking about his next business venture and a new hot blonde he was seeing "on the regular." Over the next two hours, he continued to expel every detail of his day as Marco remained unengaged, except to hand him another drink.

Marco's thoughts were spinning as he robotically responded to Don's comments and questions while mindlessly wiping down the counters and refilling orders. It wasn't that Marco didn't love his daughter; it was that he had loved his wife and her memory more.

Since Isabelle's passing, Marco couldn't stomach the thought of doing the woman's work of raising a child. His responsibility as a man was to provide for himself and pay back his debts—that was it. This child was another human who meant nothing more and nothing less to him than anyone else he saw on a daily basis. The love in his heart for his wife had been completely shattered, and he'd replaced her memory with greed and drunkenness.

Throughout the evening, Marco had managed to keep his composure, at least until he could get his hands on a handle of liquor. Like an addict waiting to be freed into their natural habitat. He was one of them.

"Well, Marco, it's been fun," Don murmured as he excused himself from the bar. "I hope you have a good evenin' and I'll see ya tomorrow." Marco graciously nodded, but as soon as Don walked out of the building Marco flipped him off, both middle fingers high above his head.

There were still a few cups in the sink when Marco locked up, but he was too drunk at this point to care. He left JT's right before dawn, driving himself home, where he could liberate the anger inside him and drink away the pain he had buried so deep inside his bones.

This level of anger hadn't been present in Marco for several months. And in less than one sentence, all the progress he'd made was destroyed.

1955
NINE YEARS OLD

Annie wasn't much taller than she'd been the year before, but she did have more teeth and her boots fit better. Other than that, her curls remained a mess and she was still a bundle of bliss. It was difficult not to fall in love with her—such a hard worker at such a young age and her ability to stay so positive. It was the little things that drew you to her, like her contagious giggles of joy. And everyone said her hugs were the best, like she was trying to squeeze every ounce of goodness out of you with her small arms.

Mama Jo had developed a particularly soft spot for Annie, considering her to be one of her own children. She always made sure Annie was drinking water so she wouldn't catch the heat's illness. And every now and then she'd even bring an extra handkerchief to put over Annie's neck so she wouldn't burn to a crisp. They shared a unique bond, one deeper than any other relationship Annie ever had.

It was September 15, 1955: heat waves wiggled above the cotton plants and sweat dripped down the backs of every worker. On the far west side of the field, a line of shiny black police cars peeled into the farmhouse, shooting up a cloud of dust that lingered in the air. Workers started snickering to one another, as if they were in on some secret. Confused, Annie looked around briefly but tried to ignore the distraction and continue picking cotton.

As soon as Mama Jo realized what was going on, she dropped her basket in fear and started shouting, "Annie, hurry over. We need ta talk ta ya! The police are here, hurry."

Uncertain, Annie bustled over to Mama Jo, dropping her wicker basket in between the two of them. "Yes, ma'am? What's going on?" Annie was trying to take in the words coming out of Mama Jo's mouth, but the older woman was talking so fast that it all seemed like a blur. *The farm never had visitors—this couldn't be good.*

Mama Jo looked stern as she spoke. Her face scowled and her eyes stared deep into Annie's soul. "Child, ya gonna have ta lie. The police are here looking for childrens working, among other things like working conditions." Annie's jaw dropped in shock and she giggled in discomfort. "Annie, this ain't funny. Tell them you're eighteen. Don't be acting silly and try ta crack a joke now. Whatever goes on, don't tell those bastards ya real age or ya gonna be shipped out of here and put away."

"But I'm not eighteen," Annie replied. "I'm only nine. And why would the police care how old I am if I can do my job?" As the words were coming out of her mouth, her body started to grasp the reality of the situation and her eyes filled with tears of fear. She knew better than to lie. *Lying causes pain.* "I do my part, Mama Jo. I don't want to go nowhere else. Eres mi familia. You are my family."

Mama Jo rolled her eyes in frustration and grabbed Annie's beige shirtsleeve. Her lips puckered real tight in seriousness and the two of them were now facing nose to nose. "Annie, ain't no childrens supposed to be working. Ya supposed to be in school with other childrens. Learning and stuff."

"What's school?" Annie couldn't help asking.

"Enough with all the damn questi—" An ear-piercing siren interrupted Mama Jo. She quickly tied a torn shirt around Annie's face, leaving only the girl's green eyes visible. Annie was sweating as she followed the running workers to the check-in station, where the police stood, holding their batons and intimidating the staff.

The three police officers, wearing tan uniforms with big glasses and shiny badges, were talking to Mr. Brown. *They look so strong and meaty compared to us,* Annie thought.

25

"See here, I hire the best and pay top dollar in all the south region," Mr. Brown touted, his voice loud enough for his workers to hear. "You can't find better working conditions than what I supply my staff with."

Officer Campbell—the youngest of the three, around twenty-one years old—took off his sunglasses, smiled a crooked smile, and waved his hands nonchalantly. He was a newer officer, eager to make a good impression. He had bright-blue eyes and light-brown hair, and kissing Don's ass was his specialty. "Don't worry, Mr. Brown. These are just standard procedures. I'm not worried about it and neither should you be, sir." Officer Campbell sucked the spit out of his bucked front teeth and gently twirled his mustache around his index finger and thumb. He was barely old enough to grow a real mustache; and based on the look of his hands, he wouldn't last an hour picking cotton with the rest of them.

Facing west, all thirty-six workers lined up backs to bellies. It was one hell of a sight, seeing thirty-five black workers and one small fair-skinned Hispanic girl all lined up in a row. Certainly not something you see every day, but that's the way it was.

One by one, Officer Campbell asked a series of questions: name, age, pay rate, working conditions. Annie started to analyze his voice and demeanor: *What could a man like this really know about working conditions?* She rolled her eyes, thinking of how hard the others worked, and got angry, her fingers tingling with fear. *He's probably never put in a real day of work in his life.*

Standing toward the end of the line, Annie's heart pounded faster and faster. The T-shirt covering most of her face was making sweat drip off her nose. Anxiety filled her little body. She held her hands by her side and stood as tall as possible, attempting to look older.

As Officer Campbell walked down the line asking these simple questions, he beat the baton against his left hand intimidatingly and his chest puffed up so big he couldn't see his feet. None of this made any sense to Annie. Thoughts were racing in her head so fast she felt like she was spinning: *Why am I not supposed to be here? What will happen if he knows I'm lying? Why did Mama Jo say I belonged in school? What is school?* When he approached her, Annie felt her stomach churn with fear, her eyes widen in panic.

"Well, aren't you a small one," Officer Campbell said, laughing. He slapped his hand with the baton three times as he looked her up and down. "Are you one of them religious freaks?" he asked, not expecting a response. Annie shook her head no and immediately looked down at his shiny black boots. "Tell me, missy, how old are you?"

Annie swallowed and her young voice managed to push out a relatively steady response: "Eighteen, sir." Officer Campbell looked at her giant boots and baggy clothing. He could feel Mr. Brown's eyes burning holes in the back of his head. "All righty then," he said as his face flushed and he moved to the next worker without asking her any other questions. Annie's chest deflated with relief as she exhaled. Her head was still spinning: *Was he going to come back to ask me the rest of the questions? Why did he stop? Did he know I was lying?*

All the workers were dismissed, and Annie ran over to Mama Jo for an embrace unlike any other as tears streamed down her face. "He knew I was a liar. He knew it," she said. "Are they going to come back for me?"

"No, shugah, that's all. Ya did good today, a mighty fine job indeed."

"Mama Jo," Annie asked hesitantly, "what's school?"

Mama Jo sighed, her heart breaking. In trying to protect Annie, she'd opened up a whole new world that Annie didn't know existed. And for this, Mama Jo would never forgive herself.

"Well, Annie, have ya ever seen how ya the only child here? There ain't no other childs here, and that's for a reason."

"I thought they were at home, Mama Jo. Taking care of the other kids." Annie's eyes were big, and curiosity was written all over her face.

Mama Jo wanted so badly to take back the words. She knew telling Annie about school and about other children would cause strain on Annie's young mind. But Mama Jo also knew that Annie deserved to find out about the real world. "No, Annie.

Them childrens like you, they at school. Learning. Getting the education. Something ya ain't ever done." Mama Jo looked into Annie's puzzled green eyes as she continued, "Them childrens go learn ta read and write, do math, science, and all sorts of stuff. School is where ya make friends and spend time before becoming an adult like us."

"But, Mama Jo, I'm not an adult." Annie's mind unraveled with an overwhelming sensation. Her eyes couldn't focus right. *How had I never wondered about other children?* She had always known she was the only kid working, but she never sat around long enough to wonder where those other kids were. Living out on the farm, she didn't think much else existed outside of her world of cotton picking. Her vision of the world had been distorted within moments and by someone she loved the most: Mama Jo. *Why was my life so different and what else was out there?*

"Mama Jo, if all the kids are there, then why didn't I just tell the officer that I needed to be in school?"

"Life ain't always that easy, Annie," she said, with sadness in her eyes. "Ya work at Mr. Brown's to pay off your family debts that are owed ta Mr. Brown, and ya gonna need ta be working here until all that debts is paid."

"Debts? What do you mean?" Annie asked in confusion. None of this made any sense to her.

"That's a story for another day, child. Don't go worrying now, just get back ta work and be glad that this hurdle is over with." Mama Jo waddled back to picking cotton.

That day, Annie promised herself that she would find answers, learning more about the other kids and school and how she could be a part of it. It was a sad, long day of picking for her—but she remained grateful to be where she was most comfortable: in the field with her family whom she loved more than anything else in the world.

About a mile and a half from the cotton farm sat Annie's small home. A lemon-yellow house with a wooden roof, no fence, and a gravel driveway. The yard was big, the lawn severely overgrown. You could scarcely see the mailbox because it was overshadowed by tall weeds and grass. The off-white front door had a gold-colored doorknob. The shutters were falling off and the windows looked pitch-black.

As you entered the front door, you were hit with an aroma of emptiness and dust. You could pretty much get a view of the entire house from here. Behind the living room and its single brown sofa was the kitchen, with a small stove, single sink, and a kitchen table that seated two. To the right of the kitchen was the one bedroom, and before entering the living room there was a narrow door that led to the only bathroom, with a sink, toilet, and tub. Old wallpaper was starting to peel, and the cheap linoleum floor needed to be replaced. Though the decor was insignificant, remnants suggested that at one point it was nicely decorated. There were dusty pictures of a beautiful couple filled with love and joy; a life Annie could only dream of. Her favorite, a black-and-white photo of her mother in a perfect white frame, sat propped up on the kitchen table. Her mother was stunning. Staring at her photo was like looking at the sunset on Annie's way home. Breathtaking.

Long black hair, big white teeth, and forest-green eyes that looked exactly like her own. Annie's mother was the most beautiful woman she'd ever seen. Every day when she came home from picking, she'd tell her mom everything that happened from sunup to sundown. They were best friends.

"Amá, on my way to picking, there were these two red birds playing with each other. It was like you and Apá together just picking up twigs and going to build a house for us. Fue increíble, Amá. When I got closer to el árbol, there was even a nest in there with two little eggs! A happy family like we used to be—like we still are, I mean. I wanted to grab the eggs and take them with me, but I knew if I climbed el árbol, I might end up late to work."

Continuing to chat with her mother, Annie walked into the kitchen and turned on the water in the rusted sink so it could warm up for the pot of beans. She struggled with her words every evening: should she use English or Spanish? She felt torn with how Mama Jo spoke and how her apá spoke. She even struggled with how Mama Jo spoke compared to how Mr. Williams spoke. *What was right and where did I fit in?*

"Then when I got to the fields today, I was picking as fast as I could and started singing a new song about my new amigos—the birds, of course. I was hoping they'd fly by if they heard my song, but they didn't. Pero, who knows? Maybe the birds will show up tomorrow and remember me like I remember them."

She turned on the stove and lit a match to ignite the burner. She filled the pot with water and beans, placing it over the flames. Stirring the beans gently, she kept her voice low but energetic as she spoke to her mother:

"Oh, Amá. You will never believe what happened today. It was the scariest day in my life. A deputy ranger showed up at the fields and we all had to stand in a straight line, and everyone answered a bunch of questions, except for me. I only answered one question. And, Amá, don't be angry, but I lied! I know, I know. I said don't be angry!" After a moment, Annie sighed in relief. She could feel that her mother's presence was no longer angry.

"I told the deputy I was eighteen, and guess what? He believed me! Well, kind of. Mama Jo said the reason they asked me how old I am was because cops now put children in *school*! It's this place where other kids like me go to get things for their head like reading and writing. And there's all these kids my age who don't pick cotton, but they have to learn all day." Her eyes filled with tears again.

"Amá, that's why I don't have any friends. Because they're all at school. Maybe one day I'll ask mi papi about it and see if I can go to school too, what do you think?" She knew not to expect a response—those kinds of things only happened in the movies. She continued cooking dinner in silence and let her mind relive all the events of the day. She was exhausted and it was almost too much to handle.

Annie flopped herself onto the old sofa as she ate dinner and stared at the panel walls covered in old family photos. She'd make up stories that would complete the history of the picture—that her mother was a woman full of laughter and grace. Her cooking was delicious, she was gifted in making everything from scratch, like her mother had taught her.

As the sun set, Annie's eyes got heavy. She made herself get up from the couch and prepare for the next day of work. She hung her sweaty clothes on the line to dry. Then she walked into the bathroom and wet a washcloth to clean her face, hands, armpits, and feet. The cool water made her skin coil, bringing a brisk feeling across her body that released tension and allowed her to fully relax.

Her bed was a pallet of cushions in the corner of the living room, her blanket a thin towel. The cushions were old, you could see the inner foam sloping down as if they'd been sat on by elephants for years, but she made sure her bed was nice and tidy before lying down in her underwear and falling deep into sleep. If you've never heard a nine-year-old snore, there's nothing more rewarding than seeing their little bodies fully recover from a hard day's work.

At night was when Annie was most free. She experienced the most vivid dreams, creating a world all her own. It was during these eight hours that her mind would wander and her soul would be fed. She'd play in the cotton fields wearing a beautiful dress, her hair blowing in the wind. There wouldn't be blisters on her feet or cuts on her hands from all the picking. She'd enjoy a home-cooked meal with her entire family and would serve everyone dessert while laughing over a game of Lotería.

Tonight's dream was unlike any other, though. She was surrounded by other boys and girls her age, in what she perceived as school: A big building in the downtown square of Big Spring. She was wearing her Sunday best: an old green dress with lace at the bottom and shiny white shoes. She hadn't worn that dress in four years, but somehow it still fit like a glove. At home, she had patted down her brown curls with a large splash of water and slid bobby pins along just the top of her ears to make sure her hair stayed neat, her face perfectly visible.

Looking in the mirror, she'd practiced her best smile, lifting her chin and demonstrating excitement and confidence all at once. Her heels clicked on the linoleum floor as she'd run into the kitchen to pack her lunch and head out for school.

"Amá, I'm going to school and it's going to be amazing. I'm going to make lots of friends and learn to read and write and other stuff." To no surprise, Amá had walked out of the bedroom with a calm smile and a gentle presence.

"Mija, te miras muy bonita. You look beautiful and you're going to have a wonderful time at school. Hurry up or you're going to be late on your first day." And like any mother would, she gave Antonia a hug and sent her on her way with a big kiss.

Holding Mama Jo's buttery hand, Antonia walked into the school building with a smile from ear to ear. She looked up at her, taking in the beauty of Mama Jo's face: full lips, soft cheeks, with a glow in her deep brown eyes. Mama Jo was wearing a knee-length navy dress and had her hair pinned back—looking just like Marian Anderson herself. They walked down the hall hand in hand as Antonia soaked in all her surroundings. Kids—kids everywhere. Some playing cards, others jumping rope, some licking ice cream, while others uncontrollably giggled and ran around. The rooms were bright with decorations and filled with happiness. Mama Jo gently kissed Antonia on the top head and whispered, "Go on, child. Be a good girl and ask lots of questions."

Antonia held on tight to her lunch sack. "Mama Jo, I'm scared to ask questions. What if the other kids don't like me?"

"Honey, they're gonna love you. Be you and enjoy every minute of school." And just like that, she turned around and left Antonia to her own adventure.

Annie awoke to the rooster's crow, covered by an old towel and wearing the same underwear she went to bed in. Her make-believe life was stripped away with the morning's welcome. She sat up, a string of drool coming off the side of her mouth, which was stretched into a big smile. Without hesitating she stood up, wiped her eyes, and headed into her father's bedroom.

Annie didn't have a strong relationship with her father. His work kept him out all night and so their interactions were minimal. When they did occasionally meet face to face, he was still half drunk and holding on to a bottle of tequila from the night before. It was like he was a baby who needed a bottle to survive.

Annie knew that her dad blamed her for the death of Amá. He made it very clear that it was her fault, constantly reminding her that he couldn't stand to look at his own daughter because of the pain that resurfaced every single day. As a solution, they lived separate lives. Ate separate meals. And together they had no resemblance of a family whatsoever.

Annie walked into the musky bedroom where her father lay on his stomach, passed out on top of the blankets in his black pants and button-down white shirt. Tiptoeing over to his sleeping body, she placed her sore hands on the corner of his right shoulder, held gently, and wiggled them back and forth.

"Apá, I gots to tell you something," she whispered with courage. "I want to go to school." After seconds of no response, she shook her hands a little harder. "Apá, wake up!"

He opened his eyes slowly, as if he was dreaming. "Who the hell do you think you are coming in here and waking me up." His speech was slurred, and he closed his eyes again, moving his face away from Annie's. "No way in hell you're going to school. That's for smart kids and you aren't one of them. Don't ask me again or I'll beat the shit out of you. Now get out."

Annie stood there, unphased. "Please, Apá. I'll do whatever you ask if I can go to school." Without hesitating, her father grabbed the white ashtray from his bedside table and smashed it on the top of her small head. She didn't see it coming and immediately fell to the floor.

Moments later, Annie slowly peeled her eyes open and awoke to a throbbing headache and blood everywhere. Her father had passed out again. Instead of staying home, she cleaned up all the blood, tied a shirt around her head, and carried on her workday as if nothing had happened.

No one in the fields had to ask what happened to her—they all knew there had been trouble at home. During a water break,

Mama Jo wet a cloth and helped clean Annie up a bit. Annie laid her head in the old woman's lap and cried quietly for what felt like hours. Crying was so painful that it was better to just stay silent.

"Baby, it's okay. Mama Jo is here." She soothed Annie as she cleaned the nasty wound on her head. "Don't ever let him put a finger on ya again. Understand me? Next time it happens, ya run; run as far as you can and don't ever look back." Annie's eyes were filled with tears as she nodded her head and blinked slowly, taking in all the sympathy and compassion she could.

Every day after that for six long and grueling months, Annie worked with a massive headache. It was almost unbearable. Sometimes she couldn't even see straight. But each day that she woke up with a headache was a reminder never to ever ask her father about going to school again.

1958
TWELVE YEARS OLD

n the middle of the night, Annie woke up, feeling as if she was being stabbed in the stomach. She curled up, knees to her chest, sweat rolling down her head, her eyes tense, squeezed shut in pain. She'd never felt anything like this before and knew she needed to go to a hospital. Annie knew she was about to die.

It took every ounce of strength she had to stand up and walk into the kitchen to scrounge for any pain medication she could get her hands on, anything to stop this agony. As she'd anticipated, the cabinets were empty except for a few cups and plates. Another punch to the stomach made Annie bend over as she teetered into the bathroom to splash cool water on her face and catch her breath.

She lit a candle and lay on the bathroom floor, trying to soothe herself. She prayed for the pain to stop: "Amá, what do I do? I feel terrible. I need some help." The dizziness overcame her and the pain subsided as she gradually fell back asleep.

At the rooster's crow, Annie awoke on the bathroom floor, the candle having melted down to its core. She stood up slowly to go pee and noticed blood in the toilet when she went to flush. Her eyes blinked slowly, taking it in. It was official: she was dying and didn't know what to do. The stabbing pain in her body had stopped but clearly something was very, very wrong.

Sitting on the toilet, she reached into the sink cabinet for a plastic baggie and clean rag, with which she created a small diaper. Whatever was going on with her was going to have to wait, or she'd be late for work.

With every step on the way to work, she could hear the swish of the plastic bag between her legs. It was very uncomfortable. The stabbing pain in her stomach came and went, but now she had to deal with this discomfort—wearing a plastic diaper—and it was unlike anything she'd ever experienced. When she finally saw Mama Jo, she told her the news and was anticipating sorrow and tears. Maybe even a goodbye ceremony before she left work.

However, after Annie confided her truths, Mama Jo and Ruth could not have laughed any harder! "Good Lord, ya not dying! It's your cycle, ya joined womanhood now!"

Shocked, embarrassed, and very uncomfortable, Annie shook her head. "No, I'm sick. I had stabbing pains and this morning there was actual blood coming out of me. This is not a celebration.

You aren't listening to me." Annie was clenching her jaw, holding her fists tight in frustration.

"Miss Annie, keep it down. We don't have ta tell everyone out here that ya on that time of the month. Some things are kept private. Didn't nobody ever tell ya what it means ta become a woman?"

"No, no one told me. How am I supposed to know? My mother is dead, remember?" Annie started pacing back and forth—the *swish, swish, swish* of plastic with every step.

"Why, yes," replied Ruth. "All women go through it. But we don't go yelling about it, and we sure as hell don't think we're dying. I'll bring you a book tomorrow and you go home and read it."

Annie bowed her head low in annoyance. "Ruth, I can't read, remember. I don't know how."

Ruth paused for a moment. "Don't worry then, Annie. I'll just tell you everything you need to know."

Annie nodded.

"Are you wearing a cloth or something now?" Ruth asked.

"Yes, I didn't want to bleed through my pants."

"Okay, well, once a month for a few days this same thing will happen. Be sure to take a bath at home and use a clean rag every day."

"And now," chimed in Mama Jo, "don't be acting a fool with

any boys or ya gonna catch yourself pregnant. And stay away from bananas and hot dogs during the cycle. Ya finally a woman now and need to be acting like a lady and not some animal."

Annie blushed. She was grateful she wasn't dying but almost wished that she was. Going through this every single month sounded awful. She had so many questions but kept them to herself. If this is what it takes to be a woman, then so be it. It was another long day at work, but the swishing of the plastic bag between her legs kept the other women smiling and giggling— proud of the young woman Annie had become and impressed at how creative Annie was at finding solutions to her problems. Who would have thought to wear a plastic bag?

On the way home from work, Annie laughed at the fact that she actually thought she was dying. *This will be a funny story to tell my kids someday.*

It was that evening that Annie tried Mama Jo's wonderful advice to help with the pain. Using a plastic bag and some rocks, she created a small water stopper for the bathtub and poured herself a warm bath. Her curly hair pulled back in a low bun, she undressed and examined her body for the first time in her life.

It was as if her body was a warzone that had endured far more than it was ever meant to. Cigarette burns on her body from her father when she misbehaved as a child, a scar on the crease of her left elbow from a beer bottle he broke on her when she missed a spot cleaning the toilet at six years old, and a missing baby toe that was cut off as punishment for wetting her bed. As she moved her hands across her body, she started to realize that what Mama Jo and Ruth said was right—she was turning into a woman. Developing breasts and having hair in more places than she ever remembered having. She was a woman and one day she would have a family, with children, and she'd make sure they never felt the way she did at this very moment—used.

The steamy water felt amazing on her weak stomach and limp body. She sat in the tub as her body relaxed, enjoying the moments of silence while her mind drifted away. A place where she had a mother who was alive, a place that was safe, where she felt smart and could read and write, and have friends like other girls and boys.

"God, why do you do this to me?" She closed her eyes and prayed. "Why do I want to go to school, and read, and write? Why do I have to live this way, when so many other people have it better than me? I'm a good girl, I listen, I work hard, I follow the rules. What have I done that I deserve a life this painful? I feel so ugly and mad. God, thank you for Mama Jo. Thank you for this bath. But please, God, help me from this life I have and take me to a better one."

Annie toweled off and made herself another clean pad to soak up her cycle, putting herself to bed with a heavy heart. *One day,* she promised herself, *one day I'm going to change everything so that my life is nothing like this life. I'm going to go to school, I'm going to learn everything that I can, and I'm going to have a family who loves me and children whom I love with all my heart.*

She fell asleep that night feeling empowered, knowing that this was going to be a short portion of her life. Working in the fields was not her forever. She promised herself to grow up to be smart and go to school, to learn to read and write and be smarter than anyone she knew. She was in charge of her forever, and she needed to figure out what that was and how she would get there. It was a big world out there, and she wanted every piece of it—her mind was strong, even though she cried herself to sleep. She was trying to convince herself to continue moving forward and that life would get better because, at this point, it really didn't seem possible that it could get any worse.

Don and Veronica had been seeing each other for nearly six months before she broke it off. A lovely woman with light-brown hair and brown eyes, Veronica was originally from up north, where the women are known for being sassy and strong. It was a dramatic breakup. In the middle of Don's five-star kitchen, she threw his finest china set on the ground while tears streamed down her face and she yelled uncontrollably in Hebrew. Shortly after her outburst, Veronica packed her bags and headed back north to be with her family. At her core, Veronica had a servant's heart, but she was not raised to be weak. No man, no matter how powerful, would play her as a fool.

Being with Veronica was the closest thing Don had ever experienced to true love. She served him breakfast every day, would comfort him after a long day of work, and most importantly she was amazingly smart and kept him on his toes—which, honestly, he liked. She was a challenge and days with her were never boring. All she needed in return was honesty and loyalty: qualities Don didn't have.

Veronica is smart enough to know the difference between sex and love, Don thought. He was the real victim here, losing the love of his life over a measly one-night stand. *No one should be restricted to one person, it's not human nature.* He'd miss Veronica. The way she'd rub his back and kiss his neck. She had a way with her hands and a heart of gold. *She'll want me back.* But she never called, she never wrote. She was out of his life forever. Don started to realize it was his loss and his broken heart. His anger and sadness were out of control, and everyone else around him felt the brunt of it.

Don was at JT's more than usual, trying to move on from Veronica. He'd tell himself he'd only stay for one drink, but one drink turned into five, six … sometimes up to twelve cocktails.

Every night would end the same.

Don would spot a woman in the bar and decide that she was the lucky winner for the night. He'd drunkenly strut over with his slurred speech and the romantic aroma of alcohol radiating from his every pore.

"Evening, miss. I'd love to take you home tonight and show you a good time. I may not be the biggest bull in the pen, but I am the most reliable." He'd wink and get too close to his prey, swaying oh so subtly. She'd flirtatiously say no—but mean it.

"Oh, that sounds wonderful, but I can't tonight. Girls' night. Thank you, though." Don would be pissed, humiliated—he'd start cussing and yelling. Marco would have to step in and call a cab to get Don home safely.

Hopeless thoughts circled Don's mind like water around a drain. As a pragmatic man, love didn't make sense to him. He had everything a woman could and should want: money, power, influence, wit. What was so wrong with Veronica that she couldn't forgive his one little mistake and look at the bigger picture of everything he provided her? She had the finest clothes, he got her the best gifts, and he made sure she lived a very comfortable life in just a short six months. He gave her everything, and she had the audacity to think she could find someone who even came close to him? She was a fool and he'd be an even bigger fool to waste any more time and energy on a bimbo like her.

A few weeks post-breakup, Don headed to JT's for his customary round of drinks and chaos. Wearing a short-sleeved white-pearl snap and light-wash jeans, with his hair combed back, he finally looked put together—the first time in a while since Veronica had left.

As he entered JT's, he made eye contact with Marco, immediately feeling an aura of control come over him. It was like he was being hypnotized—a wicked smile took over his face. He had the perfect solution to curing his broken heart.

"Marco, my man. How's it going today?" Don asked, feeling sly. Marco smiled and made Don's usual cocktail, this time with less alcohol than the recipe recommended. "I have a proposition for you that is going to be absolutely irresistible. Something that is going to change your life and mine."

By this time, Marco was losing himself to his own demons: his own alcohol addiction and his tendency to make bad financial decisions with a desire to get rich quick. Don's proposition already had a lot of promise. Even before the pitch, Marco was in. It's like money was his god, and no moral conscience would get in the way of his dreams to be the man he thought he'd always be. Powerful and rich—just like Don.

"I'm all ears," Marco said as he passed Don his drink.

"So, you and I both know that you owe me more money than I can count. You're borrowing from me, I heard you borrowed some from Lewis a few months back, and you're in way over your head, am I right?"

"Tell me something I don't know, Don," Marco said with glassy eyes. "What do you got for me?"

"Well, I've been thinking about the girl. And I know, I know. I'm not supposed to mention it. But I was thinking, we can put everything behind us if you'll give her to me for a couple of evenings a week."

Marco was not fazed by this proposition at all. Anything to help him out of his own mess was going to be a win for him—plus, he'd had well over a handle of tequila over the past couple of hours and his thinking wasn't as sharp as it should have been for a conversation this powerful.

"Don, whatever you need. But something as important as my own *daughter* is actually going to cost you." Marco's eyes were dark and empty. His heart pounded and his hands stayed calm. He had waited a lifetime to make a statement this audacious. This was the first time in all their years of knowing each other that Marco had the upper hand on a business decision—and it felt good. Real fucking good.

They went back and forth on the details and what it would cost Don. Both men agreed and a date was set. The following week, in the middle of the night, Annie was taken from the only safe place she knew. Blindfolded with a red hankie and abused in the back of

Don's old pickup truck and dropped off right before sunrise so she could tidy up and get ready for work.

Picking had been the same routine day in and day out, with a couple new faces here and there, while others had decided to leave the fields and head out of town for a better life. Times were changing and Mama Jo figured her time in the fields wasn't going to last much longer. The only thing that kept her holding on was Annie.

Annie hadn't been her usual giggly, smiley self for a while. She seemed to keep to herself and always walked with her head down, looking at the ground. Mama Jo knew something was up, but in the interest of keeping spirits high and Annie's mind on something else, she never asked what was going on. Instead, she focused on the one thing they could control: their future.

"Miss Annie, are times a-changing or what?"

Annie looked up, curious but unsure of what Mama Jo was referring to.

"People ain't staying in town as much as they used ta. Finding work in new towns and starting a whole new life for their family. I bet ya could get a new job pretty easily—ya could wait tables or help nanny childrens for a richer family down in the south."

"Mama Jo, I have nowhere to go and hardly any money saved up."

Wiping the sweat off her brow, Mama Jo laid into Annie. "Look, I know ya ain't happy, and I don't know what's going on. But what I do know is ya gonna need ta change your attitude and take life by the damn horns. We all tired, but ya young, Annie. Ya need ta be looking ta the future and how to get out of here while ya still can."

Annie hadn't thought about the future in a while. She was numb for so many reasons, accepting the life she had been given. Having hope only became exhausting. Anytime she felt she was about to get a win, life would strike her back down to reality with a situation so far out of her control.

"Mama Jo, I can't read or write. How am I supposed to get any other job than the one I have right now?" Annie's eyes looked so defeated, her spirit crushed. She continued picking as Mama Jo stood there in silence, disappointed that Annie's soul was no longer the young vibrant one it used to be. The child who would pick and make everyone laugh as she made images out of the clouds. The child who always had a story about the birds or the squirrels on her daily commutes to work. Where was the child whose spirit was so bright and had so much to give the world?

"Annie, look at me now. What I'm about ta say ain't very nice, but somebody's gotta tell ya." Mama Jo's brown eyes pierced Annie's soul. She looked angry and frustrated with Annie's attitude. "Ya gonna have got ta quit playing this sad story. Life sure as hell is hard. But what's worse is giving up. Ya want ta go ta school? Figure out a way ta make it happen. If you don't, nobody else is gone do it for ya. Get ya spirits off the floor and start making a plan ta make ya dreams come ta life."

The words stung Annie's heart, and she instinctively curled her shoulders in to protect her soul. Instead of responding to Mama Jo, she allowed the words to creep in and settle there for a while. Had she really just let life slap her around? Is there a way out of this mess into a better life? Maybe? But also, maybe not? Was this just another path to disappointment that she wasn't ready to face? Probably.

That afternoon was the first time Annie had prayed in many months. She had prayed that something bigger than her, God, was still there listening to her pleas and cries. "God, if there's a way out, please help me find it. Help me to go to school and get out of here and never, ever look back."

The long oak dining table was set for six: three white plates with beautiful blue Italian designs lined the right and left side. A green vase filled with baby's breath was placed in the center of the table next to a pitcher of ice water and lemonade. The dining room had a magnificent light fixture that created a gentle ambiance. Three small children ran around the house, in and out of the dining room and through the kitchen. An aroma of Mexican food had them asking, "Mama, when is dinner, tenemos hambre!"

Annie looked up at the young boy, who was close to five years old. Her untamed brown curls were held back by a bright-green scarf, which accentuated her beautiful eyes. Wearing an apron, plaid polyester pants, and a three-quarter-sleeved white shirt, Annie smiled and said, "Be patient, it's almost ready." Then, as all three children sat at the table, she served her beautiful family homemade enchiladas with rice and beans and atole de arroz for dessert.

She sat at the table, slowly taking everything in. The oldest boy started a prayer and the rest chimed in as if this routine was the same as always. Her mind was completely still, and tears streamed down her face. Thank you, God, she said quietly and watched them enjoy their meal as messy young children always do.

Analyzing the beauty of each child, she wanted this moment to last forever. They were perfect. She loved these children whom she felt were her own. Even though she'd never seen them before in real life, she knew they were hers. She loved every inch of them, from their gapped smiles, tousled hair, and food-stained clothes to their little hands and fingernails.

Annie woke up that morning with a feeling of empowerment stemming from her stomach and extending into her face and limbs. It had been months since she'd had a dream that was beautiful and vivid. She knew it was God's way of answering her prayers and giving her something she had missed for a long time: hope.

When she arrived in the fields that day, hot and sticky, she gave Mama Jo a big hug for the tough love. Though the words had hurt Annie, they were words that would help her grow and continue to see the light in a world that was filled with darkness. She didn't know when she would leave the fields, but she was confident that when the time was right, God and her amá would give her a sign that was undeniable.

1963
SEVENTEEN YEARS OLD

Annie walked toward the barn doors to find Mama Jo and Ruth standing there waiting for her in the late hours of the evening. Choked up, with tears streaming down their faces, both Annie and Mama Jo squeezed each other, knowing they'd never spend another day picking cotton together. There wasn't enough time in the world to prepare their hearts for this moment.

Mama Jo took a step back to compose herself, giving Annie a look that said, *Honey, I am so proud of the strong woman you have become.* Memories flooded both of their minds, each one bringing more tears than the one before. Annie had grown so much over the past nine years, and Mama Jo felt truly blessed to have Annie as a part of her family. Together they shared such joy and laughter, even during the hard times—they would always figure out a way to push through the hardship and make a joke for the benefit of everyone else.

They shared a final laugh as Mama Jo reminded Annie of one of her favorite memories together. "Remember when ya made Old Williams think the fields had caught fire. I ain't ever seen that man move so fast in twenty-five years. Ya might be going to hell for that one!"

"We can't be forgetting the time after picking when Annie sat out by the barn and ate three jalapeños raw, for a measly fifty cents," Ruth chimed in, shaking her head in disbelief. "Poor thing had the runs for days!"

"You know how to bring a person back down to earth, no?" Annie laughed as she wiped the tears from her face.

Mama Jo winked and kissed Annie on the forehead. Annie opened her mouth to say one last thank you but decided to just smile and close her eyes instead, appreciating Mama Jo and showing gratitude in the only way she knew how. Mama Jo made Annie feel like she was one of her own, and there were no words to thank her for everything she had given Annie. And no words were necessary.

Over the past couple of years, Annie had finally been able to make a small income working on Mr. Brown's farms. One day the paychecks just stopped going to her father and were given to the person who earned the money in the first place. Annie never questioned why she had started receiving the money, but she sure did appreciate it.

With Ruth's help, she was able to open up both a checking and savings account at the local bank. It would take time, but Annie knew that every penny saved would be her only ticket out of the life she was living and the misery her father had sold her into.

Mama Jo and Ruth were the masterminds behind helping her find a new city to call home. They'd read through the local papers and talked to their community of friends to figure out what the best towns were and what would be a good fit for her to succeed.

"Annie, what you got in mind for your new home? Do you want mountains or beaches? The opportunities are endless, I tell you." Ruth always had a way of asking Annie questions that made her heart skip a beat and her mind restless. *Where would I go if I could go anywhere?* Annie thought.

"Calm down, calm down. I know you all want the best for me, but I don't want to go too far in case things don't work out." Annie looked up with a sly smile. "But a beach does sound nice right about now. Putting my toes in the cold water and learning to swim."

Ruth laughed, knowing that Annie was reasonable enough to plan but still young enough to dream.

A few months later, Annie made her decision final: the best place to start her new life would be somewhere she'd always dreamed of going—to the beach. Port Isabel had a lot to offer, with tourists coming in and out and job opportunities ranging from serving tables to cleaning motels. It wasn't a very expensive town, like those places in New York or California. Port Isabel had the perfect mix of everything she wanted—and it was just a bus ride away.

The time had come for Annie to make her way into her new life. Her savings account was stacked, and she could live on her own for at least six weeks with no job and a motel stay. She knew if she didn't make her move now, she'd probably never have the guts to do it. With a one-way bus ticket purchased and her small gray bag packed, Annie was ready to make her dreams a reality.

She woke up close to 4:30 a.m. to walk to her neighbor's house, where she called a cab. Her neighbor knew she'd be coming and was happy to help aid in her move. Every minute outside of her house, she worried that her father would catch on and stop her in her tracks. The pulsing of her heart reverberated in her ears and throughout her body as she waited outside for the cab. *Please don't come outside, please don't come outside*, she repeated, as though praying for something bigger than her to help her toward her destiny.

At exactly 4:45 a.m., the small yellow cab pulled up, and she finally released her breath as she climbed into the backseat.

"Take me to the bus station off I79, please," Annie instructed confidently, as she wanted the cab to leave as quickly as possible.

"You got it, miss," the driver replied quietly.

She headed to the next town over to catch the bus at 5:15 a.m. The station looked like a concrete zoo. People of all walks of life walked in and out of the station with their belongings. She'd never ridden a bus before and didn't know what to expect. She'd heard horror stories of how people were treated on the bus and wanted to stay out of trouble. Her left foot tapped uncontrollably as her face remained calm and alert. A few minutes after five, a large silver bullet pulled into the station, looking more dazzling than a bus should ever look. Annie clutched her small gray suitcase, swallowed a deep breath, and made her way to the bus's double doors.

Step by step, Annie told herself that this was the right decision and that she was in charge of the future she wanted. As she climbed inside the bus, she made eye contact with the little white driver, who looked old enough to be a great-grandfather. He wore a black hat and a blue button-down with a crooked black tie and rusty tie clip. She took another deep inhale and the interior smell was less than attractive, but she figured she could manage. With a big smile, she handed the bus ticket to the driver.

Before picking her seat, she paused at the front of the aisle and took in the moment and all it represented. She stood there with everything she owned, wearing a new outfit bought from Sears by

58

a few of the ladies in the field as a goodbye gift: a white silk blouse with black polka dots and a black skirt that fell mid-calf. Her eyes quickly gazed through all the rows and a smile crept over her scared face. This was it.

"Uh, miss, we're gonna need you to hurry the hell up," the driver said, interrupting Annie's thoughts. Startled and embarrassed, she immediately took the first seat available.

She sat in the second row, closest to the window, and allowed herself to relax for the next several hours. The driver, who introduced himself as Dale, made it clear that this was his bus and therefore his rules and his music. Period. No requests, no complaining.

The songs were new to Annie, but she enjoyed them as did the others on the bus. Johnny Cash was apparently a big star and someone whose music she became very fond of—especially after hearing it on the bus for more than seven hours straight.

Waves of energy would overcome her fellow passengers. At times they'd all be quiet, and you'd hear only a few snores in the background. Other times people would be singing and laughing and making new friends. At one point, everyone started chiming in and clapping their hands to a popular Cash song:

> *Who was it everybody*
> *Who was it everybody*
> *Who was it everybody*

It was Jesus Christ, our Lord

The whole trip felt like a party, the bus filled with hooting and hollering. Some of the folks in the back stretched their arms and torso out the bus windows, waving at passing cars. It was as if everyone on the bus had left their sorrows behind and let the music take over their soul. It was the first time in years Annie felt herself bellowing laughs so hard she couldn't catch her breath. The trip to Port Isabel, Texas, really was the ride of her life.

A few bus stops and several hours later, Annie finally arrived in the town she would call home for the next thirty years. The brakes screeched as the bus pulled to a stop in the empty station. It was rather anticlimactic, if we're being honest. It wasn't as if she expected anyone there to cheer her on, but an empty parking lot wasn't what she had in mind—it was a little deserted. Where was the beach and all the promise she had kept envisioning?

She picked up her five empty Ruffles chip bags and started to stretch her limbs in preparation for exiting the bus. She rolled her neck in a circle and took a deep breath in. *Welcome home*, she told herself.

Annie said goodbye to the driver and went inside the bus station, where she asked the station attendant, an older woman, for assistance calling a cab.

"Sure, miss, where do you want to go?" the attendant asked as she dialed the numbers.

Annie took a small folded-up piece of paper out of her skirt pocket and handed it to the woman. Ruth knew it would be hard for Annie to remember all the details and had written down some reminders.

"All right, 2nd Street, it is. Cab will be here in about fifteen minutes. Just relax."

Relax, ha. What does that word even mean? Annie thought as she smiled and nodded. Relaxing was the last thing Annie could think about. She needed to land a job and a place to live as quickly as possible.

The taxi ride was hot and bumpy and smelled of Indian spices. But as her ride continued, her fear of desolation in an unknown town started to drift away. Although the bus station certainly wasn't the best first impression, the town itself was actually quite beautiful. Families of all races, ages, and sizes strolled the streets in their summer clothes. Some ate corn on a stick, while others enjoyed ice cream cones bought from vendors pushing carts up and down the strip. So many different kinds of restaurants lined the streets, interspersed with tourist shops with surf boards and swimsuits displayed in the windows.

As they made their way into Port Isabel, Annie kept the window rolled down to feel the sticky air brush up against her face and smell the salt of the ocean. Her brown curls rioted in the wind, tickling her face. She had never felt so free. She asked the cab to stop at the first restaurant that caught her true attention: perched atop a forty-foot-tall signpost for Uncle Clam's was a neon-lit mermaid posing inside a giant clam. *This is definitely not like Big Spring.*

Annie shook her head and smiled in disbelief. Her new home was also home to the biggest clam she'd ever seen. She got out of the cab, paid the driver, and walked up to the restaurant. She gently placed her luggage on the sidewalk and put her hands and face up to the window of Uncle Clam's to see tables of noisy teens enjoying themselves over large milkshakes and fries. Biting her lip, she picked up her bag and moved to the entrance, pulling the glass door open and walking into the restaurant to meet eyes with the most beautiful girl she'd ever seen.

She was around five-foot-nine with long blond hair and lean tan legs, wearing a hot-pink dress, white apron, and white roller skates. Momentarily stunned, Annie lost her train of thought, looking like a deer in headlights. "Um, hi there, I was wanting to see if you all needed help?" Annie placed her bag at her feet and started fidgeting with her hands. She quickly reverted to her childlike self: shy and insecure but sweet in her gesture and smile. "I'm available to work any time—night and day."

Unphased, the young blonde took a good look at Annie before saying anything. She leaned down and pulled out a piece of paper from behind the wooden hostess stand before she rolled slowly toward her. "Nifty, we're always looking for help around here. Are you afraid of cleaning a few toilets?"

Annie laughed at the thought of someone being scared to clean a toilet.

"No, I'm serious," the young woman snapped. Her voice was high, and she articulated every word precisely. "We need help with janitorial duties in the evenings. You know, cleaning tables, washing dishes, tidying up bathrooms. Is this something you could help with?" She handed Annie the job application.

"Yes, yes, of course. I'll do whatever you need," Annie said, accepting the paper.

"Boss. Well, come back tomorrow around noon for an interview and we'll let you know if you've got the job. My name's Hannah, by the way."

"Hannah, mucho gusto. Thank you very much," Annie replied graciously as she walked to the corner of the diner to take a good look at the place and get a real meal into her starving body. Ruffles chips were delicious, but they couldn't hold her over anymore.

Sitting in the corner booth, she had the best seat in the house. The ceilings were low, the plastic booths were black, and the lighting seemed very yellow compared to the natural light she always worked in back home. Pictures of cartoon sea creatures and mermaids covered the walls, looking more cluttered than artfully arranged. The place smelled of fried seafood, which was slightly overwhelming at first, but the pungency lost its power after the first few minutes. Annie sat there alone with a giant plastic menu and her first-ever job application.

Staring at the paperwork, the adrenaline began to wear off. Annie's hands were trembling as doubt crept into her mind—like a whisper turning into a scream. The words on the application were nothing more to her than odd shapes and squiggles. Without the ability to read or write, she knew she'd never be qualified or even considered for the job. *What the hell was I thinking coming here?* Pounding anxiety took over her head and the room began to shrink: *There's no way I can fucking do this. Nobody will ever hire someone like me.* Annie's hands gripped the application, defeat written all over her face. Before making eye contact with her waitress, she stood up, grabbed her things, and walked swiftly to the front of the restaurant, trying not to make a scene. She handed the application back to Hannah and muttered, "Thank you, but I can't fill this out."

Dumbfounded, Hannah cocked her head to the right. "If you needed a pen, you could have just asked for one. No need to beat feet." She pulled a blue pen out from her apron pocket and pointed it at Annie, who shook her head slowly in shame while staring at the ground.

"No, I, I can't." Her hands were curled into fists and she bit her lip even harder.

"You can't what?" retorted Hannah with a piss attitude.

"I can't read or write," Annie confessed, teeth clenched, trying to get it through to Hannah how grave the situation was.

"Oh, be serious."

Annie shook her head, attempting to comprehend whatever words came out of Hannah's mouth. *Seems like the English down here is different too.*

"You sweet thing. You must be in so much grief. How did this happen? It's 1963—everyone goes to school." Hannah was genuinely curious how someone Annie's age couldn't write or even read.

Annie still had no idea what Hannah was talking about, but before she could mutter a response Hannah kindly grabbed her left arm and accompanied her back to the big booth in the corner.

"No sweat. I can help you fill out your application." Annie thought Hannah looked like she was gliding on air in those damn roller skates. She was so cool. Both girls settled into the plastic booth, the application on the tabletop in front of them.

"So here's an easy one—what's your name?" Hannah didn't realize she was being patronizing.

"Antonia—uh, Annie."

"Um, like, which is it?"

Annie realized her indecision didn't help her case of not being able to read or write. She certainly wasn't an idiot, but she hadn't

65

considered how she'd present herself in this new town. *Damnit, I haven't even thought of how to introduce myself and who I'd be.*

"Antonia. My name is Antonia, but people call me Annie for short."

"Cool. Annie, it is—nice to meet you!" Hannah moved along the list of questions, scribbling down Annie's answers. They giggled over personal details and the lack thereof.

What a life, Annie thought. *To be able to write and read whatever you want without any help at all.* Within ten minutes, Hannah had made an impossible task so seamless and easy.

"See, that wasn't so bad, was it?" Hannah commented as she rolled away on her skates. "You'll get the job. I just know it. You're a little sweetie pie!"

Annie smiled in appreciation as Hannah went back to manning the front of the restaurant. Admiring from a distance, Annie couldn't believe what just happened. Help from an absolute stranger was not common where she was from. Annie closed her eyes and said a quick prayer: *God, thank you for keeping me safe and allowing me to be here. Thank you for Hannah's help with the job papers. Please help me to get the job tomorrow and let my interview go great. I promise I will do my best. Amá, please keep sending your guardian angels to look after me. I love you, Amá. Amen.*

As Annie opened her eyes post-prayer, she saw the waitress standing in front of her, staring at her like she was some sort of alien.

"What can I get for you, miss?" she said, her right hip out and arms crossed.

"I'll take fried shrimp, fries, and one of those chocolate milkshakes," Annie ordered, feeling confident in her meal choices after reading the room quickly to see what looked most appetizing.

"Sure thing, miss."

After dinner, it was a busy couple of hours walking the town and finding the right long-term motel that would be cheap enough to live in but safe enough to stay. She finally found the right fit, owned by an older Asian couple, Mr. and Mrs. Chang. Because Annie was so young, they decided that charging her full price wouldn't be necessary. *Two more angels in disguise*, Annie thought.

Walking into the motel room, Annie dropped her bag right next to the front door, turned on the AC, and launched herself into bed with a running start, legs sprawled and arms above her head trying to reach for each corner. She took a deep breath in and focused on this moment and this feeling—true gratitude and appreciation.

To most, the motel room would have appeared to be anything but extravagant: the beige walls complemented by outdated wallpaper, the red-and-blue comforter made of an itchy fabric, and the smell of cigarette smoke that lingered from the previous occupant. However, this was the first time in Annie's life where she had her own bed, a real bed, to herself.

Annie's petite body lay in the bed like it was sewn to the sheets. Her face was so soft and tired and her muscles fully relaxed, like she used to sleep when she was a young girl. She woke up peacefully, keeping her eyes shut and lying there motionless. The loud air conditioner reminded her that she was still in the motel room and she had successfully completed her first night away from home. Her grin was bright and beautiful, like she was performing to a crowd of thousands.

There was a tingling in her stomach, full of excitement. A new day with new opportunities lay ahead. Today was her first job interview and she had no idea what to expect.

Even though the restaurant interview wasn't until noon, Annie was ready by 7 a.m., as per usual. She paced her room like a ping-pong ball being bounced from one end to the other. Her body couldn't physically be still. Grabbing her purse, she decided she'd head down to the motel lobby and see if Mr. and Mrs. Chang needed any help with duties around the facility—they were old and could likely use her assistance for some tasks.

Mr. Gutierrez had golden brown eyes and deep brown skin. He was a short but muscular man with a stout mustache that complemented his friendly dimples. You could tell he never went a day without eating at Uncle Clam's. He had been running the family business for the past ten years and was constantly bustling around the restaurant. He was quiet, but his stern face suggested that his mind was not. There were too many things to get done in too little time. He knew where everything in the restaurant was at every minute of the day, could memorize most of his customers' orders without writing down a single word, and he knew the inventory list like the back of his hand.

"Congratulations, Annie, we'd love to have you work here." Mr. Gutierrez held out his short hairy arm to shake hands with his newest employee. "You start tonight, if you're available. It's vacationer season, so we're often real empacado in the evenings. The more help we can get, the better. We're a big family at Uncle Clam's, so ask lots of questions and the most important thing is to show up. Man, other than that—I look forward to working with you." The speech had certainly been rehearsed a time or two. It felt anything but authentic, but Annie didn't mind. She was too overwhelmed by the thought of a new job, a job she had interviewed for and could successfully claim as her own.

"Yes sir, gracias, señor!" Annie said as she shook Mr. Gutierrez's hand firmly and accepted her bright-pink uniform and white slip-on sneakers. She ran back to the motel as quick as she could to try on the new uniform.

Cheers! she said to herself in the mirror as she raised a bottle of Coke from the motel fridge. *What would Mama Jo and the rest of them say about me now?*

Annie showed up an hour and a half before her scheduled shift. Who could blame her? She looked like a young child on her first day of school, with a smile from ear to ear and proudly wearing her new uniform for everyone to see. Though she felt amazing in her work outfit, she quickly realized it didn't exactly fit like Hannah's; her friend's long tan legs and silky blond hair were far more appealing in the uniform. It didn't matter. This was the beginning of a new job and a fresh start.

As Annie arrived at Uncle Clam's, Mr. Gutierrez looked at his watch and then back up at Annie with a shocked expression. "You know you're early, right?"

"Si, señor," Annie replied enthusiastically. "I just didn't want to be late on my first day."

"Well, your trainer isn't going to be here for a while, so go sit in the staff room and when he gets here you can get started," Mr. Gutierrez directed. He got the attention of another waitress to take Annie to the back.

Annie nodded and kept her big smile as the other waitress led her through the restaurant to a small room with lockers and some tables and chairs, its walls decorated with pictures of all the employees. Annie walked around the room and inspected each picture slowly. Everyone who worked there appeared so full of joy and had a life beyond work. She found an empty locker partially open and placed her belongings in there, then waited in the gray rolling chair for what felt like forever.

"Name's Jaime. I'll be training you." He walked in abruptly with a strong demeanor and grabbed his clipboard to read up on his newest employee. Annie read him quickly and realized he wasn't a threat. She simply nodded and smiled.

"Glad to have you, Anne. Shit's pretty easy around here. Get your shit done and it'll be as easy as that. Don't get your shit done and I'll make sure you get fired. We all have to do our part. Got it?" He smelled of cigarette smoke and Clorox. He handed Annie a list of responsibilities that she would need to complete before the end of every night.

"Thank you, sir," Annie replied sternly as she grabbed the list. It was work time and her face demonstrated focus and grit.

"Oh, none of that *sir* shit. It's Jaime."

"Claro, okay, sir. I mean, Jaime." Annie looked at the list and took a deep breath. "Also, I am called Annie, not Anne. Can you review the list with me?"

"Kid, it's simple. Just read the list and do what it says. We don't got complicated stuff around here."

"Can you review it with me, please? I have a strong memory, so you only need to tell me once, promise." Annie didn't back down and wasn't going to look weak. She knew that she couldn't reveal her biggest weakness in front of everyone. She'd already let Hannah see it and that was enough.

Jaime took a deep breath and went through the list with her. "One: Make sure bathrooms are always tidy. There's a pink spray under the sink if you need to wipe anything down and the scrubber is in the stall. The bathrooms need to be checked every hour. Understand?" Without stopping, he moved on down the list. "Okay. Two: Make sure the floors stay clean. No food on the floors, ever. This can be hard during busy hours, but typically we just walk around with a broom and sweep high-traffic areas. Three: Wipe down the windows—the spray is in the back closet. Four: Make sure the common-area trash cans are never overflowing. I take them out, but I always need extra eyes to make sure the place is clean. Five: Wipe down the booths. Six: Roll the utensils in the napkins and make sure there is always plenty in the hostess stand with Hannah or Margaret. Seven: Make sure the kitchen staff have all the help they need during closing times—wash dishes, clean up the grease pits, or offer to throw out the scraps. Whatever they need, you're their go-to person at the end of the night. Eight: No sitting. Nine: Your free meal can be eaten during your break, which is thirty minutes after you've been here for at least three hours. Ten: Have fun! The last one is kind of a joke, but it's on all the onboarding papers." His voice got sluggish at the end and he was definitely done with the pretend *Welcome to work* tone.

"Claro. Thanks again, Jaime."

"There are the gloves." He pointed over in the corner, where the yellow mop bucket sat along with a pair of new yellow rubber gloves.

The work wasn't difficult at all for Annie. There were times when she almost felt guilty that people thought of this as "work." You couldn't even compare this to the pain and exhaustion of picking cotton all day in the heat with limited breaks: a hard, backbreaking job. Uncle Clam's had the air conditioning on blast so that tourists coming in from the beach could feel refreshed and calm. Apparently nothing is worse than hot and hungry customers. And Annie could get free drinks anytime she wanted—Coke on ice was her favorite. Oh and the best part, she got to split tips with the rest of the staff, which could range anywhere from an extra $5 to $15 a night. *Mama Jo, you'd be laughing at these fools, saying they'd never worked a day in their lives.*

After a few weeks of "working" at Uncle Clam's, Annie had developed a steady routine and made a few friends. She was true to herself in that she kept quiet, more of an observer than a loud attention-seeker. Annie was always watching and learning from the other employees. The waitresses loved to flirt with the beach boys who would come in after a surf lesson. It seemed a little promiscuous at first, but the waitresses always seemed to get extra tips for a cute wink here and there. Annie wasn't a prude, but flirting with boys her age seemed rather intimidating; plus, why would they be interested in her when they had Hannah to stare at?

Annie enjoyed hearing the latest gossip in the staff room and living vicariously through the other waitresses: the way they'd flip their hair and add lipstick to make their smiles appear even bigger. It was all new to Annie; a part of her turned away this desire to be wanted, but another part of her wanted attention so badly, she even craved it sometimes.

Every now and then while Annie was cleaning the bathrooms, she'd catch herself in the mirror mimicking the movements and embodying the aura of her female coworkers. Spraying the mirror then wiping, Annie would make eye contact with herself and imagine she was catching the attention of a hot young man. Pretending to be shy, she'd giggle and flip her hair, her hearing heightened in case anyone was walking in while she practiced her moves. This was a new side of Annie that she'd never explored— and it was fun embracing herself as a woman—even if it was only in the bathroom mirror.

While the rest of the young ladies wooed their way from table to table, Annie was scrubbing toilets and degreasing ovens to keep the restaurant in tip-top shape.

It was a busy Monday afternoon, which wasn't typical for Uncle Clam's. Mr. Gutierrez was in quite a mood, frustrated with all the workers who had called in sick at the last minute. As he walked back to the kitchen to clean up a bit, he realized he would have to lean on his most consistent employee to keep things afloat. "Annie, can you please put on an apron and serve tables ahora. We had three people call out today. I think you can handle it. And wash your hands first."

Annie was hunched over, stacking dishes in the back-kitchen corner. Her head turned and she immediately said yes, knowing that whatever work needed to be done, she could figure out a way to do it. She took off the long yellow rubber gloves and washed her hands for what felt like forever. She hustled over to her closest companion at Uncle Clam's, her voice frantic but quiet. "Hannah, I need your help. I'm supposed to take down orders today because we're short-staffed."

"Cool your jets, hunny," Hannah said, loudly smacking her gum. "The customers will tell you their orders, then can you remember to tell it to the kitchen staff? Ask one of the cooks, maybe? Yeah, ask Dennis to write it down for you once you yell it over the counter. Got it?"

Annie blinked several times, taking it all in, and tried to compose herself while walking slowly to her first table. Nervous sweat culminated all over her body. She took a deep breath and faked a smile. She'd been practicing for a moment like this— though the mirror was far less intimidating than a family of four.

"Welcome to Uncle Cl—" She froze as she made eye contact with the most handsome young man she'd ever seen. "Uncle Clam's. Welcome!" She smiled through her awkwardness, holding the black pen tight like a knife while the pad was upside down.

The young man was sitting with two other boys and a young woman, presumably the little sister of the bunch. He was husky, in his early twenties, and had perfectly manicured hair, dark-brown skin, and light-brown eyes. *Get it together, Annie,* she told herself as his sailor suit made her swoon a little inside.

"Can I take your drink order?" she said, squeezing the pen tighter and tighter.

His steady eyes looked up from the menu and his tense demeanor softened. "Afternoon. Sweet tea, little ice, and an extra lemon, please."

"Absolutely!" Annie ran over to the kitchen counter to not forget a word he said, leaving the other three guests confused. "Extra lemon, sweet ice, little tea," Annie shouted over to Dennis. Then she ran back to the table to get the rest of the drink orders and blushed when she realized what she had done. *Well, that's off to a bumpy start.*

Once Annie got into the groove of waitressing, she was stunning. Order in, order out. She was busting her tail remembering all the requests and keeping her mind as sharp as possible.

The tables were packed, families had crying babies and

squabbling kids, and orders weren't always prepped based on her requests, which never felt good. Though things seemed chaotic, she moved throughout the restaurant like a ballerina carrying a tray with hot meals, always keeping her eyes peeled for potential hazards, and still smiling.

After the first couple hours, Annie had a hard time understanding why people were complaining about everything. Most of the customers didn't even realize how lucky they were to be eating dinner with their entire family after enjoying a day out on the beach. One gentleman complained that his shrimp was "too hot"; another woman, who was around five hundred pounds, said her french fries were undercooked so she wanted a new basket but refused to return the current basket of fries; and the worst was the teen who claimed her milkshake wasn't chocolatey enough. What was wrong with these people?

"Yo, Annie, what's the tears for?" Dennis asked as she took a deep breath in the back.

"I don't understand. These people who have so much find so many things to complain about. I want to throw the food in their lap and tell them they have so much to be thankful for." Annie was frustrated and generally didn't feel this way toward people—but her perception of the customers was shifting. Was everyone who had money this selfish and inconsiderate?

"Annie, serving is about making people feel special. They want to enjoy a great meal and feel like they are the only table you care about at that moment. Once you realize that nothing's going to be perfect, you'll do fine. But in the meantime, take a deep breath." Annie took Dennis's advice to heart and the evening changed for the better. Instead of being mad at the kitchen every time an order was incorrect, she sympathized with the customer and told them she understood their frustration. It was amazing how her different tone completely changed the way her customers engaged with her. It was like she was their advocate for the best meal they could ever have, and they loved having her on their side. It wasn't all bad, either. Annie enjoyed delivering a meal that a family would eat and cherish together. She'd catch herself watching the young children dip their french fries in the ketchup and somehow still manage to get sauce all over their face. Other customers tried to make small talk and learn about her past and future, which made Annie feel special too.

At the end of that long night, the crew sat in celebration of surviving one hell of a day. By far the busiest Monday of the year was finally over. Mr. Gutierrez made a toast to his dream team and they enjoyed milkshakes on the house. Throughout the staff's mini-celebratory evening, Annie was complimented left and right by management and the kitchen staff at her ability to remember the orders. She'd been promoted that evening to an official Uncle Clam's waitress. *Hell yes.*

Annie often served between the cleaning crew and the waitressing team, depending on the needs of Uncle Clam's that day—she was compensated for her versatility and liked the diversity of the job. Mr. Gutierrez even nicknamed Annie as Uncle Clam's Swiss Army knife: able and willing to work wherever Uncle Clam's needed help that day.

Today, Annie was back to cleaning duties, which was a nice change of pace. Things had been going a hundred miles an hour ever since the fall semester started and some of the summer staff had left.

With the yellow mop bucket in one hand, Annie swung open the men's bathroom door, ready to tackle the tile floor's grime. Instantly she realized she had forgotten to knock before entering and made eye contact with a startled man who was in the middle of washing his hands. "SORRY! I'm so SORRY," Annie shouted as ran out of the bathroom and slammed the wooden door. She banged her forehead lightly in humiliation on the cold beige tile of the wall outside the bathroom.

Before she could process what had happened, her face blushed and thoughts started racing in her mind. Tingles filled her entire body and she couldn't stop smiling. It was him—the handsome sailor she had met on her first night as a waitress.

As he walked out of the bathroom, he nodded politely in her direction as she stared at the ground in embarrassment. "Excuse me, beautiful." Annie heard the words but knew there was no way he was talking to her. She looked up and sure enough he was standing there laughing at her as she tried to blend in with the wall. "When you decide you're done cleaning men's bathrooms, I'd love to show you the world."

She dropped the bucket in disbelief and started laughing out of discomfort. Not the cute chuckle she thought this moment would include but full-blown belly laughter, as if she was being pranked.

He smiled and said, "The offer still stands" before walking back to his table to order his dinner, this time alone.

A few seconds went by and Annie realized this was, in fact, not a joke and the love of her life had just spoken to her. She'd never been in this type of situation before, so out of instinct she hissed for Hannah to meet her in the bathroom to discuss a plan. Hannah knew her way around boys and was the perfect source to coach Annie through a life-changing moment like this.

Turns out, talking to Hannah was the worst possible idea on the entire planet. She took this task on as a mission to give Annie everything she felt Annie deserved. Before Annie knew it, Mr. Gutierrez got involved, and Annie was now serving only the sailor's table "off the clock." MORTIFIED. It was as if all her coworkers were rooting her on as she delivered the fries and made small talk with Artemio—Art for short.

Since Annie was officially off for the rest of the evening, she ended up enjoying a milkshake with her dreamy sailor as they laughed about his experiences and his travels abroad. This was her first date and it couldn't have been more perfect.

He walked her home to the motel that evening and asked her out on a proper date for the following weekend, to which she agreed. After he left, she went into her motel room and squealed with joy, jumping up and down on the unsteady bed. He had heard her squealing once she went inside, but he never told her that.

As she walked into Uncle Clam's the next day, Annie was the star of the stage. Everyone was dying to know the details of her hours-long conversation over a milkshake with the sailor, whom the other waitresses thought was such a gentleman. They were truly happy to learn she had another date with him coming up. The next seven days would feel like an eternity—but it allowed plenty of time for Hannah to help Annie prepare.

That next weekend, Annie looked magnificent. Hannah had come by to help her get ready for her big date. She pressed Annie's curls and accentuated Annie's pretty features and dewy skin in the best makeup money could buy, with a new lipstick just in case Art came in for a kiss.

Art showed up at the motel early with carnations and baby's breath. He was looking spiffy in a pearl-snap button-down shirt and black dress pants. When Annie answered the door, his face broke into a huge smile, making his already small eyes seem even smaller.

Conversation was easy and Annie was an amazing listener. She loved how smart Art was and how he could do math in his head without needing a pen and paper. He even claimed to have invented a new way to do multi-ple-ca-something. She'd ask him what it was called again later, but it had something to do with numbers and he was very proud of it.

"So, Annie, you mentioned wanting to be a writer over our milkshakes last weekend. That's wonderful. What kind of writing do you enjoy? Poetry, fiction, short stories?" Art asked, as it was his turn to listen to her dreams and desires.

Nervous and intimidated, she immediately lied because she didn't want to ruin the best first date. "Well, when I save up enough money from Uncle Clam's, I'm going to leave and start writing. A book. Yes, a book. A big one with lots of characters and drama." She smiled as a woman with her level of education and confidence should. Art was impressed by her drive and dedication, but he was a little confused at her lack of clarity. He ignored his inner voice to keep pressing the question because he was one smitten kitten.

Art had ordered dinner for the both of them, as the gentleman of this time often did. He gave her his recommendations, which included deviled eggs, chicken dumplings, and a Coke. Annie was in complete and total bliss. She hardly touched her food and couldn't even take a bite of the Jell-O cake because all she could think about was how amazing Art was; this dinner, this date, this experience was better than anything she could have ever imagined.

Upon Annie's return from freshening up in the bathroom, Art reached across the table and gently held both of her hands in his. He looked into her eyes and with total conviction made the declaration of a lifetime: "Let's do it. Let's make our dreams happen together."

1964
EIGHTEEN YEARS OLD

The house was small but quaint. It smelled of lingering cologne. Anchors, boats, and Art's fishing photography adorned the white walls. Annie was wearing her well-worn Uncle Clam's uniform as she sat on the edge of her husband's bed. She examined the bedroom thoroughly as she had over the past eight months, trying to figure out what she needed to buy to finally make this room, this house, feel like home. Though the bedroom had been sprinkled with her belongings, a bobby pin here, a small picture there, it still felt like anything but hers. She was merely living as a guest in her husband's home. It would feel like years before the reality sank in that she was now a wife with a husband, in a place she barely knew.

The life Art and Annie quickly created with each other was anything but boring. Some days they'd wake up early and go sailing. On other mornings, Art would drive Annie around town to shop for elegant outfits and accessories so she always looked and felt her best. Annie had a sense of humor that would leave Art laughing for days. She had a way of making him feel like a young boy again. Together, they were magnetic.

The two of them were a balance of opposites: Art was a hopeless romantic, whereas Annie kept her focus on predictable and realistic concerns. Annie had never met a man as genuine and giving as Art. On the contrary, Art had never met a woman as confident and stubborn as Annie. They challenged each other's minds and brought new perspectives to light. Their conversations were deep, and their connection was even deeper.

The energy of their chemistry filled an entire room. Though they were both modest, there were times it was hard for them to keep their hands off each other. Art would surprise Annie at Uncle Clam's in his handsome sailor uniform and they'd share a kiss or two until Mr. Gutierrez would interrupt. The other girls would sigh in jealousy, knowing that what Annie and Art had was not only so much fun but also truly unique.

Late in the evenings, they'd lie in bed after making love for hours. Art's strong arms would hold Annie tight and they'd just snuggle in silence, their hearts full and her stomach churning with tingles of love. It was in these deep, pure intimate moments that Art would gently lift Annie's chin, look her square in the eye, and whisper, "Annie, I love you, my beautiful. I love you so much," as he kissed her forehead.

Her eyes locked on his, Annie would accept his words. She'd embrace the moment, relishing in it, her green eyes filling with happy tears, wanting to believe him with every ounce of her being. It was moments like that where Annie felt she was living in a dream, a world she couldn't have even prayed for because it was far too blissful.

Art would slowly fall asleep and Annie would lay awake, her husband's words lingering in her mind and heart. It was easy for her to understand that she was loved but difficult to comprehend why he loved her so much. It was unfathomable to Annie that she could be loved for simply being herself, not because of her contribution to society or her background or education. Art just loved her for who she was. But, like an unwelcome guest, Annie's bad thoughts creeped in and sabotaged her mind: *He can't love you. You don't deserve him. He's going to leave you.*

Sure, the insecurities were distracting, but what Annie struggled with most was the interdependence. Her entire life had been built around self-sufficiency and solitude. At times, she was skeptical of Art's ability to share his life and his belongings with another person—at no cost. Surely there had to be a cost. Surely he couldn't be this kind.

Annie took a final look around the bare bedroom and closed

her eyes, wishing Mama Jo could guide her and hug the doubt away. *I can do this*, Annie told herself, swallowing every ounce of uncertainty into the pit of her stomach. *Mama Jo would give me such grief if she saw me right now.* And with that, Annie stood up, straightened her white apron, and headed to Woolco to buy some knickknacks for her new home before heading into work.

"Hey, sweet pea," Hannah greeted Annie as she walked into Uncle Clam's. "How are you and Romeo doing? You two lovebirds make me sick!"

"Good, good. We're good," Annie responded as she looked at the ground, blushing. "He comes home tomorrow. I can't wait."

"Oh, I'm sorry, sweet stuff. I forgot he's away. How have you been doing on your own?"

"It's a little tough, but I'm okay. I miss him," Annie responded before hurrying back to the staff room to drop off her belongings.

One of the biggest contributors to Annie and Art's undeniable passion and friendship was Art's work schedule. Being a sailor, he was gone for weeks at a stretch. When the time would come, Annie would pack his bags for him and bake some treats for his journey away at sea. Since Annie didn't know how to drive, they'd take a cab together out to the port and as he'd walk confidently toward the ship, she'd wave her handkerchief dramatically in the wind and dab away her crocodile tears.

The first couple of times Art went away, Annie would smile and wave as his ship left port. However, her reaction was so painfully contrasted by the behavior of the other sailors' wives, who would cry hysterically. Annie would stare at them awkwardly, thinking, *They're coming back soon, why are you so upset?* After those first few goodbyes, Annie thought that carrying a handkerchief would be best, to play it safe—she couldn't have the other women thinking she was cold-hearted wife who wouldn't cry as her husband weighed anchor.

After waving Art a theatrical tear-filled goodbye, Annie would take a cab back home and fall into her own peaceful world. The time alone provided her the space to be with her thoughts and have the independence she had always been so accustomed to. Some days she'd go out to get her hair done at the salon or quietly walk through the park, thinking of Mama Jo and her apá—the life she used to live and had left behind. Time alone was good for her relationship with her husband, but mostly it was good for Annie's soul.

She got joy from cleaning out the cabinets and reorganizing the house. It would take time, but their home was her domain and she took pride in knowing that every crevice was as clean and organized as possible. It was like her mind was a large database that could itemize and account for the contents of every drawer, cabinet, closet, and room of their thirteen-hundred-square-foot home.

Eventually Annie's solitude would wear off and she'd find herself yearning for Art's return. Seeing him disembark from the ship with his belongings and his bright smile would send pulses down her body and a flush of color across her face. She'd count down the moments when she'd be able to make love to his strong body and have him home to shower her with affection.

Throughout the evening at Uncle Clam's, Annie laughed to herself, knowing that the key to her happiness was the fact that she and Art spent time apart. Hannah would never understand, and Annie would never dare try to explain it. It would be Annie's little secret. Though their relationship was usually rather smooth, they certainly had their hard times together, especially during the first couple months as husband and wife.

It was a cold January evening and the shift at Uncle Clam's had been frustrating, to say it nicely. Annie was having to constantly cover for the young unreliable staff whom Mr. Gutierrez continued to hire, and tonight was the last straw. It was incomprehensible to Annie that her coworkers actively chose not to show up. It's not like there was a death in the family—supposedly, some just had a light cold or a cough.

This evening, Annie had enough. Not because she was busy at work, she liked being busy, but because she felt there should be punishment for the employees who didn't pull their weight. Mr. Gutierrez, though he looked hard on the outside, knew he couldn't fire his staff on the account of absences. He just kept letting it happen, and this would put everyone else who was working in a bind: covering more tables with less employees. When Annie came home, instead of greeting her husband, who was waiting at the dinner table with food and flowers, she threw her purse on the sofa and kicked off her white sneakers, pouting like a young teen.

"Well, Annie, that's not the way to come home to your husband, is it?" Art asked, a snide tone in his voice. For some time now he'd been suggesting that Annie quit her job; she didn't need to work, he could afford a nice lifestyle for the both of them.

"Art, forgive me. It's work. I don't understand people. They want a job, they get a job, and all they have to do is show up. That's it, just show up! They wouldn't last an hour doing what I was doing as a kid. And Mr. Gutierrez doesn't have the balls to fire anyone. I would have fired them ages ago!" Becoming passionate about it, Annie started to yell at Art, who was not amused.

"Mi linda, take a deep breath," he said gently enough not to step on one of Annie's land mines. "I think this job is taking a toll on you. It's already 6:15 p.m., you're upset, and this isn't even a job you like that much. I say you leave Uncle Clam's right now—or put your notice in if it makes you feel better to give notice—and focus on your writing like you've always wanted."

Annie's face turned white. She'd been avoiding this conversation over and over again. It was evident that the truth had to be revealed, and it wasn't going to feel good. Not for her, and not for Art. Without second-guessing her decision to come clean, she spit out the truth as fast as she could. "I lied, Art. I lied to you and I'm sorry. I didn't think we'd end up here, and so soon. And you. You're so perfect and I'm not."

Annie was in such shock at her confession that she couldn't even find the tears to cry for sympathy. She just headed to the bedroom to pack her gray bag. Surely this would be the beginning of the end for them: she had lied.

"Annie, what did you lie about?" Art asked, his breathing getting heavier by the second. His hands trembled in fear as his thoughts started to spiral. *What had the love of his life lied to him about?*

"Remember when I told you that I wanted to be an author one day?" Annie said as tears started to dwell in her sad green eyes.

"Of course, and I support that, mi linda. But what—"

"I won't be an author because I never went to school and I never learned how to read or write."

His expression didn't change; he just sat there, motionless. Thoughts were buzzing through his head, and he knew that the next words to come out of his mouth would shape the future of their relationship.

Everything Annie had been saying finally made sense: her disinterest in arithmetic, her inability to express the type of books she enjoyed, the fact that she never talked about school friends or favorite subjects. She was broken and had openly poured out her heart for him to trample on. His initial reaction was to scream in anger about distrust—*that lying flake.* But he knew that wasn't who Annie was; he had to look beyond that. In that split-second, he chose kindness.

"Annie, like I said, quit your job at Uncle Clam's. I can support us now and you can focus on your writing. You can write every day and put your heart on paper."

Art stood up from the kitchen table and went to the bathroom to clean up from making dinner. Annie's tears stopped immediately, and she stood frozen. *Where was this kindness coming from? Did he not hear what I just said?* As she wiped away the last of her tears from her cheeks, she yelled, "Did you understand what I said? Why aren't you saying anything and just washing your hands?"

"Annie, you are the hardest working, most giving person I have ever met." Although his words were kind, he started to grit his teeth in frustration. "I love you and I want to support you, like we talked about. So, I'll use my inheritance and I'll get you a personal tutor. You can start next week, and you can begin your formal education. You deserve that."

That was it. Art never brought up Annie's lie again, and he didn't have to. It would be a hurdle Annie would have to overcome for the rest of her life. It was so simple for him to problem-solve and stay true to his word. The very next day, Annie quit her job at Uncle Clam's so she could focus on her education. She would be attending two to three classes a week in personal tutoring sessions at their own home or at the Port Isabel Library.

When people today ask Annie what true love is, she thinks about this moment with Art and how he saw her through her flaws and limitations. He knew that at Annie's core, she was hungry for more and eager to make her dreams come true.

A retired history and economics teacher, Joffrey Jones had worked in the Port Isabel School District for nearly forty years. Now in his late sixties, he filled his time with completing large cat puzzles and watching game shows: neither of which was good for his marriage. Mr. Jones needed more stimulation, and living a life of boredom at home was far lonelier than being responsible for a classroom of snooty teens. He missed the classroom, where he shined and could share his passion for learning.

When Art committed to providing his wife with tutoring sessions, he knew the perfect fit. Mr. Jones had taught Art in high school and always made politics, wars, and social issues come to life. After a brief conversation, Joffrey jumped at the opportunity to get out of the house and impact someone's education once again.

Annie threw up fifteen minutes before Joffrey Jones arrived at their home. She rinsed with mouthwash to rid the sour residue burning the back of her throat. Her body felt discombobulated, as if she was being dropped from a sixty-foot building and couldn't catch her breath. Formal education, learning to read and write, had felt like such a far-fetched dream but because of Art, it was finally happening in the comfort of her own home. Sure, it wasn't the school she had envisioned, but through these sessions she'd finally be seen as an equal in society: able to read and write and contribute just like everyone else. As she looked at herself in the mirror, she saw a woman with a pale-green complexion and fear-filled eyes. *Pull it together, Annie, you can do this.*

Right on schedule, Joffrey Jones rang the doorbell and Annie walked slowly to the front door, maintaining her calm facade. Strutting a big smile, Annie greeted her teacher in a light-blue dress and black loafers. Her hair was tied back, with curls highlighting her cheeks.

Gray hair covered the sides and back of Joffrey's head; his bald spot on top was extra shiny. He was tall and slim, around six-foot-three, with lanky arms and a very oval face. His nose and jaw were perfectly pointed, and he wore his reading glasses on the edge of his nose. Always dressed to impress, Joffrey stood at the door of the Garza household wearing a suit and tie, and carrying a leather briefcase, which was more formal than Annie had expected.

"Welcome, Joffrey, I mean, Señor Jones. My name's Annie. Welcome, welcome, come on in." Her voice was more high-pitched, weak, and awkward than she intended.

Joffrey Jones walked in slowly and went right toward the dining room, where Annie had anxiously prepared for a great first day of learning. The wooden dining table was covered in a surplus of unnecessary school supplies: a yellow notepad, pencils, a calculator, colored pencils, glue, scissors, tape, ruler, and a large pencil sharpener.

Art wanted her to be prepared and insisted she buy everything for her sessions to be most successful. In the center of the crochet table runner was a clear pitcher filled with bright-yellow lemonade, ice, and sliced lemons. To the right of the pitcher was a small crystal bowl filled with salted nuts.

"Well, Mrs. Garza, if you don't mind I address you as such," Joffrey Jones said, breaking the silence that had built up between them. His accent was drawn and slow.

"No, not at all, Mr. Joffrey," Annie said. "Please, call me whatever you'd like."

"Mrs. Garza, it looks like you have a fancy setup here. Art informed me of your, um, your situation, and I look forward to making progress with you. Can you tell me a bit of your background? It will help ensure that I use the best teaching methods possible for your sessions." The two of them settled into the dining-room chairs facing each other. Mr. Joffrey stared at his notepad as Annie sat up nice and tall.

"Yes, sir, of course. I'm sorry, señor, I'm very nervous today," Annie said, staring straight through his eyes. "I want to learn as much as I can so that I can be smart. In my younger years, I worked out on the cotton field, and didn't go to school like most kids do."

"So you've never had any sort of formal education, at all? Not even from your mom or dad as a child?" said Mr. Joffrey, stunned.

"That's true, no school for me. Especially from my parents—I have no real schooling." It wasn't hard for Annie to express these facts to Mr. Joffrey. The only way to move forward was to accept that this was who she was and how she was molded. There was no time to be sad and vulnerable—this was the time to learn and move forward. However, it was rather difficult for Mr. Joffrey to comprehend what kind of childhood prohibits a kid from having any sort of education, especially in the 1950s; everyone had access to education at this point, did they not? His questions stopped at that and he was no longer taking notes on "Getting to Know Mrs. Garza."

"Well then, we should start at the very beginning, shouldn't we?" Mr. Joffrey knew that Annie was not going to have a strong foundation, but he was certain that her eagerness to learn was a great start. As a formal high-school teacher, he had to channel a different part of his brain in order to articulate the simplicity of his lesson plans. The types of sessions that he was going to provide Annie seemed easier said than done.

As any good teacher would, Mr. Joffrey took a second to regain his composure and create a new lesson for the day. "Do you know the alphabet, Mrs. Garza?" he asked, anticipating her answer.

"Yes, actually, I do. I learned it with Mama Jo on the cotton fields."

"That's mighty fine. Can you please recite the alphabet?"

To the tune of the "American English Alphabet," Annie blushed as she sang to her new teacher, off-key and quieter than she used to practice: "abcd–efg–hijk–lmnop–qrs–tuv–wx, y and z."

Throughout her recitation, Mr. Joffrey wrote PATIENCE in big letters on his notepad to remind himself that Annie, though a full-grown adult, had the education level of a three-year-old. It's incomprehensible, and would often be frustrating for both parties. He smiled kindly and nodded his head in approval.

"All right, that was a breeze. Can you now write the alphabet and numbers one through ten?"

"I don't know how to do that, señor."

"All righty. Then that's where we shall start today. This will be a great first lesson and I'll have lots of things for you to work on until we meet again in, what, two days? Are you committed to putting in the work needed?"

"Yes, I'm ready. I can work harder than any other student you've ever taught. I can promise you that."

"Well then, Mrs. Garza, you're going to do just fine. Don't you worry."

Annie's chest released all the tension that had built up inside, like a balloon slowly deflating.

With his large wrinkly hands, Mr. Joffrey grabbed hold of Annie's yellow notepad and began writing down all twenty-six letters of the alphabet. "Do you know what these are? Have you seen these before?"

"Yes, but I don't know what they are or what they mean."

"Okay, the song you sang, the alphabet, includes twenty-six letters of the American English language. These letters make up all the words in the English dictionary and they will be monumental in your ability to learn to read and write. Each letter makes a specific sound and contributes to specific words. We will start at the beginning of the alphabet with the letter *A* and work our way through the end of the alphabet, with the letter *Z*."

Annie grabbed a pencil with her strong hand and held it like a knife she was about to stab in someone's chest.

Mr. Joffrey made eye contact with her as his hands gently touched her left hand. His hands shook, but it wasn't from nerves—must have been an old-man thing. "Mrs. Garza, you're going to want to put your index finger around the pencil and your other fingers will support the pencil, like this." He placed her fingers around the pencil, her thumb and index lightly touching while her ring finger, middle finger, and pinky supported the weight of her movements.

Her hand cramped from holding the pencil so tight, but along the yellow paper she followed the dashed lines that Mr. Joffrey had drawn out for her to trace the letter *A*.

"All right, Mrs. Garza, this is the first letter, *A*. *A* is a vowel and it sounds like *ah*, *aye*. *A* is included in the words *apple*, *alligator*, and *Alaska*."

Vowel, Alaska, alligator, apple. Vowel, apple, alligator, Alaska, Annie started to sing in her head to imprint it to memory. Her hands shook slightly and the cursive curves of her *A* weren't near as smooth as Mr. Joffrey's. The focus in her eyes stayed completely zoned in on the task at hand: her mind blank and her fingers doing a task that would be difficult at first. "When I picked cotton as a kid, my fingers would move so fast. It's nice using my hands again, except now it's for learning." Annie started to get comfortable in the presence of Mr. Joffrey.

"Ain't that right? My granddaddy lived on a cotton farm as a kid. That's not an easy job out there, Mrs. Garza. I'm impressed." Mr. Joffrey said kindly as he watched Annie trace her *A*'s over and over again.

"Yeah, sometimes I miss it. I miss my family out there, but I'm happy here. I'm happy to finally get to do these lessons and start learning."

"Well, the thing about family is they never go away. There's always a part of them that's with you."

Annie smiled, thinking of Mama Jo. She hadn't thought of her in a while. She would be so proud to see Annie right now: here learning to write. Looking over her right shoulder, she pictured Mama Jo standing there smiling at her.

Over the next thirty minutes, Annie continued practicing writing the letters *B*, *C*, and *D*. It was harder than she anticipated. Her mind would want her hand to do one thing and often it would do another.

"All right, Mrs. Garza. You know what you need to practice, right?" Mr. Joffrey stood up and straightened his tie.

"Yes, sir. *Alligators, bird, cat, dog.* I'll be sure to write it all down and practice my word associations."

"That's perfect. And if you have any questions, please don't hesitate to visit me in the library on Wednesdays from 4 to 6 p.m."

Nodding, her ponytail of brown curls swaying, Annie stood up and walked Mr. Joffrey out the front door. His brown shoes clapped the sidewalk and off he wandered home. As she closed the front door, she rested her back against the door, then slowly slid to the floor in exhaustion. Her head throbbed with a pounding headache from the amount of focus, but her fingers tingled with excitement.

Once Annie regained composure, she ran to Uncle Clam's to tell Hannah all the details over a chocolate milkshake and fries. Annie's brain was fried, but Hannah quizzed Annie over dinner to make word associations. It was one of many successful girls' nights out—for studying, that is.

The first six sessions with Mr. Joffrey focused solely on the memorization and understanding of the English alphabet. Annie proved to be an excellent student. She sat at the table captivated by every word that came out of Mr. Joffrey's mouth, as if everything he spoke was gospel. He had the keys to her kingdom of knowledge, and she knew that listening was the first step to understanding.

Annie would schedule time every day to practice her writing. Art would come home after a long trip out on sea to find Annie in the exact spot that he had left her in: hunched over the notepad at the dining-room table with mounds of paper scattered around her. He'd smile, kiss her on the head, and ask when dinner would be ready.

There were days when Mr. Joffrey was evidently frustrated by the slow pace at which Annie was improving. She could write her letters well, but when it came to creating words, there was an immediate halt in her progress. Every session felt painful, each minute lasted an hour.

"BUH-OH-GEE," Annie pronounced the word on the page slowly. "Buh, buh, buh, oh, oh, oh, gee, gee, gee."

"Remember that the letter *G* can also make the sound *guh*, not only *gee*. And what sound does a *D* make?"

"Duh, duh, duh," Annie replied robotically. Confused. "B-oh-g?"

"Mrs. Garza, we've talked about this. When you see the letters together, you blend them out to create a word." He pointed at the children's book with a picture of a big brown dog. "D-o-g. Duh-aw-guh. DOG."

"Yes, that makes sense. DOG." Except, in fact, it didn't make sense. The letters correlating together didn't make sense to her at all. And her insides burned, wanting to yell that it didn't make sense, but she didn't want to appear stupid. She didn't want to seem like she wasn't trying because she was trying with everything she had. Instead, she lowered her head in shame.

Mr. Joffrey could sense that Annie was no longer the eager learner she once was. At the end of the session, as she walked him to the door, he said, "Mrs. Garza, are you still interested in continuing our sessions?"

"Yes, yes, señor, of course," Annie said, caught off guard that he had seen straight through her veil.

"Well, I'm checking because you seem to be rather upset lately, and I'd like to confirm that you're doing a great job. You have a lot to overcome, and I can tell you're working hard." Mr. Joffrey's voice was low, like he was talking to his young daughter.

"Mr. Joffrey, you just get so upset with me sometimes and I don't know what to do because I'm trying my hardest."

"Mrs. Garza." Mr. Joffrey leaned over to make eye contact with her as they stood at the front door. "Nobody said learning was going to be easy. What I'm trying to instill in you is called tough love. I know how smart you are, so I'm demanding better of you. Why? Because I see how your brain works, and there's a lot in there."

Annie sighed in relief. He still believed in her and she felt her value increase. She finally felt seen and knew that he wasn't being ugly to her; rather, he was trying to encourage her. "Well, Mr. Joffrey, this is very stressful and I want to make you and my husband proud of me."

"We are all so, so proud of you. Now don't you forget that."

"Thank you, Mr. Joffrey, I'll see you next week."

"Goodnight. I'll see you next week."

Wiping her tired eyes, Annie walked to the kitchen to prepare dinner. She would leave all her stresses in the kitchen and look forward to seeing her husband for the first time in several weeks. Her learning was a challenge, but it also opened a new world of conversation for the both of them.

Art always thought Annie was so smart, and Annie loved to

show off to him when he returned—especially when it came to his expertise in math. Annie was able to show him her progress with learning addition and subtraction. Like Art, she excelled at math and it was far less complex than reading and reading comprehension. He'd ask her questions as she'd cook dinner and without using a pen and paper she would have to try to solve the problems in her head. Sometimes she'd get them wrong, but more times than not she could add the numbers quickly and confidently.

It was a journey that Annie had started but that others tried to play a supportive role in as well. From Hannah to Art to Mr. Joffrey, they all knew how important this was to Annie and wanted with their every being for her to succeed.

1965
NINETEEN YEARS OLD

The inside of the windows fogged up with humidity from all the cooking, the small house smelling of mashed potatoes and roasted vegetables. Wearing a sunny-yellow apron, Annie was preparing her specialty as Mr. Joffrey would be joining her and Art for a weeknight dinner. There was no formal occasion, other than Annie really enjoyed Mr. Joffrey's company. Every now and then Mrs. Jones would join too, but after being diagnosed with arthritis, she didn't leave the house much since it was difficult to move around in the cold weather.

"Hurry and eat, I made plenty!" Annie said as she finally sat down to feast with the men. "But the next serving is on you because I am one hungry and tired woman!"

"Well, Mrs. Garza, this looks fantastic!" Mr. Joffrey said with a bright smile on his face as he pushed his glasses up toward his brow

105

ridge. His mouth salivated over the meal, but his eyes were on the rice atole that smelled of rich cinnamon and sugar for dessert.

"Mr. Jones, how are things? I know Annie's been working hard, I see her studying all the damn time. I trust that my money is being put to good use?" Art wasn't the most smooth when it came to speaking with other men. He had this demeanor that postured, and he was naturally very loud.

"Yes, yes. Mrs. Garza is doing fine. We've got some hurdles to overcome, but nothing that can't be tackled with a couple of good techniques." Mr. Joffrey stared down at his food, too old to even care how intimidating Art was attempting to be.

"Well, I don't wake up thinking I want to be fine. And fine isn't what I want for my wife. I wake up wanting to be great, and that's what I want her to be doing: *great*. I want her progress to be *great*." Art scooped a spoonful of vegetables into his mouth, his breathing loud and uncomfortable, and his hands shaking. He evidently had a lot to get off his chest and the room suddenly shifted. There was tension, plenty of it.

Annie dropped her fork at Art's sudden change of mood. She had no idea where this was coming from, but the confrontation made her squirm in her seat. Her voice was incapable of forming words to get her husband to stop the nonsense. *Art, please don't do this. Not to Mr. Joffrey*, she thought.

True to himself, Mr. Joffrey moved slowly and spoke in a

more controlled manner than Art had expected. "Well, Art, I've worked with students like Annie in the past. I wanted to tell you sooner but couldn't find the right moment. And now's as good a moment as any, I suppose." Mr. Joffrey cleared his throat and handled the confrontation quite well. "I find that, in my personal and professional opinion, Mrs. Garza may have some sort of eye condition that inhibits her from seeing words on a page correctly."

"Are you saying she needs glasses?" Art took great offense to this, not because getting Annie glasses was unreasonable, but he felt as though Mr. Jones was making an excuse for his lack of teaching abilities.

Mr. Jones pushed his glasses up again as he slowly chewed through the meatloaf. "Not exactly. Her progress is incredibly slow compared to what is anticipated for someone at her age. Her eyes need to be looked at by a physician because she isn't progressing how she should be. I don't know the answer as to why she isn't grasping the letters, but it's become apparent that it's out of my control."

Both Art and Annie had completely lost their appetite. Annie's heart fell to the floor in embarrassment and Art couldn't control his anger and defensiveness to protect his wife. "You're telling me, that you, a man with no medical expertise, is diagnosing my wife with a disorder because she isn't progressing to your expectations? You're a shitshow of an old hag teacher. Get out, and don't come back." It was only then that Mr. Joffrey realized the severity of their conversation.

"No, Art, you don't mean that!" Annie started yelling at her husband for the disrespect he was showing her teacher. "No, Mr. Joffrey, please don't go. Please." Annie stood up to grab her husband's shoulders and physically shake the anger off him.

Mr. Joffrey kept his gaze low and he steadily gathered his belongings. He headed out to his peaceful house to finish his most recent puzzle of sleeping cats, and spend time in solitude with his lovely wife. Annie continued tugging at Art's shirt, begging him to retract his statement of firing her teacher.

"How can you do this to me, Art? Please don't have him leave, please, please. I beg you." Art looked down at Annie as she pleaded on her knees for his grace.

"Get up, now," Art demanded as he studied Annie's crying face. "You are not a dog, nor will you act like one. Not in this house."

Mr. Joffrey walked home peacefully that evening, although he was saddened by the fact that he had unintentionally offended Art so badly that he could no longer continue working with Mrs. Garza.

Many mornings and nights had come and gone, but the pain of Mr. Joffrey's words still left Annie's heart raw like they did weeks ago over dinner. On this brisk March evening, she was alone on the sofa eating dinner: a mediocre caldo de res with a few homemade tortillas.

Nearly three weeks had gone by since Annie had spoken to another person. With Art away at sea, the solitude was wearing her down. The voices in her head were getting louder and louder, deprecating her entire existence. Her soup spoon twirled around the bowl, dinging the sides lightly, as she hoped to force a desire to eat.

You're so stupid. You're such a loser. No one loves you. No one is there for you. God hates you. You're alone. Not even your own dad wanted you. You're dumb. You're fat. You're ugly. You'll never be smart. You'll never be able to read a book. You'll never become an author. Marco, that bastard of a father, was right. I'm too fucking stupid to learn. Maybe he knew this all along, maybe he was stupid too and was trying to protect me from all this anguish.

Tears escaped Annie's eyes and dropped silently into her soup. She looked around and across the hall caught sight of the yellow notepad and papers, all her hard work of practicing letters and numbers, covering the dining table. Then the anger that had been building swallowed her whole.

A loud yell escaped her soul. Not a scream of fear, but something much deeper. Every ounce of her body was releasing the frustration and anger and disappointment she felt in herself. *Why was this so fucking hard?* she thought. Her husband, her friends, her teachers: they all believed in her and cheered her on. But she was not progressing, and she knew deep down that her biggest fear had been validated by someone she trusted and respected: something was wrong with her.

In an instant, the crying stopped. With a craze in her steady green eyes, she walked into the kitchen, placed her food on the counter, opened the cabinet door to the right of the stove, and grabbed a dinner plate. One by one, Annie threw the glass plates forcefully onto the tile floor; it was as if time had stopped. With each plate she smashed, anger released from the pit of her soul and a wail escaped her tiny frame.

Minutes later, Annie awoke from the possessive anger that had overtaken her body and found herself curled up on the closet floor. She remembered running out of plates, but not how she ended up here. Her senses heightened, the carpet felt itchy on her soft face, her eyes adjusted to the deep darkness of the enclosed space, and her tongue felt scaly and dry. She continued to cry into the night. Sobs that were inconsolable that sounded purely painful. Not cries of pity or frustration, but the cries of a broken heart.

Through the crack of the closet door, the morning light gently touched Annie's face. Her head throbbing slightly, her eyes heavy and puffy, she stood up slowly and slid her feet across the clean carpet and into the bathroom. The cold tile floor sent shivers up her heels and into her legs, back, and arms; her body felt weak and tired.

Pulling back the plastic shower curtain, Annie mindlessly turned the large silver knob to draw herself a warm bath. As she undressed, she stared at the floor, trying to shake off the trauma that her body had endured the night before. As she stepped her right leg into the porcelain tub and it grazed the water, her skin recoiled and her foot instantly retracted. It was far colder than she had anticipated, but the brisk water was bringing life back to Annie's face. Slowly immersing herself into the bathtub, Annie's body was shocked as it took in the cold from every angle: her mind blank and her body motionless, shivering. Her body eventually adapted, and she ran her hands over her eyes, hoping to decrease the purple bags and puffiness that accompanied her morning look.

Her mind wandered to another place, as it had many times before. A moment of peace and joy. She started singing a song Mama Jo used to sing out in the fields. Annie's eyes were closed as she pictured the both of them laughing and singing, singing and laughing. Oh, how Annie had missed her. She hummed quietly and lay in the tub reminiscing about all the warmth and protection Mama Jo had provided.

"Anything is possible, little Annie," Mama Jo had said while she sweated in her black overalls, green undershirt, and big straw hat in the early morning heat.

"But not everything is possible. Sometimes things just don't happen," Annie had said, remembering that she had been far more snarky-sounding than she had intended. She was young at the time, so she hoped Mama Jo understood.

"Well, Annie, with an attitude like that ya absolutely right. Nothing'll ever be possible if ya always limit yourself. Remember, if ya want something bad enough, ya gonna figure out a way. And no one, absolutely no one, will stop ya."

"You're right, Mama Jo. You're right. I guess I can do anything I want to do."

"That's true, Annie. Now tell me, what's something ya want so badly that if there were no limits in this world ya would do it right away?" Mama Jo asked, continuing her lesson on drive and persistence.

"You know how you always talk about the kids in school?"

"Yes, child. What about them?"

"Well, those kids are smart. And I want to be smart so badly. More than anything in the world. And you know what I think the smartest people in the world do?"

"Now what is that, Miss Annie?"

"They write stories. They read and write until their minds explode because their brains are so big that they learn everything they can and then they write it all down."

"Well, sounds like ya wanting ta be an author one day."

Annie smiled a hopeful smile as she continued picking cotton, sweat dripping off her nose and into the basket. "I guess so, Mama Jo."

"Annie, don't ever, ever let anything stop ya. Ya gonna get out of this mess, and ya need ta go and reach for the stars, child. And don't worry, we'll be here cheering ya on."

Annie laughed out loud thinking of this conversation from nearly fifteen years ago. *Boy, what would Mama Jo say if she saw me now?* Annie thought. *She'd probably be devastated and so sad for me—to find out that not everything is possible. Turns out something's wrong with me and I'll never have my deepest dreams come true—I'll never be smart.*

Then, in the depth of her sadness, Annie envisioned Mama Jo cheering her on to keep on going, to keep on fighting. And that's exactly what Annie did.

Drying off after the bath, Annie knew that Mama Jo's words held true, even today. As bad as it hurt, Annie would continue to pursue her dreams. It would be a new day, and she would take the initiative to start her sessions back up. No more sadness, it was time to clean up her act—which would start by cleaning up the actual mess she had made in the kitchen.

Sweeping up the broken pieces of glass on the floor, Annie planned to go back to work at Uncle Clam's so she could pay for more tutoring sessions. She knew that if Art wasn't going to pay for her time with Mr. Joffrey, then she was going to find a way to make it happen. And if that upset Art, well, at this point she didn't really care. It was her decision.

Later that afternoon, Annie dolled herself up and headed out to the library with her purse, notepad, and a few of her favorite pens. It was only a fifteen-minute walk from her house, and with all the adrenaline pumping it felt like it took her less than five minutes. Each step Annie took toward the library, she envisioned her conversation with Mr. Joffrey. What she would say if he yelled at her, how would they engage? Would it feel different?

She walked into the brown-brick building. It smelled of books and cleaned carpet. The older woman at the front was busy hushing a group of teenagers while Annie headed straight to the back of the room. There, with his glasses resting on the tip of his pointy nose, was Mr. Joffrey.

His legs were crossed and he looked just as he did a few months ago: kind and gentle, old and fragile, smart and brave.

"Hi, Mr. Joffrey," Annie greeted him with a timid whisper. "I came to apologize for everything that happened. I was hoping that we could still meet up?"

Joffrey licked his finger and slowly turned the page before he even looked up at Annie.

"Hello, Mrs. Garza. I don't recall us having an appointment. Please, sit down. How can I help you?"

Annie pulled out the wooden chair and sat on the tuft of

carpeted seating. She put her bag down and leaned into Mr. Joffrey closely as if she had a secret to tell him. "Can we please start our sessions again. I'm sorry about everything Art said. He was just trying to protect me."

"Mrs. Garza, don't worry about it. Life's too short to sweat the small stuff. I'd be glad to start doing our sessions again, but unfortunately Mrs. Jones and I are going to be leaving town here soon. We're going to be moving in with our daughter who lives out in North Carolina."

A million thoughts a minute rushed into Annie's mind. *Why was he leaving? Why was he being so calm? How could this end? What should I do? Can I convince them to stay?*

"I understand. It's great to see you, Mr. Joffrey. I wish you and Mrs. Jones the best in your move. Thanks, anyways." Annie grabbed her things, took a deep breath, and headed toward the door, her shoulders still standing tall, proud of the bravery she had to even ask Mr. Joffrey for a second chance. There would be other opportunities, she just knew it.

Just as she reached the library front door, she felt a small tap on her shoulder. When she turned around, Mr. Joffrey handed her a piece of paper.

"Mrs. Garza, please take this. It's a recommendation for another former educator in town who I think would be a great fit for your needs. Please don't give up, continue pursuing your dreams. Her name is Rosetta Mendez, and the number is on the piece of paper."

Eyes wide, Annie thanked Mr. Joffrey and hugged him goodbye. As they released from hugging, Annie grabbed the piece of paper and headed straight to the payphone down the street from the library. She inserted her two coins, dialed the number as written, and waited anxiously for an answer at the other end of the line.

Her left foot tapped as the phone continued to ring. The silver coil dangling from the handset stunk of old iron.

"Hello?" answered a young male voice.

"Hi, I was wanting to speak with Ms. Mendez."

"Yes, just a second," said the voice, followed by a scream: "MOOOOOM, phone's for you."

A second phone connected to the call. "Hello, Mendez residence, this is Rosetta," said a confident-sounding voice.

"Hi, Ms. Mendez, Mr. Joffrey Jones used to teach me. He's moving to North Carolina and said you could help?"

"Well, that's great to hear about Joffrey. Kind man, isn't he?"

"Yes, he really is," Annie said anxiously, waiting to see if Ms. Mendez would accept her request.

"To be honest, I haven't been teaching in the past couple years, so I'm truly flattered that Joffrey recommended me. I've got a house full of kids I'm watching, but let me speak to my husband.

Between me and you, it'd be great to get out of the house even two times a month."

"Great, can I call you again next week? The pay is negotiable, and I'd like to get together as much as we can."

"Yes, that would be great. Please call again next week. I look forward to it. And what was your name again?

"Annie, my name is Annie Garza."

The two hung up and Annie was hopeful to continue her one-on-one tutoring sessions. Her road hadn't ended, just merely took a turn down a different path.

1966
TWENTY YEARS OLD

Sitting across from Annie at the dining table, Mrs. Johnson was sweating profusely, huffing and puffing with every movement. She was a busty woman, wearing a Pepto Bismol–colored dress and brown sneakers. The right-side lens of her outdated cat's-eye glasses had a large crack in it. Most notably, she smelled faintly of urine: sour and pungent.

"Well, to get started, I think you can tell me a little about yourself," she said in a loud rumbly voice, lipstick smudged on her yellow front teeth. "Why do you want to start these sessions and what is the goal? What kind of books do you want to concentrate on?" Despite how focused she sounded, Mrs. Johnson didn't seem to be engaged. She was busy blotting her clammy face and trying to suck back the ice water that Annie had served her. She kept shuffling through her big purple purse looking for something.

Annie started to answer, "I'm from Big Spring and—" but was abruptly cut off.

"Oh wow, new in town, huh? I remember when I first moved here with my husband. Military family. We moved a lot. I hardly had any friends, but it's so nice once you finally get settled in. You'll get settled in no time. Do you go to church? I used to go to church down the road, but it got a bit catty, if you know what I mean. So we're currently in the market for a new church, but there aren't many to choose from. Hopefully we can be friends, I'd love to have you over for dinner and we can go shopping and head out to the salon for a little fixing up. And our husbands can get together to watch a game. Oh, I just love the thought of that."

Mrs. Johnson's mouth kept moving. Her cracked pink lipstick kept Annie's attention. Annie thought, *She's loca. She won't stop talking.* And sure enough, Mrs. Johnson didn't stop talking. Poor woman was desperate for a friend, and with a mouth that moved that fast, it was no wonder no one would listen to her. It was evident that she had completely forgotten why she was called to be here in the first place.

"I'm sorry to interrupt, Mrs. Johnson, but can we—"

"Oh, please call me Jennifer. Mrs. Johnson is my mother-in-law and, well, I surely don't need to bear that burden right now!" She laughed nervously and popped a stick of gum into her mouth.

"Jennifer, we were talking about the goal of working together,"

119

Annie continued, frustrated that this was now the fifth educator whom she had tried working with since Mr. Joffrey left town and Ms. Mendez had turned her down.

"Oh dear, yes! Continue!"

"You came highly recommended by some of my husband's friends. They said that you could help teach me to read more consistently."

"Wait, what? Oh my heavens, no!" Jennifer laughed that obnoxious laugh again. "I thought you had books that I would read and then we would discuss them over lunch and, you know, occupy each other while our husbands were gone."

"What? You aren't a teacher?" Annie had some pretty odd interactions with potential tutors over the last few months, but this surpassed all the others.

"Yes, I certainly was! A preschool teacher. I cared for kids ages two to four. They're just so fun at that age. Taught for nearly ten years, but like I said, we moved a lot so it just became easier for me to be at home with the kids."

Son of a bitch. Annie was angry and appalled. She took a deep breath before speaking. "So, you showed up thinking that I would pay you for what? Being my friend? Just reading books and talking over lunch?"

"We all need friends, don't we? I just figured you were more desperate than most."

With that, Annie sat quietly fuming, the anger boiling up inside of her. Like an eruption, she stood up and pointed at the door with a scowl on her face while Jennifer gathered herself and her things, muttering small protests. They both rose from the table, and without another word Annie escorted the fetid and perspiring rent-a-friend out the door.

She slammed the front door shut, replaying the last five minutes in pure disbelief. Instead of staying angry, Annie went to the kitchen, grabbed her belongings, and went to Uncle Clam's. *There's nothing a good milkshake can't solve.*

The walk to Uncle Clam's was just what she needed. It was warm outside: seagulls were squealing loudly as cars bustled by. It was in these beautiful moments of peaceful walking that Annie would remember just how far she'd come. Progress was slow, painfully slow at that, but she could easily leave her wonderful home and walk to get a milkshake without a worry in the world.

"Annie, buenos dias!" Mr. Gutierrez welcomed her loudly as he swept the front entryway of the restaurant. "You're not scheduled again until Friday. What are you doing here?"

"I wanted one of your delicious chocolate shakes! Is Hannah working by chance?" Annie asked as she stood at the restaurant door.

"Yeah, she's taking fifteen. I'll go on back and let her know you're here," he said as he put the broom down and patted the sweat off his mustache with a small white towel. He was wearing his usual black pants and Port Isabel Tarpons T-shirt. That man loved high-school football more than anyone else she knew.

Hannah was walking out from the back sporting a short haircut and wearing bright-green tights under her uniform. Her smile always warmed Annie's heart: they were true friends, with totally different lives. Hannah worked in order to meet people and she enjoyed Uncle Clam's atmosphere; plus, she always found herself making great tips from the male customers. Annie worked at Uncle Clam's to try to pay for tutors who continued to fail her.

"Hey, sweet stuff, what's going on?" Hannah said, concerned. "Guti mentioned you wanted a chocolate shake so that'll be out soon." Hannah scooted her thin body into the plastic booth and placed her elbows on the table.

"Another bust today," Annie said as she wiped a previous customer's crumbs off the table. It felt like the harder she tried, the harder it became to connect with a reasonable tutor who was willing and capable of committing to teaching someone to read and write.

"What? No way. I'm so sorry, sweetie." Hannah moved closer to Annie, to give her a hug.

"I know, I wanted to scream at the one today, the worst one yet, but I didn't." Annie's face was growing red, and Hannah could feel the defeat radiating from her.

"Maybe it's time you just focus on other things. Or see a doctor, like that first old guy said."

Mr. Gutierrez brought over the milkshake with a smile and a nod, and Annie twirled the shiny spoon around to get a big spoonful of deliciousness in her mouth. The shakes were so thick she often ate them like ice cream rather than using a straw. Maybe Hannah's suggestion wasn't *too* inconceivable? Maybe she did need to see a physician for confirmation?

With a mouthful of chocolate goodness, Annie continued debating with her friend and mostly with herself. "Yeah, but I just feel like that's giving up. If I see a doctor, and if the doctor does say something is wrong with me, then what?" A small drop of chocolate dotted Annie's floral blouse, and she reached for some napkins from the silver dispenser to wipe it off.

Hannah waved at Mr. Gutierrez, who knew the drill and brought a second spoon over to the table. She smiled and thanked him as he whisked himself away.

"I'm just thinking there's got to be someone who can help me. Someone in this fuckhole of a town can help me, right?" Annie said, putting another spoonful of shake into her mouth.

"Of course. But, Annie, maybe this is a sign that there are other things you should focus on?" Hannah said as she too started to indulge in Annie's shake. "Why is this so important to you when you have everything you could need? You have a husband, great clothes, a cute house, you all seem to have everything anyone could ever want. Why is this what you're so fixated on?"

"I'm not fixated, Hannah. I just want to feel like everyone else." Annie placed her spoon on the table and looked at her friend in disbelief. "Do you know how hard it is to walk down the street and not know what all the billboards around me are saying? To be unable to pick up a book and get lost in the story? To write my feelings and express what is going on in my head?"

"I never thought of it that way. I didn't mean to upset you." Hannah said as she sifted for another chocolate spoonful.

"But I am upset. Nobody knows what it's like. I pretend like I know what I'm doing, but all I ever do is pretend. Pretend to understand some of the things people talk about, some of the experiences you all have. I *can't do that*, even if I tried."

"Well, reading isn't even that much fun," Hannah said, trying to find the right thing to say to her dearest friend.

"That's not the fucking point, Hannah," Annie said as she wiped her mouth with a napkin. "It's one thing to want to read, it's another thing to not even have the ability or opportunity to know how to. If you wanted to write a story, you grab a typewriter, damnit, and you put down your thoughts on paper. You want to try out a recipe, you open the cookbook and read it." Annie's breathing was speeding up, and Hannah realized how important this was to her.

124

"Annie, I had no idea, I'm so … "

"Sorry? You're sorry? Everyone's sorry, but no one understands and I'm so tired of being dependent on others. I have dreams too. What if I have more desires than just being a wife and a mom?"

"You're right, Annie, I'm sorry. I never knew that this meant so much to you. Especially after seeing you working hard at Uncle Clam's for all these months without writing one order down. You seemed unstoppable, so I never realized how important it was to you. It seemed like you could do everything everyone else can do."

Annie was speechless. Her mind was racing, as she was feeling slapped in the face by life once again.

"I love you, Annie, and we'll do everything we can to find you the right teacher. I believe in you."

"I don't think it's going to be that easy, Hannah."

"Don't say that, Annie. We'll find a way. Give me a minute." Hannah stood up from the booth and walked to the back. She finished her last hour of work, took off her apron, and spent the rest of the afternoon with her best friend.

"Let's get out of here, Annie. Let's go to the beach for a swim and an afternoon of fun!"

Before Annie knew it, Hannah was grabbing her sad and mopey friend by the arm and off they went.

One of the biggest reasons Annie had wanted to move to Port Isabel was the beach. Mama Jo and Annie used to make-believe what it would be like: sand between her toes, the intoxicating smell of the saltwater, the sounds of the seagulls and families laughing and enjoying music. Yet, in the years that Annie had lived in Port Isabel, she hadn't ever had the courage to go for a swim in the big blue water. Sure, she'd been sailing with Art, but that was different. It was just the two of them and she could wear her regular clothes. Today would change all that.

Hannah still lived in her parents' house, where she had everything you could imagine on the island. Her father was a successful businessman who spent a lot of time away. To paint a picture of how giant their house was, there was an elevator to take you to the different levels of the home. It was loud and smelled of iron, yet there it was: an elevator in a single-family house.

Hannah's bedroom on the third floor overlooked the beautiful gulf. It was painted a dazzling turquoise and had a vivid orange shag rug smack dab in the center. Annie's eyes always hurt as they adjusted to the brightness of Hannah's things. But they were all true to Hannah's big, brilliant personality.

Hannah ran into her room and quickly took off her pink uniform and green tights, throwing them on top of the bed.

Annie's eyes clenched shut seeing Hannah undressed.

"Annie, it's just a body, calm down," Hannah said as she peeled off her bra. Standing there topless, she was so damn comfortable in her own skin; so different from Annie. Pulling off her panties, Hannah grabbed her bright-red bikini and slid right in, looking at herself in the floor-length mirror.

"Hannah, I didn't bring a swimsuit. What if we just stay here and watch TV?" Annie suggested as she started to curl her body in, already feeling anxious, comparing her body to Hannah's.

"Don't be silly. You're tiny with a great rack, you can probably fit into one of mine from last season. Living here, I literally buy a gazillion swimsuits. One for every day of summer, of course!" Hannah wasn't lying. She opened the oak dresser and sure enough she had hundreds of colored pieces jumbled together in the drawer.

Hannah picked one out and threw it over at Annie. "Here, this one will fit you perfectly!"

Annie caught the green-and-yellow one piece and stood there, frozen. "Oh, thanks," she said, sounding anything but thankful. She walked over to the bathroom and stared at herself in the mirror. She didn't generally like people to see her body, but it was time she put that behind her.

This is what you've been wanting, Annie told herself as she studied the stranger in the bright swimsuit. Instead of being excited, all she could focus on was the scars on her arms and legs.

127

I hope Hannah doesn't ask any questions.

As soon as Annie walked out of the bathroom, Hannah's eyes grew big, seeing the scarring on her best friend's body. She couldn't help but stare, though she tried to be inconspicuous.

"Girl, you look amazing in that suit! You should keep it," she said overly excited, trying to overcompensate for the shock she felt inside. Although overwhelmed with sadness, she was also finding herself inspired by her best friend's friend strength, realizing how little she actually knew about Annie.

Annie smiled bravely. Inside, her body was curling over itself from nervousness. Her hands shook. Her head was spinning. This was it. She was going to go to the beach, and nothing was going to ruin this beautiful day with her best friend.

Carrying their towels and snacks, the two women walked through the glass back door and out onto the lawn. Hannah grabbed Annie's hand and started to run toward the water, pulling Annie along until she picked up her own pace. As their feet hit the hot sand, Annie's heart melted. She looked up into the sky and felt Amá smiling down on her.

A loud laugh bellowed out of Annie's tiny body without a worry in the world. The women dropped their things and headed straight for the brisk saltwater.

Still holding Hannah's hand, Annie screamed like a little girl as the water hit her legs. "Muy frío, es muy frío!" she yelled, squealing with joy.

"Let it out, Annie!" Hannah hollered from the top of her lungs. "Just scream and let the world know that you are smart, you are amazing, don't bottle it up!"

Annie screamed and laughed and hollered. The two women splashed each other for what felt like hours. As their bodies tired, they set up their towels side by side and napped under the warm sun.

"Annie, it's a little hot, are you okay? Do we need to go back in the water?" Hannah asked as she looked at Annie all flushed and sweaty.

"No, this feeling reminds me of being back home. I can handle the heat. This is nothing."

Hannah smiled and they rested for the remainder of the afternoon, letting Annie's sorrows drift away. Their friendship was so unique and special, and so very important. Annie realized that sometimes in life, it's not about having friends who are just like you. It's about having friends who will sit with you and carry you out of your trenches and into a world that feels lighter just because they're there with you.

PART II
AUSTIN, TEXAS

2009

The pink house at 1305 was on its eighth consecutive month of being awarded the HOA's Yard of the Month. For as much as the HOA dues cost, you'd think they'd be able to afford a nicer lawn sign, but it wasn't as much about the sign as it was about the pride. 1305 had the greenest St. Augustine grass, with an assembly of elephant ears, caladiums, and banana trees aligning the edge of the house. The yard was perfectly manicured, trimmed and treated, every blade of grass upheld.

In the evenings, families walked their dogs and young children wiggled their bicycles down the concrete sidewalk. Admirers from around the neighborhood would ask questions about the secret techniques used to maintain 1305's impressive yard; secrets that are still kept to this day. As beautiful as the house was on the outside, it was a fucking riot on the inside: four kids, two distraught parents, a busy grandma, and an unfinished renovation from 2007.

2009 had been filled with a lot of darkness: a year full of yelling, fighting, crying, more fighting, and the big "D" being thrown all over the place—*Divorce*. The source of all these problems came from my family's bad financial planning and no money to cover the gaps. It went something like this:

Both of my parents being laid off caused them to be late on the house payment. So, to avoid being late on the next house payment, they'd pull out a loan to cover it. Then, we'd be late on paying the loan payment that paid for the house payment, then we'd be late on the car payment trying to cover the loan payment. This cycle continued until we'd result in getting, you guessed it, another loan. Bills dictated every ounce of our lives and it was the desperate need to keep a roof over our heads that made loans appear so damn tempting. By Christmastime, we'd end up losing our family home at 1305, our family's cars, and every day I just prayed for a way out. I wanted something positive to have in our lives despite this chaos, before we became homeless living out of my aunt's garage.

It was a cold October evening and my five-foot-two stature strutted an oversized gray Nike T-shirt and black spandex shorts, with my long brown hair sitting on top of my head in a sloppy bun. My demeanor was as defeated as anyone would be in my situation. We only had a few more weeks left in the house before we'd be evicted. Belongings I'd grown so fond of were boxed away or thrown in the trash, preparing for our homelessness. At times I became so sad that the only thing I looked forward to was checking the mail and enjoying the evening sounds of crickets and kids playing.

As I walked to the mailbox, I quietly looked up at the stars and asked God why my family had to be in this situation. I wanted to cry, but had no tears left to shed. My heart was turning bitter, a bit sad, and I became more and more isolated. Our life circumstances were not something we shared with other people; it was private and no one needed to know the pain of what we were experiencing within the walls of our beautiful home.

By the time I arrived at the mailbox, a small breeze brushed my face. I took the tiny gold key from the large keychain and slowly inserted it into mailbox #4. As the little door opened, I peeked inside to see an overwhelming number of flyers, furniture magazines, and then at the bottom was a large manila envelope. I fingered my way through the mail until I realized the envelope had my name on the front. My heart dropped; immediately I knew what was inside.

I galloped home as quickly as I could, my body shivering from the cold and building excitement from within my bones. This was the moment I had been dreaming of my entire life. As soon as I walked in the house, I dropped the excess mail at the foot of the wooden front door onto the green tile. Time felt still as I stared down at the envelope and walked straight into the kitchen.

Slowly and unsteadily, my index finger slid across the top of the envelope, gently breaking the seal, my hands quivering in apprehension. I pulled out the thick packet inside and read the first sentence of the letter on top: *Congratulations! You've been accepted to The University of Texas at Austin.*

My head spun in disbelief and my body tingled with overwhelming joy. I kept reading the first sentence over and over again, making sure I wasn't imagining things.

"I'm going to UT, baby!" I shouted from the kitchen as my voice echoed through the almost-empty house. Like a stampede I heard my family rush from all corners of the house to congratulate me with hugs and kisses. As my siblings hugged me, I kept my eyes open for the back hallway, and slowly but surely my grandmother came over with a big smile.

As she squeezed me tightly, my nanny whispered in my ear, "I knew you were smart like me." And a big smirk crossed her face. We locked eyes and I knew I had made her proud.

In continued celebration, I ran into my halfway packed-up bedroom and turned my stereo on to play the marching band rendition of "The Eyes of Texas." I stood there alone, gripping the acceptance letter in my left hand as I raised my right arm up in the air with my fingers making the longhorn hand sign. My eyes were closed tight and I pictured myself living the life of a college student: studying, learning, evolving. I felt joy for the first time in so long, full of gratitude as the music vibrated throughout the house.

There was infinite relief in finally receiving the validation I'd been praying for. I knew that this was my opportunity to help my family and get out of this vicious financial cycle we'd been drowning in for generations.

As excited as I felt about being accepted into college, I knew that my family's situation of being evicted was just another strike against me. As we were celebrating in the kitchen, my father looked at the acceptance letter and sighed in disbelief:

"To accept, a first semester deposit is due by April 2010." What a mood-killer.

"Don't worry," Nanny said dismissively. "She will get the money she needs."

I'm not sure why she believed in me so much. I had no savings, no rich uncle who had left me millions, and, to top it all off, no driver's license, which made commuting to and from work that much more difficult. But my nanny was right. If there's anything I've learned from my parents, and especially my grandmother, it's that if there's a will, there's a way. I needed to spend the next several months creating a plan to ensure that I would be able to afford college.

My conflicting emotions from joy to strategic thinking kept me occupied for the remainder of the evening. It was a tug-of-war with myself. I pulled out my green journal and at the very top wrote *If there's a will, there's a way* and jotted down all the topics I felt I needed to research in order to accurately calculate my college finances.

Being the first in my family to attend college, I had no idea what to expect—truth was, no one in my family knew what to expect either. It's not that they didn't want me to succeed, it's that I knew I needed to depend on myself to make it happen.

For weeks after receiving my acceptance letter, I spent every moment manipulating numbers, estimating paychecks, and calculating expenses. I'd get online in the middle of the night and look for jobs that paid the best with the smallest amount of experience. I'd research and compare how much insurance would cost for the car I had been illegally driving the past five months. I'd research how to afford used tires so that I could make it to and from work. I'd Google "used books for college" and "FAFSA."

Every scholarship possible I'd apply for, which was far more time-consuming than one would have hoped. Being at a big school like UT, I was far too average to get any special recognition or scholarship. That didn't stop me from applying though. I applied for everything imaginable—left-handed scholarships, athletic scholarships for sports I'd never even heard of, let alone played. There were even scholarships for new ideas to contribute to society; hell, I even tried to pitch a new business idea. When I wasn't filling out scholarship applications at the library, I was applying for jobs.

Of course, 2009 was a rough year in the Austin market. We weren't the only family who lost our home and so many employers were spending more time laying off workers than bringing in new talent. From personal assistant to nanny to waitress, I applied for nearly a hundred different jobs.

My inbox flooded with rejection letters to my scholarship applications. Each one I deleted with a little more angst than the one before. I became numb to the rejection and wondered what type of person would actually qualify for these scholarships if I wasn't able to.

Day in and day out, I would remind myself of the seven little words that kept popping up in my head: *If there's a will, there's a way.*

"Thank you so much for the opportunity." I would smile and nod as I finished yet another job interview. As I walked away, I would pray that this would finally be the last one.

"No, I don't actually have any experience serving, but I am a quick learner and very coachable." I tried to convince yet another restaurant manager that I could be a fit into their food family.

"I don't have any CPR training, but I'm great with kids. The eldest of four in my family. I can be as structured as you need me to be and I'll be sure to adhere to your parenting style." Parents were always my worst nightmare with their ridiculous expectations. *Are YOU CPR certified?* I wanted to ask them.

Rejection is an ugly beast, but I had learned from my nanny how to work hard; all I needed was the opportunity to show an employer that I was worth the investment.

I had only ten months to prepare for my first semester of college, and I was hell-bent on finding a way to pay for it, no matter what. My family is not built on quitters and sure enough— if there's a will, there's a way.

2010

got the job! Working as a gym janitor wasn't a particularly sexy career. No one loves waking up to scrub a toilet and take out an overflowing trash can, but my grandma has been a janitor for many years and anything I could do to be more like her was a win in my book. People would often ask me why I was so happy all the time, and the truth was, I wasn't happy, I was grateful. Grateful for a job, grateful for the future, and grateful for life. Without this job, my life wouldn't have been the same. The day they hired me, I promised myself to be their best employee. I wanted job security and outworking my coworkers and bringing a positive attitude was my only key to perseverance. I may not have been their smartest worker, but I knew I would work harder than anyone else they'd hire.

My first few months on the job were eye-opening. As I was

cleaning stacks of paper behind the front desk, I came across the gym membership fees. The cost was close to $350 a month, private lessons were $100 an hour, and that didn't include the luxury workout wear that everyone invested in at $80 a sports bra. I didn't realize people lived this way and it fascinated me. I wanted to learn and dissect everything about their lives. Not because of wealth, but because this kind of lifestyle was so new to me.

I wanted to learn how they made money, more importantly, how they managed it, and where did they learn to manage money? Who knew that working as a janitor would lead to so many questions that piqued my interest.

I wanted to find the courage to introduce myself to these clients and learn about them, but it was so daunting. *There was this invisible wall that told me people with this much money would not want to associate with someone like me.* The little voice inside my head said, *Keep to yourself,* but I tried to ignore it. I knew that eventually I would meet members of the gym and I made it my goal to do so. Sure enough, it only took me three months to make it happen.

It was the middle of summer and I had been running in and out of the gym taking out the trash, mopping the lobby, and I was sweating profusely. Not the cute glistening sweat, but the kind where your hair looks all frizzy and your upper lip carries a disgusting wet mustache. Yeah, that kind of sweating. Anyways,

I was mopping the lobby with the fabulous yellow bucket and watching a group of spunky women workout in the far corner of the gym. They snickered in their little Lululemon sports bras and spandex while they ran circuits and timed one another on their fancy watches. It was nice to see people have fun for a change. I was so used to the negativity at home that sometimes I lost sight of what life was really about.

As I watched them, I knew that my work here would pay off. After attending college, and graduating, I would be able to work out at a gym like this without a worry in the world. Not as a free perk (all employees could use the equipment) but as a paying, high-end member. I appreciated the exterior motives like this. I wasn't jealous, merely observing women with a totally different lifestyle, one that I wanted to achieve.

"What's got you all wound up, buttercup?" Brad, the owner of the gym, approached me calmly with a concerned look in his bright sea-colored eyes. He was small in stature with thick salt-and-pepper hair and a smile as big as Texas itself. Always standing confident and alive, his aura helped snap me out of my daze and brought me back to reality.

"Hi! Yeah, sorry. I was watching those girls work out. Gosh, they're so fit! I was thinking of introducing myself since I know they work out here a bunch."

"Yes, you should! They go to UT so that'll be perfect for you.

Put the mop down and go say hi," Brad said as more of a command than he probably intended.

"No, no, I'll wait until I'm dressed a little nicer. I'm a hot mess today." I was wearing my red gym shirt and gray Nike shorts. And in case you forgot, that ponytail on my head wasn't looking too good with all the frizzies everywhere.

Brad wrapped his arm around my shoulders gently, as if giving me a side hug. As I was under his wing, he started walking me toward the end of the lobby. I dropped the mop out of discomfort, not knowing where to put it. We walked side by side as if in a three-legged race across the gym floor, growing closer and closer to the three ladies. I could smell his delicious cologne and feel his warm energy permeate through my body and almost forgot what was happening.

"Hi, ladies, I wanted to introduce you to a great employee of mine." Brad was talking to the group with such ease and confidence. He gave me no time to contemplate my outfit and my sweaty hair. Honestly, I was horrified. "She's attending the university in the fall and I wanted y'all to connect. I think y'all will be great friends." Brad winked at me slyly as he walked away.

Without skipping a beat, the tall young woman wiped her hands on her plush pink towel and kindly held it out for a proper introduction. I stared at Brad, feeling helpless. I may have mouthed

143

the words *"I hate you."* Even in the middle of a full workout, these women all looked fabulous with their big eyelashes and sparkly blush.

"Brad, thank you!" one of the ladies shouted as he headed back to his office. Her big brown eyes twinkled as she genuinely looked excited and interested in learning about me. "It's nice to meet you! My name's Whitney, and this is Rachel and Capri. What classes are you signed up for this coming semester and what's your major going to be?"

"Hi, it's great to meet y'all too," I said as I stood there pigeon-toed and my arms dangling. "I saw you and your friends working out from across the gym. Y'all are really going hard." I could feel my face blushing out of pure nerves. "I wasn't being creepy though, just recognizing all the athletic moves over here." *Get it together, stop rambling,* I told myself as I continued talking. "I'm going to be taking the basics—general freshman courses: English, math, chemistry, and two others that I can't remember right now. You?" I spoke so quickly I felt like I was talking a thousand words a minute.

"I'm an English major, hoping to attend law school in the next couple of years," said Whitney. My eyes grew three sizes. *She was going to be a real lawyer, that sounded so prestigious and intimidating and how freaking cool?* "So, how often do you work out here, maybe we can work out together sometime," Whitney looked like she could whip anyone in shape. She had so much bubbly energy and was full of fire. I doubt I'd last five minutes in her guidance.

"Oh, no. I don't actually work—" *out here.* I couldn't finish my sentence before it was interrupted by someone yelling my name across the gym.

"A, we got some vomit. Can you please come help?" Tyler requested my help from behind the front desk. His high-pitched voice could be heard a mile away.

My face couldn't get any redder at this point. "Sorry, Whitney, I'd love to catch up next time. But duty calls." I laughed uncomfortably and ran quickly across the gym floor. She nodded, and the departure took me out of my complete and total embarrassment.

As I mopped the vomit from the lobby, Whitney and her two friends waved goodbye and drove off in their luxury SUVs. I waved, overexcitedly, trying to compensate for the fact that I was a janitor at the gym they attended. I was generally unashamed of myself, but at that moment I definitely wanted to be anyone but me.

Though there were tough interactions like my first with Whitney, Capri, and Rachel, that summer working at the gym was one of the most rewarding summers in my life. I worked hard to meet people who lived different lives than I did and were from different socioeconomic backgrounds. Instead of being intimidated by the unknown, I embraced it, with the help of Brad and some of the other coaches I worked with. My coworkers helped create this bridge for me to not feel so inferior to others. It was the perception I needed to feel confident going into my first semester at college, not knowing what to expect. What I did know was that I could talk to just about anyone; and really, that's all I needed. I had made friends while cleaning the gym: asking questions about members' families, how work was going, how summer school was. I asked business owners how they got involved in their trade. I learned about their drive and commitment.

There were so many jobs out there that I didn't even know existed: a software project manager, supply chain management director, and risk analyst were among the topmost interesting, in my opinion. I loved learning about people and their stories, it inspired me in more ways than I could have ever imagined. It's not like I grew up in a box or anything, it was just that the only real jobs I was aware of were the ones that the school district shoved down our throats as children: lawyers, doctors, accountants, teachers, and service professionals.

By the time my freshman semester would start, I felt so confident. I had saved up enough money and met enough people to know that college wasn't going to be as scary as I had built it up in my head to be. It wasn't going to be an easy road ahead, but I was sure as hell ready to give it my all.

I was wearing navy shorts with a white button-down and brown sandals. My book bag was camel brown and my hair was pulled back in a low ponytail. I had arrived at my first college class fifteen minutes before it was supposed to start. As students piled up before the double doors, I began introducing myself, which went against every fiber in my body. Based on all the *Harvard Business Review* articles I'd read, I learned that in order to be successful, I needed to build a network of students who (to my assumption) were smarter and more capable than me. *Surround yourself with people who are smarter than you.*

The wooden doors opened to an auditorium that felt like a theatre. More than six hundred seats would be filled with eager students; I jetted to the front row, picked a seat right in the middle, and opened my notebook to a fresh new sheet while the students around me propped up shiny new laptops. I tapped my pen aggressively, fighting the urge to feel ill-equipped. My foot shook in nervousness, yet I continued to smile and introduce myself to students sitting around me.

Dr. Laude was tall and confident. The way he spoke inspired me and I could tell he was so passionate and brilliant about the world of chemistry. His jet-black hair was combed to the right side, and he had a somewhat Dracula aura to him. Towering, pale, formally dressed, and a little cryptic.

"Students, I hope you all had a great summer. I am going to need the results of your summer assignments by this Friday at 5:00 p.m.," Dr. Laude directed at the class in a low voice that matched his demeanor. I subtly began looking around to see the reactions of my peers. Were they as confused as I was? It appeared that I was the only one who had no idea about the damn assignment. This was a great start.

Instead of panicking, I tried to remain calm. I opened up my camel book bag, pulled out my 2010 school planner, and wrote neatly, *Complete Chemistry Assignment ASAP*. I hoped that the work the rest of the class had finished in three months, I could complete in just three days. Boy, was I wrong, so very very wrong.

I'd be lying if I said my first semester of college went well. I was barely holding on. I nearly failed every class and I spent so much time moving from one place to the next that I was never fully present, always filled with exhaustion. Little things that I took for granted in high school became so overwhelming to me. *How does anyone have the balls to ask a question with nearly five hundred other students in the room? How do I know what to study if the test is over nine chapters? Who can memorize nine chapters? How do people memorize where all their classes are? There are so many damn buildings I'm lost every minute of the day.*

It's not like I didn't try, I just couldn't get into the swing of things. I was constantly moving, working, studying, and every day was a battle against the clock. If only I had more time, I'd be able to get more done.

Everyone else around me just seemed to get it. They knew where to go and how to have an easygoing routine. Me, on the other hand, I felt like a crazy squirrel trying to plan out every minute of the day. I was so spacey that I even got lost finding my dorm room. No, seriously, turns out that I need to be told how to get places and I can't read a map for the life of me. The forty acres of campus felt like the Black Forest at times and my crazy schedule didn't help:

> 5 a.m. wake up and get dressed for work
> Work from 6–8:30 a.m.
> Sit in Austin traffic from 8:30–9:30 a.m. and eat breakfast in the car
> Fight for a parking spot in the closest lot near my class. (Cars would drive around like sharks waiting for someone to leave their spot.)
> 10 a.m. first class (usually late due to no parking)
> 11 a.m. second class (across campus)
> 2 p.m. third class
> 3 p.m. leave for the gym
> 9:45 p.m. arrive back home from work

> Shower, eat dinner
> Homework 11–2 a.m.
> Repeat.

It was a Sunday afternoon toward the end of my first semester of college. I had a painfully long day cleaning the gym, and an even longer week at school. Finals were around the corner and all I could think about was how much studying I needed to cram in before the big test tomorrow morning.

As I walked into my dorm room, shoulders slouched, smelling like sweat, I was greeted by my roommate, who was slightly inebriated. Her golden skin was covered in a shimmery pink bathrobe, her strawberry-blond hair was held back by a cheetah-print spa headband, her face was covered in a seaweed face mask, and she was holding a stemless glass of her favorite sauvignon blanc.

"I'm so glad you're back!" she shouted as I walked through the door and threw my bag on the couch. "I'm having the worst day imaginable!"

"What's going on?" I asked with concern in my eyes. I worried that someone had died as I'd never seen my roommate so distraught—though we weren't very close for me to know

150

otherwise.

"It's just." She sniffled as she tried to control her emotions. "It's that my sorority sisters didn't like the shirt design I submitted. And, and, they picked this wretched out-of-style bullshit. And it's mandatory that we buy it." She hugged me and sobbed as I stood there frozen. I would be lying if I told you I wasn't speechless. I felt as though I was on the scene of a housewife television show.

As she let go of our embrace, I could see the sadness in her eyes.

"Girl, that sounds awful. I am so sorry." I lied between my teeth as I tried to find this part deep within my being that could become empathetic toward her grief.

"I feel like no one likes me and they went against my design just because I'm the one who submitted it." She continued to sob inconsolably.

"No, that can't be." I rubbed her back calmly "What is it about the shirt design that has you so upset? It's just a shirt, right? Or am I missing something here?" I questioned her, trying to really understand where this pain was coming from.

"I am always left out. And I thought that maybe if they liked my shirt design, I would feel like a part of them. You know?" She stopped crying as she realized her face mask was melting off.

"I know. We all want to feel included," I whispered as I sat on the bed and held her close. "I'm sorry that happened to you."

"I'm sorry I'm crying like this. I just feel so lonely sometimes and it makes me mad because I'm doing everything possible to feel included. The other day all the girls had a study hall and I didn't get invited. I just sat there waiting and inching closer, thinking they'd want to include me. And they didn't."

It was in that moment that I realized we both felt the same pain of wanting to be accepted and cared for. I started crying too, realizing that what she was experiencing wasn't as foreign as I had once thought.

"Go wash your face because I can't decide if I'm going to keep crying or start laughing." I said as tears streamed down my face. It was the icebreaker we needed from our hot and heavy tears.

She laughed gently as she looked in the mirror and realized what a mess she was. It was a beautiful moment for both of us. I remember thinking to myself that I felt just as lonely and unknown as she had felt. Everyone is just treading water, day by day to get by. Her life, which on the outside seemed so much more glamorous than mine, was not far different from the pain I experienced.

Instead of studying for my exam that evening, I did something far more important: I made a friend. We each got dressed in our pajamas and shared deep stories of pain that we had been experiencing through our first semester. She opened up about feeling inadequate to the people she was surrounded by. I shared my overwhelming exhaustion from working constantly to make ends meet. We cried together, we drank wine together, and we talked about our lives and experiences.

We couldn't have been more different on the outside, but over time we would become the best of friends—a friend I so desperately needed throughout my college journey.

2011

The sun brilliantly lit up the empty gym through the large warehouse windows. Little specks of dust gleamed through the air while the artificial scent of lavender permeated the space. An eerie atmosphere filled the gym: it was never this quiet on a Saturday morning. But after a long week of school and work, it was nice to have a little bit of quiet.

Brad was in the back offices doing payroll while one of the gym's regulars, Kyle, worked out in the far corner. I made a point to walk around the lobby several times looking for things to clean and wipe down. My head moved back and forth a few times to see if anyone was watching me and, finally, I gave in and just sat behind the front desk.

My head was barely visible from the tall walls that protected me, like a queen sitting behind a fortress. The desk was large and gray, with several manila folders on top. I crossed my arms and placed my forehead on my forearm. Eyes closed, my pulse vibrated through my legs, enjoying the moments of relaxation and peace. It felt like so long since I had been alone with my thoughts in a quiet room.

My mind wandered off to a place where it didn't typically go. A desolate vacuum of unhappiness: wishing, wanting, needing. Wishing for more rest. Wanting to be somebody. Needing more time. The seedling of negativity grew into a suffocating forest. The reason I didn't give myself these moments of rest was because my mind didn't know what rest was. Even when it looked like I was resting on the outside, I often stayed silent not because I was at peace but because the thoughts in my head moved so fast I didn't know where to start.

Racing from one thing to the next: payments I was late on, things I forgot to do, and papers I needed to get started on. Like a volcano erupting, all the exhaustion caught up with me. I started crying behind the desk, in the comfort of those big walls protecting me. It had been a while since I had let out tears this deep and painful. So many thoughts consumed me: *How do I ensure that the decisions I make are the right ones? Is spending my last dollar on my education the right investment? Should I have settled for living a simple life with the kids back home? Am I living a life toward greed? Will all this work ever really pay off?*

Amid my heavy, painful, and quiet tears, I heard Brad's bouncy footsteps make their way across the gym floor. I shimmed up to proper posture and wiped my eyes excessively with the neck of my gym T-shirt.

"Woah, are you all right?" Brad asked in a voice that was far too loud.

I slowly shook my head and closed my eyes, insinuating that I did not want to talk about "it," whatever "it" was.

"Well, sweetie, it's empty here. Go home."

I stood up, nervous that he would think I wasn't working (which I wasn't, I had just cried for ten minutes behind the front desk). Though "trouble" never existed at the gym; it was just something I made up in my head. "Oh, I was just sitting waiting for more people to show. Bathrooms are already cleaned, trash is taken out, and I vacuumed."

Brad smiled a mischievous smile, knowing I was having a shitty day, or a shitty life—I'm not sure which crossed his mind. He reached into his navy cargo shorts and pulled out two long tickets that shimmered with silver holographic stickers. "You should get out of here and go to the big game. That's where everyone's at."

"What game?" I asked with confusion.

"Honey, do you live under a rock? The big game is today, you need to get out of here, get yourself dolled up, and go. Take these two tickets and have a nice time. I can't wait to hear how it goes."

Football tickets were so expensive at the university. It was a dream for me to attend a game, but with all the other things I had in my life, having fun wasn't one that made the top of the list. Swollen eyes and all, I gently grabbed those two tickets and hugged Brad with everything that I could. He laughed as I inhaled his calming scent of Kenneth Cole Black. He always smelled so good. That hug meant everything to me that afternoon. I grabbed my keychain from the counter and ran out with my belongings to the empty gym parking lot.

As I unlocked Oliver, my green 2001 Sport Ford Explorer, my heart pounded with excitement. Oliver wasn't the sexiest ride in town, but I was grateful for a fast getaway to get me to the game right on time.

I parked in the garage closest to my dorm and ran in my room as fast as I could. I knew I didn't have any outfits that would be game-day ready, so I had called my roommate on the way home to get permission to borrow an outfit in exchange for a free ticket. She was ecstatic!

I remember slipping on a blue-jean skirt and a tiny white tank top with a cute pair of cowboy boots. I was astonished at Jenny's ability to make me feel beautiful with the makeup she had. I felt so pretty that I even sprayed a little perfume for the special occasion. On top of my dresser was a package of facial tattoos with the longhorn emblem. Slowly and meticulously Jenny wet a paper towel and pressed the tattoo into my right cheekbone. She peeled the back off the tattoo and a big smile crossed my face: it was perfect! Returning the favor, I placed the tattoo on her face and felt my breathing stop. As we completed our looks, we glanced in the mirror together and winked at each other, feeling fabulous and hyped up for the big game.

The game-day atmosphere on campus was one I had never really experienced. Spending so many Saturdays away at work, I never realized how contagious the energy became. Hooting and hollering and throwing up the longhorn hand sign was a part of the culture. It felt so invigorating to just be walking the same streets as so many excited fans, students, and alumni.

As Jenny and I stood before the stadium, waiting to get our tickets checked, I looked at the seats that felt as high as heaven. The roar of the crowd continued to grow louder and louder over the incredible stereo system. I loved taking in every moment, every scent, every vibration of sound that hit my body.

Walking into the stadium I felt like a little sardine. Person by person filtered in through the concrete building to get to their assigned seat. I had jitters running down my body and no words could communicate the thrill I was living. I looked over at Jenny, who was leading the way; she walked in like she knew the place and suggested we hold hands to avoid getting lost in the shuffle.

The atmosphere penetrated my soul and built this energy

within me. No one would have known that just a few hours earlier I was crying my heart out at work.

"WAHOOO!" I shouted as we made our way to our seats. The energy was so positively overwhelming that I had to let it escape. A yell that felt so good and full of life. A few fans near us turned around and high-fived me. I'm sure they assumed I was a little drunk, but the truth was, I was just so overjoyed.

"This is what it's all about!" Jenny yelled over the pre-game music.

"Are all games like this?" I shouted back.

"Every single one."

I shook my head in disbelief as we stood in our seats at the fifty-yard line, Row 2. Though Jenny had been to several games, she'd admittedly never had seats this incredible before. We jumped up and down among the old and wealthy alumni who surrounded us.

We screamed the songs that played throughout the stadium and laughed at the commercials on the Jumbotron. Minute by minute the stadium continued to grow bigger than my mind could even conceive. More than 100,000 fans had gathered; some were shirtless with fat and hairy painted bellies and way too much alcohol running through their blood, while others were eating hotdogs as a family and wearing matching jerseys. There were a few fans who stayed rather quiet, but you could tell they had all the heart. They're the fans who have been cheering on this same team for forty-plus years in the exact same seat, year in and year out.

Jenny and I stood in front of our seats with big smiles covering our faces. Our bodies wiggled with excitement as we waited for kickoff. A drumroll ignited chills throughout my body as 100,000 fans proudly lifted our arms in the sky and showed off the longhorn hand sign. In unison, we all sang "The Eyes of Texas."

It was at this moment that I appreciated all the hard times I had been working through. This moment signified that there was something bigger than me. To commit to something I never thought possible. I was here in this moment, and this was the honor I had earned: to sing this song with so many of my peers.

Just two years ago I was jumping and screaming around my house playing this song on my stereo as loud as possible. I was finally experiencing this in real life. The Texas flag waving in the wind. I remembered what it felt like to get that acceptance letter. This was why I was here.

I don't remember much of the game that day, other than Jenny and I enjoying every second of it.

We walked home together, talking about our favorite moments. I knew I had to get up early for work the next day, but I did it with far more gusto and passion than I had before. I couldn't give up on my dream, I had to keep going. Not just for me, but for my family.

2013

During the fall semester of my senior year, I lived in an apartment off-campus nestled between work and school. Although Jenny and I were no longer sharing a dorm room, we kept in touch mostly through FaceTime since my schedule was still a mess. I missed her a lot, but I was fortunate to find cheaper housing living with two other UT students who excelled at baking. I could always count on the smell of fresh cookies and chocolate treats wafting through our two-bedroom apartment with its beautiful wooden floors, dark cabinets, and luxurious countertops.

The college semesters had flown by and little by little I excelled at my coursework. I developed strong time management skills and a knack for prioritizing. I was finally turning the corner to graduation. Seven semesters down, only one more to go. Next step was to secure a job.

My years working at the gym provided a broad range of individuals for me to learn from. Most notably, Angie. In short, Angie was a total badass. With the small interactions I had with her, I knew she had a feisty personality and never took anyone's shit. Angie was the queen bee of marketing and I yearned for her to be my mentor and inspiration. Based on the phone calls she had in the lobby, I could tell she was a mover and shaker of her industry.

Angie was a tall woman with wonderful curves. A short blond haircut and bangs framed her round face and bright-blue eyes. She always looked kissed by the sun and walked to and from the gym like she was on a mission.

After a year of building up the courage to ask Angie for an internship, I finally did it. She was one of the best things that ever happened to me.

In between working at the gym and school, I spent my time interning for Angie. I didn't do the usual things like get coffee and order lunches; Angie gave me the opportunity to fail. She challenged me in more ways than I thought possible and I am so grateful for that. I pulled monthly metrics from the sales team, learned how to pitch a business to a group of executives, and managed a small marketing project. What I learned most from Angie was how to be a great leader. She was incredible and the first woman I had ever seen kick ass in a work setting.

I wanted to be just like Angie, and it would be my dream for me to work with her post-graduation. Fortunately for her, but unfortunately for me, she got a great gig in a big city and I was still in Austin. There'd be hope for a position down the line, but Angie needed to make her mark before bringing in a new graduate. I didn't have that kind of time on my hands: I needed something secure and I needed it now.

In just four months I would be graduating with a degree in communications. Every day felt like one step closer to the finish line and no part of me was willing to give up this close to the end. I spent any available second I had researching entry-level positions that I felt I would enjoy and thrive in. I knew that the odds of college students graduating without a job was increasing, but I would not allow myself to become another statistic.

I sat on my bed staring at my references and praying for a win. I had a job interview over the phone in less than thirty minutes for what felt like a breakthrough position. As soon as the word *Amen* came out of my mouth, I started pacing my small bedroom back and forth, my thumbs rubbing against the outsides of my fingers as I squeezed them nervously in fists. Angie had taught me the importance of a good pitch, and I needed to perfect it for this call. I could hear it now: *"Welcome to our team, you're exactly what we're looking for!"*

I knew that I had gone above and beyond during my college years. Some of my classmates were looking for their first internship while I was nailing my third one. I wanted to get experience interning to apply my knowledge to the real world. Yes, it made my schedule a little more hectic, but I knew it was a sacrifice I wanted to make for success in the long run.

"—Ma'am, I'm sorry to interrupt you, but let me stop you here," said a cold female voice during the middle of my introductory pitch. "I think you need to do some more searching because my instincts tell me that you just aren't a good fit for the industry."

My jaw dropped and my eyes grew wide in shock. Luckily she couldn't see the look on my face. I had sucked all the air out in front of me. I could somewhat understand not being a good candidate for the position she was offering, but to say I shouldn't be considered in the industry felt absolutely heartbreaking. All I could mutter out was a muffled "Thank you" and I hung up immediately.

I lay flat on my bed as the air in my lungs inhaled and exhaled faster and faster. My palms were sweating and my face was hot, fuming with anger. *How can someone who has only heard me pitch myself for fifteen seconds claim that I needed to be in an entirely different industry?*

I have worked so hard to get here, to this single point in my life, and NOW I'm told that I'm not a good fit. Is this degree just going to go in the trash because I'm not good enough to serve the people I'm supposed to?

I was drowning in my thoughts. I kept tangoing with the feedback she had provided. On the one hand, I disregarded what she said, knowing in my gut that I would be a great employee. On the other hand, this person was a successful CEO of a marketing agency that achieved considerable accolades. Was I being stubborn by ignoring her? If this woman had made it and knew what it took to be successful, then I'd be a fool not to listen to her.

Needless to say, the interview was a bust. One big fucking bust. I would need to wait to hear back from the other seventy applications that I had filled out for jobs all over the country.

Luckily for me, I spent that evening enjoying a tub of 1905 vanilla ice cream and shared my horrible experience with my roommates. Nobody knew what to think of the wild encounter I just went through.

I knew I had worked through worse things in my life. Though this one was up there for "most traumatic." Mostly because I feared she was right. *Maybe I wasn't a good fit for the industry?*

As part of my therapy session that evening, I applied for more positions. I reviewed every line in my résumé and tweaked it to perfectly fit the job that I felt I would be a strong asset for. When I clicked *SUBMIT APPLICATION*, I would shout "Screw You!" to the CEO lady as if she could hear me. It's not that I *actually* meant it, but the exercise served my own ego, which she'd trampled all over. Sure, she was probably a nice person, but the fact was, I believed in myself. Or at least I needed to fake it until I made it. Even sometimes today her words still haunt me.

Also, I'm 99% sure all the applications I submitted that evening were a lost cause. I was far too angry to think straight—another lesson learned. Don't submit applications under the intoxication of an entire tub of ice cream. Noted.

Only time would tell if I was truly meant for the plan that I had cultivated in my own mind. Sure, it sucked not getting hired, but I felt it deep in my bones that the right job was out there. I just needed to be patient. And sure enough, I wasn't wrong.

2014

Hot water stung my body as I entered the steamy shower. My skin clenched tight as the water rolled down my back. I bit my lip, gently trying to prevent myself from losing control; a smile crept onto my face and my heart was beating faster and faster. A tiny shrill moved up my body and I finally let out a loud squeal. As I massaged shampoo into my hair, I danced to the beat of the music that played within my head. I was able to finally celebrate my hard work. Graduation day was here: I freaking did it!

Every movement I made had a little more pep than before. My cheeks were cramping from the large smile that was cemented on my face. As I exited the shower and toweled off, I imagined what I'd look like walking across that big beautiful stage. I wrapped the towel around my body, tied my hair up in a small wrap, and took my time prepping for one of the biggest moments in my life.

Delicately I painted every toenail for the first time in months, making sure every stroke was neat and smooth. I lathered on cucumber melon lotion onto my tan legs, arms, and belly. I looked at myself in the mirror and appreciated the woman I had become. I felt unstoppable.

As I blow dried my hair, I teared up thinking about every heartache and painful moment that I worked through to get here. I knew it was going to be hard, but I never imagined it being this hard. Sure, I missed out on parties, traveling, and studying abroad like many of my peers. But what I learned over the past four years was determination and perseverance unlike anything I could have ever imagined. There were so many times when I thought I was going to get dropped from classes because I didn't have the funds to pay for it. One semester I did get dropped because I didn't get the money in time. But sure enough, I grinded hard and graduated in four years. Hard work and a degree well worth it.

On top of graduating, I had also just landed a job that would set the foundation for a career I hoped to create in the marketing industry. INK was the perfect fit for me. A marketing agency working with some of the biggest tech giants in the industry and I was going to join their tiny but mighty team. Somebody pinch me, is this real life?

As I walked my way to the colosseum holding my cap and

gown, I knew that this moment was important not only to me but to my family. We would no longer be a family without college graduates. I would set the precedent that anything is possible: *If there's a will, there's a way.* So many students made the same walk that I had that afternoon. We waved at one another as we filled the streets all heading in the same direction, to complete that walk across the stage.

As I entered the Frank Erwin Center, I felt a sensation of peace overwhelm me. I knew my family would be cheering me on from the stands, and though they didn't know the intricacies of my experiences, they would get to celebrate one of the biggest moments in my life—and that's all I could ever hope for.

The colosseum was filled with so many people: some carrying large signs adorned with glitter, others holding the forbidden airhorns, all so proud of their loved one who was about to complete this huge accomplishment. Tears filled my eyes thinking of how important this was for me; to be the first in my family to get this level of education and to start a new legacy for the family members who were to follow in my footsteps. This was no small task, and something that was so much bigger than me.

I didn't graduate with honors, I didn't make a speech, I didn't even have all the fancy graduation cords that so many other students had. But what I determined that day was that I had grit. I had been able to push through more obstacles than I had anticipated to graduate in four years and land a dream job.

Walking that stage was everything I had hoped for and so much more. It all happened in slow motion, and I zoned in on my breathing and remembered all the things I had to be grateful for: being accepted into the university, Brad hiring me, Angie believing in me, failing and passing classes. With each step I took across the stage, the crowd grew wild for me (so I told myself) and I had a smile that was so big I could barely see straight. As I accepted my diploma and shook the hands of the headmaster of the College of Communications at The University of Texas at Austin, I looked out into the crowd and for the first time in my life, I felt truly proud of myself.

Oliver was barely holding on, but my trusty Ford Explorer got me to work forty-five minutes early on my first day. The three-story limestone house sat on the top of a beautiful summit overlooking the Austin hill country. I was way overdressed, but fortunately no one held it against me. The building smelled of fresh Mrs. Meyer's basil candles and the fun spunky interior colors had my heart melting in pure joy. At the top of the second story was my corner office with an incredible view. I sat at my desk in awe, staring at my yellow notepad and new work laptop.

The first day I couldn't stop smiling, I held my notepad open the entire day so I could take notes of everything everyone was saying, including their hometown, kids' names, and birthdays. I wanted to make a great impression and grow as quickly as possible.

I had much to learn and so much I wanted to take in. My manager was wonderful, stern but incredibly patient. She had a knack for writing and taught me the ropes of being a strong account coordinator. I had a long way to go until I'd ever reach her level of expertise, but I wanted to learn from her. I could see the way clients respected her and wanted to gain her perspective—she was brilliant. She made me think of Angie in a lot of ways, which was exciting to be surrounded by a bunch of badass women. A few rock-star men too! (There were only two men at the time of my employment here.)

Week in and week out I was starting to make progress as the new hire. I wanted to be the first one at the office and the last one to leave: something that wasn't difficult for me to do. Hell, I could finally focus on just one thing and it was pretty nice, to say the least. I wasn't having to run around town going from one place to the next. I just had to focus on the job at hand. In just a few months I had a pretty solid routine set. Some mornings were busier than others, but the days were always interesting and kept me on my toes.

It was a busy September morning at work. I had a massive

headache and I was trying to get a report delivered to a client by 10 a.m. As I walked into my office to shut the door and zone out on the timely project, I received a heartbreaking call. I had to leave work urgently. A piece of my heart was about to visit heaven, and I had to be there to say goodbye.

PART III

1967
TWENTY-ONE YEARS OLD

The phone rang for what seemed like an eternity before anyone picked up the other line.

"What?" an old man answered, irritation reverberating through his scratchy voice.

"Hi, this is Annie," she said. "I worked with Mama Jo in Mr. Brown's fields. Do I have the right number?"

"Little Annie, is that you? It's Robbie Jackson. How the hell are ya, shugah" He sounded more excited than he'd originally let on.

Robert "Robbie" Jackson was Josephine "Mama Jo" Jackson's treasured husband, and Annie had only heard stories about him and his contagious sense of humor. She'd never once spoken to him in real life, so this was quite the treat. Hearing his voice for

176

the first time made Annie's heart beat fast. She had finally tapped into the life of someone she missed so much.

"Yes, it's me. My friend helped me look through all the Jacksons in the phone book," Annie said. "Can Mama Jo call me when she's back from the farm?"

"Aw, shugah, I'll be sure ta tell her. She's gone be real glad ta hear from ya. Lot's changing around here, and I'm sure things are different for you too, over yonder. What's ya number, wait let me get a pen, let me get a pen, hold on there."

Annie listened to the commotion on the other end of the line as he kept yelling, "Don't hang up, hold on, there's a damn pen 'round here somewhere. Oh, found the pen, found the pen. Hold on, now, I need paper ta write down the number."

Annie laughed to herself, excited to share her number and hopefully talk to Mama Jo sooner than later. She repeated the number four times before Mr. Jackson got it right, but it was worth the effort. Annie felt one step closer to catching up with Mama Jo, and the thought of hearing her voice for the first time in years brought warmth to her soul.

"Thank you, Mr. Jackson. I'm going out with a friend now, but I'll be home tonight, so have her call me anytime. Muchas gracias and hugs to you and the family." Annie hung up the phone and squealed with joy.

"Told you we'd eventually find them! I'm so excited for you,

Annie," Hannah said as she lay in relief on the bright-blue sofa, her arms flailing above her head and her legs perched up to let her feet breathe.

"My heart is racing," Annie said with a giant smile. "I can't believe we called Mama Jo's casita. I hope she calls soon, we have so much to talk about." And then, with her big eyes looking sly, "Hannah, are you hungry?"

"Not really, but I can tell you are."

"Great, let's go to our usual spot. I'll grab my purse and you'll drive!" Annie exclaimed.

"I guess," Hannah moaned as she sat up slowly and patted down her blond curls. "Just 'cause I love you."

Every day was a fiesta at Los Deliciosos. The restaurant smelled of savory Mexican food: homemade tortillas with authentic sauces and spices. Colored paper lanterns were strung across the ceiling along with bright triangular flags in pinks, oranges, yellows, and greens. The wooden tables were small and had a single freshly picked flower placed in a clear vase with yellow napkins folded around the silverware. The waitresses, dressed in long off-the-shoulder white dresses embellished with green-and-red threaded flowers, appeared as though they were gliding across the restaurant floor while mariachi music played in the background.

Hannah loved trying new Mexican restaurants in town, but this was her and Annie's spot. Los Deliciosos made some incredible cocktails. The drinks were so good, the two women didn't even ask what was in them! Every couple of weeks, they would enjoy a wonderful meal while Annie caught Hannah up on the latest drama from Uncle Clam's as well as some of the juicy details of the affair happening at a house down the street that Annie cleaned twice a month. Hannah had officially left the restaurant business and was focusing on her nursing studies.

Annie enjoyed telling detailed stories and using her facial expressions and big arm gestures to demonstrate how dramatic the moments felt. She was an entertaining storyteller who could keep Hannah laughing for hours.

The two friends took a seat at their favorite table. Their young waitress, her dark hair pinned back and her beautifully smooth skin resembling chocolate, immediately served them water and chips and salsa. Annie instinctively added salt to all the chips while Hannah scanned the plastic menu for the thousandth time, even though she always ended up ordering the exact same thing.

"I just love eating here with you," Hannah said as she held up the menu in front of her. All you could see was her white-blond hair.

"You need to marry into a Mexican family so you can learn to cook like we do." Annie was always poking fun at her friend's inability to prepare a good meal.

"Add that to the list of requirements," Hannah said, putting down the menu. Her seriousness broke into a broad grin.

Hannah's checklist for the perfect man was one that always made Annie shake her head and think, *She's so crazy.*

"When you were little, Hannah," Annie began in a peculiar tone, "what did you imagine your future to look like?"

"Oh, I love these question games," Hannah said as she readjusted herself in her seat and popped another chip in her mouth. "When I was little, I wanted to be a nurse, fall in love with a doctor, then live as a stay-at-home mom and raise five well-behaved and smart children."

"You're almost halfway there, aren't you?" Annie laughed lightly as she sipped her water.

"Sure am! Just need the kids and the man. Not sure which will come first though." The two of them laughed knowing that Hannah had a pregnancy scare a few months back. "What about you, Annie? What did you dream of when you were little?"

The waitress walked up to the table to get their order. Sensing that these two women were engaged in good conversation, she asked, "Should I come back in five or ten?"

Annie said no at the same time as Hannah said yes. The waitress stood with a blank stare while Hannah and Annie laughed and wiped the salt from the addictive chips off their fingers.

"Yes, we're ready," Annie agreed. She could hear her stomach growling, wanting something more satiating than the appetizer could deliver. The young waitress pulled out her notepad and waited to write down their orders. Annie asked for an enchilada combo while Hannah requested the tortilla soup and a cocktail for each of them. The waitress repeated the order slowly, then nodded and walked back to the kitchen, returning a few minutes later with their drinks and more water. As the two ladies waited for the main courses to arrive, they dove right back into their banter.

"You know, when I was a kid out on the cotton fields, we would tell stories for hours. I would make them up and have all my family on the field laughing, saying I had the best stories they'd ever heard. I didn't know then how important it'd be to me, but my dream has been to write stories to make other people happier. Just like I used to when I was a kid."

"Annie, that cotton field sure did make an impact on you," Hannah said as she squeezed lime into her fresh cocktail, stirring it gently with the small straw so not to spill any over the salted rim. "Makes sense as to why you're always stressing about tutors, though. I didn't realize writing was so important to you." She took a large swirl of margarita in her mouth and swallowed, making a sour face.

"In the fields, Mama Jo would always tell me 'if there's a will, there's a way,' and I think of those words often. I just feel like I've done everything I can when it comes to learning to read. But who knows? Then I look at my life, and I see us eating a beautiful lunch, I have a good husband, a nice home, and I feel guilty for wanting more. And sometimes I hear you talk about how much you want to be a mom and stay at home, and that sounds scary to me."

"I mean, I want to be a mom, but that's after I have some of my own experiences," Hannah explained. "I still want to work as a nurse and learn as much as I can. I just don't see me doing that forever. I guess I know nursing is something that will be for me, and then my life will be focused on my family."

"Maybe." Annie compared that statement to her own life. What was *hers*? What did she do to make herself feel complete? Perhaps the difference was that Hannah was achieving her dreams, and Annie felt so very far away from hers.

After their meal, Hannah stood up and hugged Annie tightly. "I love you, friend," she whispered in Annie's ear. Annie whispered it back. The two of them always managed to have wonderful conversation. Even though Annie wasn't comfortable sharing her every thought, she appreciated the perspective of someone with so much gusto and experience. Hannah was similar to Art in that way.

As they headed to the car, Hannah could tell that Annie had a lot on her mind. Instead of pressing, she decided their time together should continue.

"Where are you going?" Annie asked as Hannah turned right

out of the parking lot instead of turning left toward home.

"We can't end the day without a little shopping," Hannah said with a big smile. "Let's go to Woolco!"

"But what if I miss Mama Jo's call?" Annie asked.

"Then you can call her again tonight!"

Satisfied with that answer, Annie smiled too as Hannah blasted the stereo in the small blue Pontiac. With all the windows rolled down, Hannah's blond hair and Annie's brown hair whipped around like crazy as the wind hit their faces.

Shopping that afternoon was wonderful: therapeutic in a sense. Section by section, the women fingered through nearly every clothing rack at Woolco. Clearance items, seasonal top picks, and home decor. With arms full of bright colors, Hannah marched confidently to the dressing room. Trying on outfits was like trying on personalities; she had to see if it made her feel a certain way—sexy, fun, cute, vulnerable, sporty. A lot of thought went into selecting an outfit: it had to be perfect and hug her body in all the right ways without being too revealing.

Annie took a more pragmatic approach. Clothes were fun to look at, to keep up with the latest styles and see how women presented themselves, but it all felt so excessive to her. More than anything, spending time at Woolco was a way to be out of the house; she didn't need anything, she just appreciated looking at all the items and supporting Hannah in her newest personality picks.

As Annie moved through the department store, the far-right corner, the children's section, was calling her name. Mindlessly, she walked over to the racks and glided her hands across the hundreds of onesies all coordinated by size and gender. A centerpiece of plush teddy bears filled a sectional sofa and posters of happy families adorned the walls. The soft fabrics tickled her hands and warmed her soul. She looked at her reflection in the mirror and saw her short body, brown hair, and the small salsa stain on her white blouse. Her mind drifted, dreaming of what having a family would be like one day.

They'd always be well dressed, she thought as she pictured them in the adorable ducky pajamas displayed in front of her. *When we go out to church, we'll even color-coordinate so that everyone knows we are a strong unit. And, good God, their manners will be impeccable, always saying "yes, sir" and "no, ma'am." None of that yelling in a store, and no tantrums. They will always obey without having to be abused like I was. Education will be a top priority; none of my kids will ever miss a day of school.*

Annie smiled to herself. *Maybe Hannah was right?* Maybe focusing on a family was the way to move forward. Surprisingly, her stomach fizzed with butterflies at the thought, her face becoming warm with love. But a part of Annie was still fighting back the idea that being a parent meant no future for her own education—for her own dreams.

She stood frozen in the baby section of the department store, contemplating these life-changing thoughts. Her eyes focused and face still, Annie gently rubbed her stomach and looked down.

"Hey, what are you doing over here?" Hannah interrupted Annie's deep thoughts.

"Just looking," Annie pulled out a small blue fuzzy pajama outfit to show Hannah.

"Ugh, my body just melts!" Hannah said. "I love this stuff." They both giggled and continued to browse through the store.

Around three hours later, Annie and Hannah made it out of Woolco with seven big white bags full of bright outfits. Annie didn't make any purchases, but after a full day of shopping and a big meal, she felt exhausted.

The car ride home was quiet as both women decompressed from a long but productive day of sifting through the phone book, catching up over lunch, and shopping for every occasion possible. Hannah dropped her off, and they promised each other they'd talk again later in the week.

Annie walked into the front entrance of her home and inhaled deeply the scent of vanilla, which made her tired body relax. As she took off her shoes, the telephone rang on the other side of the house. It had to be Mama Jo.

Annie went from zero to one hundred, suddenly having all the energy you could imagine to answer the phone in the kitchen.

Gripping the beige handset with both hands, Annie leaned on the edge of the kitchen table, waiting to savor every word Mama Jo had to say.

"Hi," Annie said as her face tensed in anticipation.

"Child, how are ya? I see you're making it out okay down south. It's so lovely ta hear that beautiful voice and sweet accent of yours again," said Mama Jo.

Annie's shoulders relaxed and she closed her eyes, picturing her Mama Jo.

"Yes, same to you, Mama Jo. I've been okay. I spend a lot of time cleaning, whether it be my house or a house of one of the neighbors. And I work at a restaurant, Uncle Clam's. I love it there, lots of cleaning and helping customers get their orders."

"Oh hell, child. Ya sound busy. Missing us in the cotton fields though, right?"

"Of course, missing you all every day. Oh and ... I got married! To a very smart, hardworking, and handsome man. I said yes on our first official date."

"Ya always had a way of taking life by the horns. He makin' a fine woman out of ya?"

"No, no, I think you mean I'm making a fine man out of him, Mama Jo." The two laughed hard. "I'm very glad I spoke to Mr. Jackson this morning to leave you a message. I wasn't sure if you were still working at Mr. Brown's or if you were finally at home."

"Annie, there sure as hell ain't no time ta be at home. I'm barely fifty-seven, or something like that—still got plenty of time out here. I hope … last week I done and fainted out there near the shed. Doc said it was dehydration and that I needed rest. Kept me in the hospital for damn near four days."

The image of Mama Jo lying on the hot gravel, her body limp and helpless, made Annie weak in the stomach. It was evident in her trembling voice that Mama Jo wasn't feeling well.

"In all the time I've known you, you never once took a day off. How are you feeling now? Drinking more water and staying in the shade, no? You need to take care of yourself, Mama Jo."

"Now don't ya come start babying me. I got enough of that from everyone else around here. Ya just worry about yaself, child. I'm fine. They gone have ta drag me off those fields before I throw in the towel. They ain't getting rid of me that easily."

"And los otros? Ruth and Grumpy Gerry?" Silence hit the other end of the line and Annie could hear Mama Jo sigh loudly.

"Gerry didn't make it much longer after ya left. He had a heart attack and died in his sleep."

"I'm sorry to hear that. Sounds funny to say, but I bet everyone misses his grumpiness," Annie offered.

"You know it, shugah," Mama Jo said. "He was one of a kind. Funeral was nice, and I still keep in touch with the family. Ruth is good, though. She still loud and crazy, ya know her."

Annie hummed in agreement. "I've missed you so much, Mama Jo. It's so great to hear your voice."

"I will say that it made my whole day ta hear from ya. When Robbie told me ya called, I couldn't get on the phone any faster. What else is keeping ya busy down there? Are you doing good, you happy?

"I'm doing okay."

"Okay? You didn't move halfway across the state ta just be okay, baby. Gimme the details."

"Well, I have a beautiful house, small but nicer than anything I could have wished for as a kid. My husband, Art, is a sailor, very smart and hardworking. You'd like him."

"What more could you want? Sounds like ya doing a hell of a lot better than okay."

"You're right. Remember when I was younger, and you told me that if I wanted to move I could make it happen?"

"Keep going."

"I started school a few years ago, and to put it simply, it isn't going very well. My teacher said I had something wrong with my eyes that made it hard for me to remember and read well. Just makes me think that no matter how hard I try, I'll never be smart."

"Hmm. Now, Annie, I have known you since ya was a little one, and if there's anything I know about ya it's that there ain't no quit in ya. Ya a fighter. Ain't that right?"

"Yeah."

"And there's nothing ya can't do. So if ya want to learn ta read and ya want ta get educated, then, damnit, don't give up. Ya gonna be a better wife and a better person for it. I promise you that much."

"You're right. Gracias, Mama Jo."

"Keep ya chin up, child. I can hear the failure in ya voice. Don't let that in 'cause once it creeps in, ya gone have one hell of a time getting it out of there."

"Mama Jo, can I tell you a secret?"

"Of course, child, ya can tell me anything ya want."

"I'm pregnant."

"I'll be damned, child! Congratulations! Though you ain't a child no more, but ya always gone be my child, now don't ya forget that." Mama Jo sounded so full of love. You could hear her smile through the phone.

Annie smiled so hard it pained her face. She hadn't told anyone else that she was pregnant and so many different emotions were resurfacing.

"I just don't want to let my child down. I want to give them more than what I had. I want to be a great, smart mom, and I want my kids to know I can help them."

"Annie, it's what's in ya heart that counts and ya got a heart of gold." Robbie started yelling in the background that he was hungry and dinner was ready. "Miss Annie, I want ya ta know, ya always welcome back here if ya ever want ta come by. I want ta meet my grandbabies."

"Mama Jo, we can talk every day now that I have your number. This won't be the last you hear from me. And I promise, once Art and I save up, we'll visit. It'll be a pretty expensive bus trip, so I'll let you know. And, Mama Jo, te amo, and I want to thank you for loving me."

"Child, don't make me cry. Ya something special, ya know that?" Mama Jo was sniffling on the other end. "Good night, little Annie. I'll talk ta ya tomorrow."

After they had hung up, Annie stood in the kitchen, staring at the phone receiver. She had a stillness come over her and a feeling of calmness flowing through her body. Everything was going to be okay, she was sure of it. She walked into the bathroom to give herself the celebration she'd wanted—a nice warm bath.

Steam was rising gently from the bathtub and the mirror was covered in fog. The silver spout dripped slowly into the bathwater. *Drip, drip, drip.* Annie laid her head on the ceramic edge of the tub and dazed off, looking past the shower curtain to envision the child she had inside her: she was no longer alone. She started singing and humming to the little one in her belly.

As her melodious hum drifted into silence, Annie closed her eyes to pray. It had been a while since she'd done so, but it was time; time to talk to the woman who she desired to talk to the most, her amá. It was only through prayer and guidance that she and Art could be the best parents possible. Now, more than ever, she felt complete. Yes, there were doubts about her abilities to be a great mom, but she knew deep down that she loved this baby more than anything else in the world.

"Amá." Annie opened her eyes and stared into the distance beyond the shower curtain, hoping her mother would reappear before her eyes. "Please guide me to be the best mother I can be. Allow me to be gentle and kind. Give me the strength to be an amazing mother and to get to be there for my baby. I wish you were here to guide me through everything. I love you so much, Amá, and I pray that you will be our guardian angel through it all. Amen."

Embracing the silence, Annie lay in the tub for fifteen minutes, listening only to the sound of her own breathing. But slowly, as she lay there envisioning her future, her confidence as a soon-to-be parent started to deteriorate.

Memories of her own childhood crept in, making their way into the serene bath. Flashes of beatings and cigarette burns to the skin overpowered her. The desire she had to be like everyone else and her shame in her education, or lack thereof. The fear started to sink in: *What if it was inevitable that she would become just like him? Was it even possible that those evil tendencies existed within her too? What if her children would be incapable of learning, just like she was? What then?*

Her face started to redden as she tried to push those feelings away. How she hated when the memories crept in, and she wished with all her might that they would just evaporate from her thoughts.

As Annie stepped out of the tub, she remembered a dream she had many years ago, where she had a beautiful family and kids running around—the family she would create, not allowing her past to dictate her future.

Blood wasn't everything. Yes, her father was an evil and sick man. He was, more than anything, a terrible father. But Mama Jo had taught Annie how to love. How to stay true to herself and follow her dreams. All Annie had to do was to keep Mama Jo's spirit alive. How she loved that woman very much.

Annie toweled off and walked to the bedroom, where she lay down and thought of the future with her family—a future where she committed to do anything to protect her children and to love them with every ounce of her being.

1968
TWENTY-ONE YEARS OLD

T he small yellow house in Big Spring looked as if it had been abandoned for years: cobwebs blanketed the porch and broken front windows were left untouched. Like an eerie warning, a dark cloud hovered over the place. There, in the front of the gravel driveway, sat a white 1960 Corolla. The house that used to be Annie's home was almost unrecognizable. It was no wonder Apá never had friends—his home was far too unkempt to welcome any visitors.

Sitting among low lighting with a cold beer was Apá, painted with a lifeless expression. The small color television was featuring a Houston basketball game, but his eyes and thoughts were focused elsewhere. It was as though he was ruminating in the past and escaping the present and future.

With arms full of groceries and luggage, Annie burst through the front door with her three beautiful children: all color-coordinated in navy blue, white, and red; their hair perfectly brushed. She had been anticipating this moment for so long. Her estranged father would finally meet his grandchildren, the children she and Art were raising successfully. Smart, well mannered, and full of energy.

Annie shouted a big hello to her father as she placed the groceries on the small kitchen table and started to peel the nervous children from her legs. This place that Mommy had been so excited to arrive at was new and uncomfortable to them. As all this was going on, Apá never stood up to greet them and his expression never changed—it was as if they were ghosts and didn't exist. Instead, he groaned, irritated at the inconvenience they were imposing on his quiet Saturday. Annie's heart started to sink as she realized his inability to even fake excitement— not just for her but for his own grandchildren.

"What are you doing here, Antonia?" Apá asked as he stood up to throw his beer can in the sink. Flies swarmed the nasty kitchen, briefly touching down on the pile of dishes and trash he hadn't cleaned up. His clothes were covered with stains and holes, so worn out, and his once handsome face had been marred by sadness and emptiness. Like an intruder, addiction had overtaken his soul; it started with the urge to consume one drink and made its final siege within the emptiness of his eyes. Annie could take one look at him and know he wasn't even there.

"Apá, I wanted to stop by for you to meet your beautiful grandkids. Kids, say hi to your abuelo." The kids didn't move from behind

Mommy's legs, but that was no surprise to her. She affirmed that the children would warm up to him after their shyness had dissipated.

Anger started churning in Apá's stomach. The pulse of his heartbeat was screaming in his ears, his face tingling from disbelief. With his jaw clenched tight and his hands sweating, he said, "These are not my fucking grandkids. You left me, and when you left, you cost me my job. So, fuck you and fuck your little family." He grabbed an empty beer bottle and threw it across the room. Everyone ducked in fear as it hit the wall and shattered. He continued throwing bottles aggressively, hoping to knock one of the kids out and scare them from ever returning again. It felt like they had walked into a war zone—even though their intentions were nothing but good, they were being punished for purely existing.

Annie's arms protected her children as they ran out the front door and into the cab they'd arrived in. She was so grateful that the driver hadn't left yet. Rage overcame her face as she got back out of the cab and ran inside the house to grab the gun stashed in the side table. Between her fingers, the metal felt heavy and cold. Without taking another second to think, she pointed the gun at her father, closed her eyes, and angrily pulled the trigger.

"Fuck you, Marco." She stood above him, covered in his blood. The rest went black.

"Annie! Annie!" Art shouted, attempting to awaken his wife from the paralysis of her nightmares. "It's just a dream. Wake up,

Annie." She kept screaming in the depth of her sleep, tears flowing down her face.

It was as if she'd been punched in the stomach a hundred times. Annie's eyes finally opened, and she fought to catch her breath as she sat up, her chest rising and falling faster and faster. Tears kept streaming down her soft cheeks, reminding her that everything she had just experienced wasn't real. She was here now, in her bed, at home. She was safe. Her newborn son in the other room, he was safe too, Art assured her.

She sat up, lifeless. Her body was physically exhausted: her green eyes ringed with dark circles, her face pale. It was the third time this month that Annie had been traumatized by nightmares that felt so real she often struggled to understand if they were imaginings or memories of her past life intersecting with the life she and Art had worked so hard to create. She once used to be so grateful for her ability to find peace and freedom in her sleep; now it was suffocating her with the past she ran so far away from.

She lay on her left side, pulled the blankets over her head, and felt completely numb. Though she had just woken up, it felt like she'd need another five hours of sleep before being able to function properly. Disoriented, distraught, and disgusted.

Art's large hands grazed softly over the comforter. "Annie, this can't keep happening. We have to get you help," he asserted, small brown eyes full of concern for his wife's well-being. "I'm trying to help you, but we're out of solutions at this point. It's out of my hands."

"Art, I'm fine." Annie pulled a pillow over her head to quiet him out and silently pray away the negative thoughts. *Why is this happening to me? Why does it feel so real?* Ever since the birth of her son, sleep became harder for Annie. Not in the normal way, which most new parents experience, but something far worse. Anytime Annie closed her eyes, she feared the nightmares that would take over her mind. She was becoming weak and vulnerable to bad thoughts.

As she lay there, she realized how much hatred she still had sitting in her chest. The way her father threw the beer bottle at her family, the way he sat there full of himself, unable to greet them as they walked in. All of this was made up in her dreams, but the anger, that was real, and she continued to fight it off. She reminded herself one hundred times that this was just a dream, but it didn't feel that way at all. In fact, it felt very real.

Becoming a mother was one of the best things that ever happened to Annie. The inadequacies of the world she would so heavily focus on in her past life, and sometimes in her dreams, disintegrated as she visualized the future of her family, particularly that of her son, Greg.

It was in these moments of peace, rocking her baby back and forth and back and forth, that Annie's heart would grow with love. As she'd soothe him to sleep, she'd envision a future for him: *Would he be a sailor, a teacher, a firefighter? Would he grow up to love his wife and be kind and gentle?*

Sitting on the wooden ottoman, she'd think of how far she'd come in this world and the overwhelming sensation of gratefulness would fill her body. She knew in these quiet moments that it was her amá watching over her, guiding her to stay afloat through the tireless nights of an infant's cry and her own battles of metamorphosizing into motherhood.

In an effort to help Annie adjust to her new life, Hannah would pop by when Art was away at sea to help out. She'd drop off a few groceries and watch Greg while Annie showered and cleaned up. It was always hard to get things done alone.

"Annie?" Hannah asked from the sofa where she was watching Greg sleep on the living-room floor. A thick pallet of blankets made a perfectly square bed for his swaddled body.

"Yes," Annie shouted as she toweled off in the bathroom, hurriedly put on deodorant, and brushed out her wet curls.

"Why don't we teach you how to drive? I think it would be so good for you to get out of the house with Greg. You know, go to doctor's appointments on your own time, get groceries when you need it, and just feel independent now that you have a child to look after."

"Are you planning to teach me?" Annie said, with slight sarcasm in her voice.

"Well, of course, Annie! We can pack up Greg when he's asleep and practice two to three hours a week. I promise it'll make your life so much easier."

"Okay, let's go now!" Annie said with enthusiasm in her voice. If she could have a baby alone in a hospital (Art had been at sea when Greg finally arrived), she could learn to drive down the street. *How hard could it be?*

Though illegal, she and Hannah spent hours in the evenings and on weekends navigating through the school parking lot with Art's old Cadillac. Carrying precious cargo in the backseat, Annie always made sure to focus and drive slowly. There was no way she'd be responsible for putting her son in danger. In just three weeks, Annie was confidently driving across town feeling, more alive than ever before.

1970
TWENTY-THREE YEARS OLD

Art's time away at sea had gotten the best of him. Promoted to captain of the shrimp boat, he started to drink more and struggled to adjust to life as a father. Many long nights ended with Annie and Art fighting over his behavior—and eventually calling Art's brother and sister to help extinguish the yelling. The fighting had to end or Annie would not hesitate to leave; the safety of her son came first.

Art suggested that in an effort to change his ways once and for all, he needed a new foundation for their family, one that focused on God and His ways. Art knew that going to back to religion would not only help him but could also help Annie with the terrible nightmares she continued to experience.

This particular weekend's car ride to the Hall was a frustrating one; both boys cried the entire time, their little bodies still recovering from a bad winter cold. Greg, now three years old, and Paul, his seventeen-month-old baby brother, wanted nothing more than to lie in bed and sleep. All the while, Art was holding a death grip on the steering wheel, trying not to lose his temper. Earlier that morning, he had tripped over a toy car that Greg had left out on the living-room floor, spilling half of his breakfast all over his new dress shirt. Annie sat silently in the backseat, exhausted, with her eyes closed as she sang gently to try to soothe her sons. The only thing that could make this morning worse would be to arrive late to the Hall.

Kingdom Hall was a long brown-brick building with two beige front doors and a brown roof. The beige doors were propped open, as they were every Saturday and Sunday, and two small women wearing ankle-length blue dresses and thick scarves stood there, smiling and welcoming witnesses into today's meetings of worship and study.

Annie let out a sigh of relief knowing that the doors hadn't been closed yet. She hustled out of the vehicle with the boys, Art trailing closely behind, still fuming.

"Welcome, bienvenidos," the women said as Annie and her sons walked through the doors. Inside the Hall, it smelled of old cologne and freshly vacuumed floors. The gray carpet did little to contrast the beige walls. Thankfully, the heater was on full blast so walking in felt like a warm hug. She smiled, grateful that her family was not late, and walked past the poinsettia arrangements and straight into the main room. Annie filed her small family into their usual seats in the fifth row.

Art would have killed me if we'd been late, she thought.

On the red-carpeted stage behind a wooden lectern stood an elder wearing an olive-green suit, yellow dress shirt, and checkered tie. As he began to speak, Annie's mind focused on his every word:

"Life is full of challenges," Elder Martinez said, beginning his opening remarks. "We cannot conform to the ways of this world. We are supposed to be challenged so that we can lean on our Lord, to save us and get us through these hard times."

Annie started to have moments of self-reflection. Her life as a mom was wonderful, she loved Greg and Paul more than anything else in the world. It was hard, though, to understand God and His will and relate it to her own life: *Why would God allow her to have been treated so poorly as a child? Why would God make learning so difficult for her? And why would God permit her nightmares to paralyze her for months at a time?* It was easy to get lost in reflection during the meetings.

"Lord willing, you can overcome all the hurdles in your life. The healing you experience is a direct correlation of your faith but can also be a precise demonstration of your lack of faith. It is when you truly believe, and when the Lord chooses to favor you, that you will be healed," he continued.

In her long gray dress with her curls tied back in a low ponytail and wearing no makeup, Annie listened attentively. Her thumbs fidgeted as Elder Martinez shared his words of wisdom. Sometimes she felt like the sermons were directed only toward her. Did everyone at the Hall know what she was struggling with at home? She continued to think, *God, I am faithful. I really am. Please allow me to be healed. Allow me to wake up and be able to read and be able to sleep comfortably. Allow me to be a better mom and a better wife.*

Annie and Art had been attending the Hall three days a week for the past three years. It was the only way Art knew how to get Annie help with all her nightmares, and Annie wanted to do whatever it took to feel better, especially for her boys.

Though a lot of the scripture seemed confusing to her, she did appreciate the guidance that it added to her life and it was nice having such a strong community associated with the Hall. This was the closest thing to family she had experienced since working in Mr. Brown's fields.

When Annie or one of the boys was sick, an elder or another witness from the Hall would stop by with a warm casserole. Or if money was tight, Art would be sure to tithe first, knowing that the Hall would step in and help them pay all their bills if need be. It was all a true blessing, but it didn't come without a cost.

The Hall and serving as a witness became the only focus in their marriage, in Annie's life, and laid the foundation for the lives of their two boys. You see, Art had made some bad financial decisions in 1967. He started gambling the family money, drinking a little too much while he was away at sea, all while Annie struggled with severe nightmares, panic attacks, and a hard pregnancy with Greg. Art only had one solution to all his problems: God.

Now, there's no wrong in believing in God, as Annie had done so her whole life—except without ever attending church. She'd talk to her amá, who was in heaven, knowing that she was with her. But this was different. This didn't feel like God to Annie; this entire experience at the Hall felt far more controlling. Every action had a consequence; every thought was considered. It was overwhelming and exhausting. And, after giving this religion her all (time, money, energy), she still had terrible nightmares but now slept in another room so that Art wouldn't know. As the elders would say, her nightmares were a direct correlation of her lack of faith.

As she sat in the meeting, Annie's thoughts wandered again. She would go back to a time that was difficult but comfortable.

The cotton plants stood taller than her, swaying discretely in the light breeze. Her fingers moved quickly as she focused on the balls of cotton nested between the prickly leaves. She could hear the faint hums of Mama Jo and Ruth as they meticulously pulled the cotton and shared stories with each other. She felt completely at peace and satisfied

204

with everything surrounding her. Annie moved her lips around as she remembered the salty taste of the sweat dripping down her face. She missed home, and she missed the routine she once had.

She pictured her apá. His jet-black hair and his beautiful eyes. The way he smelled when I would hug him. She could count the number of hugs they had shared on one hand, but those hugs were unforgettable. She looked over at her sleeping boys, their heads on either side of her lap, and wondered what it would be like for them to meet their abuelo. When I look at Greg, he reminds me of Apá. Sometimes his smile is stern, waiting for a response. Or sometimes it's his actions that are a mirror to my father's. I want my family to be whole but I'm not sure that will ever be a possibility. I forgive you, Apá, she tells herself.

"Amen." Art's loud finale to the prayer brought Annie back. Gently picking up their sleeping boys, they left the Hall after greeting everyone with big smiles. Annie knew the usual routine but still hated the superficial conversations. Art often debriefed the teachings while driving home, and Annie stayed quiet as she thought about how fake she had become: going through the motions one day at a time.

As the white Cadillac pulled into the driveway, the boys were bouncing back with some much-needed energy. Annie looked at Art through the rearview mirror and smiled at him as their sons— both rambunctious personalities—started chatting up a storm.

Greg had curly jet-black hair while Paul's was board straight; both with round brown eyes. The older boy had light skin like Annie, and the youngest was of a darker complexion, with beautiful skin like Art. Annie picked up both sons, who seemed so big and full compared to her small stature.

"All right, mijos. You know what time it is!" Annie said with a motherly level of excitement.

Greg ran through the front door with Paul following closely behind his big brother. They went straight to their room and jumped on top of their small white bed, which was decorated with a light-blue Thomas the Train comforter. They jumped up and down, waiting to get undressed out of their suits and into more comfortable clothing. They each lifted their arms above their head and Annie slid off their dress clothes and pulled on pants and long-sleeved shirts. She then kindly asked them to play in the room knowing they'd tire out and be ready for a nap shortly thereafter.

Luckily, the boys got along. Greg was a great older brother and liked to teach Paul all about trucks and cars. After a few minutes of watching her boys play together, Annie made her way into the kitchen and sat at the table to enjoy her weekly call with Mama Jo. She picked up the beige phone and used the rotary dialer to call her favorite person.

"Hola, Mama Jo, it's Annie."

"Hi, shugah, it's so good ta hear from ya." Mama Jo's voice

sounded tired and she had a hard time talking.

"You too. We just got home from the Hall and the boys napped the whole time, gracias dios. They're playing trucks in their bedroom; they're crazy, those two. I'm ready for a little girl. One who listens and behaves and doesn't bounce up and down all the time." Mama Jo and Annie laughed.

"Keep dreamin', child. It doesn't get easier. Girls have their own set of buttons they like ta push."

"That's what you keep telling me, but maybe she'll be like me. Maybe her and I will be best friends?"

"Now, another Annie would be a dream come true, but I don't think this world can handle two of ya! Do ya think y'all ever gone make your way down ta visit? I'd love ta meet the family."

Annie sighed loudly. "I worry if we go visit, I won't want to come back here."

"Oh, Annie. It can't be that bad? Just have you and Art take a few days off work and come visit. Maybe that's what ya need ta get ya out of the funk?"

"I want nothing more than for you to meet them, but it isn't that easy."

"All right, all right, I'll stop pushing."

"Thank you, Mama Jo. I promise, one day you'll meet them. How are you holding up?"

"As good as I can be. I miss my husband. And it's just too

damn quiet now. And well, I'm just an angry woman."

"I'm angry too. I think about it a lot at the Hall. I can't believe Robbie's just ... gone. Forever. It's horrible that none of those young police officers have to hold any responsibility. 'Accident' isn't a good enough excuse."

"Annie, we can't expect anythin' from other people. We have ta work within ourselves ta forgive. But right now, I'm not in that place." Mama Jo sighed audibly. The conversation struck a nerve. Her heart was still healing from the sudden death of her husband and best friend at the hands of the police.

"You don't sound too good. Are you sure you're okay, Mama Jo?"

"I'm just fine. Anyways, how's ya teachings going. Any luck with the new tutor?"

"Actually, I'm taking some time away from that. I'm staying focused on Paul and Greg right now and waiting until we have a little more money in the bank before we spend money on that again."

"Well, that's okay too, isn't it? It's wonderful ta be able ta just focus on your kids. It might take some of the pressure off. Then one day it'll just click."

"Maybe."

There was a long silence at the other end of the line. "Well, Annie, I was gonna tell ya last week, but I guess I have ta tell ya now. I was asked ta stay home from now on. Too much of a risk for the farm. Sons of bitches. So, I just have ta be on welfare and wait until I die, I guess. Them assholes want me ta rot here alone."

"What? That's horrible. You shouldn't have kept this burden to yourself. You should have told me right away."

"I know. I know. Don't go yelling at me. Just know that my time here isn't long. I'm sick of this. And I can hardly move anymore."

"Yeah, well who's taking care of you at home? If it's that serious, you probably need some help."

"Don't you go babying me now. I'm just fine. I don't need nobody. Just don't forget ta keep calling. I look forward ta hearing ya voice."

Annie could hear one of the kids crying in the background. "I'm sorry, Mama, but I've got to go. I hear one of the boys crying and I still have so much to do for lunch before Art gets upset."

"Talk ta ya next Sunday, Annie. I love you." Mama Jo hung up.

Annie walked into her sons' room and stared at them. Paul had tears running down his face, his hair was a mess, and he looked uncomfortable, so she lifted him up and held him tightly. Greg was sitting up, looking ready for a much-needed nap.

While she consoled Paul by hugging him close to her chest, she thought of Mama Jo living all alone, after losing her husband so tragically. There was not ever going to be a perfect time to make the trek back to Big Spring. Annie squinted her eyes in focus as she calculated how much money they had saved up.

Without discussing her plans with Art, she started packing a bag for the boys. She called the local bus station and purchased one bus ticket for them all to travel back to Big Spring, Texas. This time, it was Mama Jo who needed help and Annie wasn't going to let her suffer alone.

The bus ride to Big Spring felt much longer with two young boys than it had many years before. The seats were itchy and uncomfortable, and the boys were not in the right state to be sitting on a bus for that long. They cried and fought for the first three hours, mostly due to hunger and discomfort. Annie stood up and rocked them, she fed them grapes and pretzels, she walked up and down the bus aisle with them. Nothing would make them stop crying, and she was exhausted before she had even arrived.

Annie quietly prayed, wondering if she had made the wrong decision bringing her two sons across the state. She became numb to their ear-piercing screams and images of Art flashed in her mind: his loud screaming and furrowed eyebrows as he threatened against Annie's departure. She ignored him and waved awkwardly as she and the boys rushed into the cab: *"You're going to regret this more than anything else, Annie. Mark my words."* Spit came spewing out of his mouth.

She knew deep down that the Hall wouldn't allow Art to just leave her and the boys—and truthfully she found comfort in that. Annie needed space and rather than communicating that, she took Mama Jo's need for help and ran with it. There would be nothing more devastating to Annie than missing the opportunity for her boys to meet the woman she loved and admired more than anyone else.

Annie kept lying to herself and blaming a lack of money, but the truth was that Annie feared going back to Big Spring to face the reality of her nightmares. She feared running into her rapist and feared seeing her evil father. She had so much anger built up against them; after all she had endured, she was now strong enough to give them a piece of her mind. Once and for all.

She decided to face her past with the two things in her life that made her stronger than she could have ever imagined: her two beautiful boys. She'd be back home by next weekend, right in time to attend the Hall as a wholesome family. *It's only a quick trip*, she reminded herself as they got closer and closer to the destination.

Familiar roads now covered with brighter, newer signs made Annie's heart sink. There was no amount of paint, brick, and concrete that could mask the disturbing memories drowning her

211

thoughts. She looked down at her two sleeping boys and swallowed the sour taste of nausea that filled her mouth. It was too late to go back, she had to face her past.

Cabs surrounded the bus station parking lot like vultures. Annie gently rubbed the backs of her boys to wake them up as passengers stood up impatiently to exit the bus. She quickly dressed them in their oversized earmuffs, warm jackets, and gloves and grabbed her bags, rushing her sons into an old black cab. They headed straight to Mama Jo's house, where she'd be surprising the woman whom she'd missed for nearly seven years.

It was an expensive twenty-minute cab ride to the other side of Big Spring. Annie had never been to Mama Jo's before but had memorized the address by repeating it hundreds of times while bathing the boys and putting up dishes at home.

As the cab turned on to the two-way street into the old neighborhood, Annie could sense Mama Jo's presence. Knots consumed her stomach and her hands began to sweat profusely. For the first time in years, Annie looked like a little girl; joy spread across her face and excitement filled her chest.

The house was small but had Mama Jo's personality written all over it. It was painted a dazzling orange with white trim, with brightly colored Christmas decorations and lights in the yard. Her favorite rose garden, though dormant during the winter, lined the front of the house. Their neighbor's yard was overwhelmingly neglected and filled with junk, making Mama Jo's place look even more quaint.

The cab pulled up, and Annie gathered her things and got the boys ready to exit the car. As they made the cold walk to the small front door, she said quietly, "Mijos, you are going to have so much fun these next couple of days, but please, please behave." They nodded as she knocked loudly three times.

"Mama Jo, buenas tardes! It's us— estamos contentos de estar aquí!"

"Annie, is that you?" Mama Jo said, peering through the door's top window. She couldn't see well, but she knew Annie's Spanish from a mile away. "And ya boys?"

"Yes, open up! It's freezing," Annie said as she bounced on her toes from the cold. The door opened slowly as Mama Jo coughed loudly. Her hair was tangled and her face resembled that of a young child. She wrapped her robe tighter around her body to keep warm.

"Oh my Lord, whatcha doin' here!" Mama Jo said, shocked.

"I missed you so much," Annie said, kissing Mama Jo gently on the cheek. She wanted so badly to squeeze her, but she looked far too fragile for a deep hug. Greg and Paul stood there wide-eyed, holding a red toy airplane and toy soldiers in their hands.

Mama Jo waddled back to her wooden rocker and smiled a big smile. "My legs are weak, but bring those boys closer to Mama Jo.

213

I'm too tired ta hold them up."

"Mama Jo, this is Greggy and Paul. Boys, say hi to Mama Jo. She used to help take care of me when I was a little girl." The boys, well mannered, went to kiss Mama Jo and shyly hug her. Their diapers needed to be changed and they needed to be dressed in more comfortable clothes. Annie ignored all those details for the time being and focused on memorizing the new face of the woman before her.

"Mama, I hope you don't mind, but we'd love to stay with you for a few days. I am so happy to be here. You have no idea."

"Child, it's my pleasure. Forgive me, I haven't cleaned in a while with Robbie gone and my body failing me. Go into the room over there and drop ya things off. I'm not going nowhere."

"I'm so happy to see you, I'm speechless. Let me get the boys settled and I'll be right back."

Annie reached for a hand from each son and took in every detail of the home as they made their way back to the second bedroom to change. In this room there was a narrow bed with white sheets and a single pillow on top. She reached for the silver chain hanging from the fan and a dim light turned on. She placed Paul in the middle of the bed and took off his many warm layers of clothing. Greg did so on his own, and in no time Annie had both boys cleaned up. As a self-proclaimed neat freak, Annie had to organize the bedroom and their belongings slightly before she and the boys joined Mama Jo again in the living room.

The house had a faint smell of coffee and felt a little dirty. Annie nodded slowly to herself as she walked back into the living room, making mental notes of what needed to be addressed: the sink, the kitchen, the bathroom, the floors, the lights, the dust, and the smell. It was a real shame that Mama Jo's two kids had left her here all alone to fend for herself after Mr. Jackson's death. She deserved better, and Annie felt grateful that she was able to help Mama Jo, even if it was only for a couple of days.

The orange sofa adorned with yellow flowers was adjacent to a laminate wood-paneling wall covered in pictures of Mama Jo's family—photos from family reunions throughout the years and school portraits of her children growing a little more in each one. It was here that Annie sat the boys comfortably with a few of their favorite trucks, moving all the reachable candles and fragile items to the kitchen table so they wouldn't find themselves breaking a vase. Life with two toddlers always made Annie think twice about safety. The more entertained and safe the boys could be, the more Annie could enjoy her time with Mama Jo.

Because of the loss of her husband and having to stay home alone, Mama Jo needed a friend more now than ever. As soon as the boys were playing happily on the couch, Annie's dear friend kicked off what felt like an hour-long monologue. The two were so caught up in discussion that Mama Jo couldn't tell how fast

Annie was cleaning and scrubbing. They had talked every Sunday for more than three years but seeing each other face to face was entirely different. Annie couldn't fathom how different Mama Jo looked, how broken and weak she appeared.

Mama Jo's eyes were yellow and her hair completely white. The once steady hands that used to pick cotton meticulously had a severe tremble when she tried to grab anything. Annie had to help her drink so she wouldn't spill her water and even had to spoon-feed her at times at dinner. Mama Jo downplayed the entire situation, but Annie felt part of her soul shatter that first evening.

The two of them laughed so hard they cried: sharing memories and stories about each other. Paul and Greg kept it fun too. They were so wonderfully behaved and brought a new energy to Mama Jo that she needed.

After the boys were tucked into the bed together, Annie made herself comfortable on the orange sofa and watched as Mama Jo rocked in her chair back and forth.

"I am so proud of ya, Annie. I never once doubted you'd do amazing things with ya life. Ya always had big dreams as a child."

"Thanks, Mama. It's great to be back with you. I avoided this for a while, but it was time. I needed to make time, and I'm sorry I didn't come sooner. It's just with the Hall and the boys I hardly have time for anything."

"How is that church thing you're always gone ta?"

"I hate it," Annie blurted out. "Wow, that felt good to say." Her eyes grew in shock as she finally admitted to herself what she'd been denying for years. A rebellious laugh escaped from her mouth. "I pray all the time for these nightmares to be taken away. They're horrible, Mama. Just horrible."

"Well, you can pray all you want. But if ya ain't takin' action, nothing ever is gonna change. There's something deep in your soul holding ya back. Ya have ta let it go."

"Loca!" Annie said, continuing with her lighthearted demeanor.

"The God I know ain't just gonna fix everything for ya. He's gone ta test ya and make ya work for it. And if ya not fully committed and allowing ya heart to move forward, then ya never gone change. Just think about that."

The two of them sat in silence as Annie's face reddened in embarrassment. "I don't understand."

"To hell with what everyone else says or thinks. Ain't nobody ever walked a mile in your shoes. I ain't ever seen someone deal with as much as you have. Instead of acknowledging the pain y'all been through, ya just bury that shit down deep. And it'll haunt ya, forever, if ya don't let it go. Allow yaself ta be healed."

"Easier said, I guess."

"I know, child. I know. Just don't give up." Mama Jo's eyes were getting heavy in her rocking chair and Annie covered her with

217

a blanket before saying goodnight. Annie didn't sleep at all that entire night; she felt every ounce of fear that she had ever felt times a thousand. It was as if the voices in her head were getting louder and louder. The fear of everything she had ever experienced was coming to life. She worried that this was actually all a nightmare, that she actually wasn't in Big Spring. She just needed to wake up. Wake up.

The next morning, Annie was dressed and ready before the sun came up. She gently tapped Mama Jo on the shoulder in an effort not to startle her from sleep. "Mama Jo, I'm going to head into town to get some groceries for the next couple of days. Will you watch the boys while I'm out?"

"'Course. Will you grab me some licorice as well? I been wanting some of those, but Robbie always forgets."

Robbie's gone, though, Annie thought.

"Yes, I'll get you that. Be back within the hour, I've already called a cab and he's outside."

"Okay, just be careful."

The grocery store hadn't changed a bit. Annie remembered her young six-year-old self walking through the aisles, picking up beans or tomatoes to try to make it through the rest of the week. She grabbed a green basket by the front of the store and headed straight to the produce section. Picking out the ripest tomatoes, onions, and cilantro, Annie was going to whip up salsa with eggs for breakfast—one of Art's favorites.

It had been far too long since she'd been to the grocery store without the boys. Annie found that she was walking slower than usual, squeezing all the fruits and vegetables she passed. It was euphoric almost, to be alone in a grocery store—no nagging, no crying, just picking out delicious food to make a meal worth slaving over a hot stove.

The store was rather empty and quiet. With all the items she needed in her basket, Annie walked toward the checkout line. As she approached the customer in front of her, she could smell cigarettes and alcohol. Clearly he had no sense of hygiene. He was a mess.

Annie stood back, allowing him to organize his cans of evaporated milk and rice, and a large bag of dog food. Once the items had been scanned, she started to unload her basket of fresh foods and meats. The man in front of her decided last minute that he wanted a pack of gum, so he turned around and they made eye contact. Immediately Annie dropped the basket on top of the conveyor belt and looked down, trying to focus on taking the items out.

"Isabelle? Is that you?" the man asked, confused, standing there frozen. His eyes were wide as he stared intensely at her.

Emotions raced back and forth across Annie's mind and within her body in a matter of milliseconds. Without thinking,

219

she reacted.

"No," she replied with an angry confidence. "My name is Antonia Garza. I'm your daughter." Her hands were shaking and her face went numb, but she stood there tall and proud.

You could see the look of fear cross this old man's face. His hair was still jet-black, his shirt old and mangy. "Wow, mija, forgive me. You look just like your mother. It's been so long. How are you?"

His kindness was so off-putting. Annie had spent the past couple of years envisioning their first encounter together. First, she'd scream at him. She'd yell at him and maybe even beat the shit out of him if he made her angry enough. But she never envisioned this.

"Thanks, Apá." The words slid out of her like butter. She smiled kindly as she fought her own mind. *No, give him hell. Tell him how much he hurt you. Fuck him. Tell him off.* "It's good to see you. I'm in town with my boys for a few days. Maybe we can stop by the house."

As the words came out of her mouth, she regretted it. The man she hated more than anyone in the world she was now treating with such respect and love. She couldn't be mean to him.

"I'll be at the tavern tonight, but come by tomorrow afternoon for lunch so I can meet my grandkids."

"That sounds great, Apá." Annie's heart fluttered with an

overwhelming sensation. This is *not* how she pictured their connection after all these years. What was wrong with her?

He paid for his items and left without another word. She took her time organizing her groceries, paying, and bagging her items, to create some distance from him. As she sat silently in the cab back to Mama Jo's house, she replayed the scene over and over, seething with anger as she felt disappointed in herself.

Annie walked into the small house robotically, and the boys met her at the door cheering on her arrival. Usually the boys could distract her from anything, but the surrealness of what had happened at the grocery store was something she could have never prepared for. Annie aggressively put away the groceries and began cooking an elaborate breakfast for the four of them.

"What got into y'all panties?" Mama Jo yelled from the living room over the blaring TV. "I can hear you chopping from way out here."

"Nothing, Mama. I'm cooking."

"Okay, don't cut your finger in my kitchen. I don't have time ta clean up the blood." Annie rolled her eyes and laughed slightly, knowing Mama Jo couldn't clean anything up even if she wanted to. "Are ya still pissy from what I said last night?" Mama Jo continued yelling over the television. "I'm sorry if it upset ya. I just don't want ya being bitter bones."

"I know, Mama Jo. I know," Annie said, looking up at the

221

boys playing in the living room. She stayed focused on the task at hand, not wanting to bring up the incident at the grocery store. She made breakfast for everyone and played a game of dominoes with Mama Jo at the table for several hours.

Annie thought this trip was going to be far more rewarding than how she was feeling. It was as if a beautiful puzzle had been broken apart and all the pieces looked gray and meaningless. Sipping on her black coffee, Annie contemplated what she should do.

"Ya seem off, Annie. What's wrong? Ever since ya went ta the store this morning, ya been short with me."

"I'm sorry, Mama. It's nothing. I'm just missing Art. That's all."

"Well, next time bring him too. There's always room at Mama Jo's for anyone who needs it."

"He had to work. Maybe next time, though." Annie knew there'd never be a next time. The two-minute interaction in the grocery lineup was not something she'd want to experience with Art. His temper could be so unpredictable. She felt like a failure— she felt weak and insecure.

Annie put the boys to bed around 8 p.m. and Mama Jo fell asleep shortly after. Lying on the sofa and staring at the popcorn ceiling, Annie tried to play out every possible situation of visiting her apá for lunch the next day. A part of her was excited, as he had seemed kind and genuine. He'd be so thrilled to see how handsome his grandsons were. The other part of her was angry: how could he dare invite her over after trying to get rid of her for so long, wishing she was dead at every opportunity he had?

Closing her eyes, she pictured a childhood more full of love and peace than she had experienced. She pictured a loving home with Mama Jo and her father visiting and loving her with all his might. She pictured being smart, writing stories, and running free outside as the wind hit her big brown curls and soft golden skin. She pictured that peace as she soothed herself to sleep.

Waking up the next morning, she could hear Mama Jo groaning for help. Annie quickly grabbed a glass of water and walked into Mama Jo's bedroom, where she lay awake and in pain, with a large plaid blanket over her.

"Call 911, Annie. I'm having. I'm having … "

"Tell me, what's going on? Is it your hand? Your head? What's wrong?" Annie asked, panicking as she saw Mama Jo fade in and out.

She ran over to the phone in the living room and called 911. The boys came out of the bedroom in their diapers, crying and causing far more chaos than Annie was ready for. It was all happening in slow motion. She tried to calm the boys down before ushering them back into bed and closing the door. She hurried back to Mama Jo's bedroom.

Her dear friend's eyes rolled back as her body shook ferociously. Annie held Mama Jo tight, trying to stop the convulsions, slowly screaming as she felt Mama Jo lose consciousness.

The ambulance arrived, but the attendants said there was nothing else they could do and that her time of death was 6:12 a.m.

Annie fell to her knees, holding Mama Jo's hand tightly. She cried out, begging her to come back. She needed more time, she needed more guidance, she wasn't ready to say goodbye. The ambulance attendants had notified the coroner before leaving the house, and Mama Jo's neighbors started poking their heads in as they had assumed the worst. Within the hour, Mama Jo's pastor came in and he was able to contact Robbie Jr. and Bethany to let them know their mother had died. They'd be arriving at the house shortly to relive the loss of another parent.

As Annie sat on the orange sofa, her boys came back into the living room and tapped her shoulder, asking, "Mamita, que paso? Where's Mama Jo?"

Finally, she shook herself back into the moment, wiped her eyes, and embraced her two boys with all her might. She knew this day would come but had never dreamed it would be under these circumstances.

When the coroner arrived, the attendants covered Mama Jo's cold body with a white sheet, placed her on a stretcher, and wheeled it out of the house and into the awaiting hearse.

As the commotion in the front yard was settling, Annie made her way to the kitchen to call for a cab. Their visit at Big Spring had ended abruptly, and it was time to go back home. She also phoned Art, gracefully asking him to pick them up at the Port Isabel bus station in ten hours.

Though he was angry at Annie's sudden departure, he was so sad that she had lost the only mother figure she ever had. His kind words assured Annie that everything would be okay.

It was a quiet bus ride home. It was as if Greg and Paul could sense the devastation in their mother's soul. They entertained each other with poking games and running up and down the empty bus aisle, sleeping, and eating as Annie stared out the window, numb. There was no music to distract her, no task to keep her mind busy. Just the realization of the depressing silence and missing the sound and laughter of Mama Jo's voice.

"Mama Jo and Amá," Annie sniffled as she prayed to the two people she loved more than anyone else. "I hope you keep each other company and make me stronger day by day. I know that with you two by my side, anything is possible. Please help me be a better mom. Help my marriage, help me. Amen."

Art graciously picked up his family from the station. He had a giant bouquet of roses and a big smile on his face, wearing his Sunday best. Life would go back to the same routine.

"It's so traumatic what happened to you and the boys. I'm so glad to have you all home," Art said as he guided them into the Cadillac, the boys rushing to give their papa a big hug and kiss.

"Thank you, Art. It was so sad," Annie said, no emotion in her voice.

"At least you got to say your goodbyes and close that chapter of your life officially." Art didn't realize how broken Annie had been. Not merely by the loss of Mama Jo, but also by the fact that she never gave Marco another chance. She had stood him up, and that guilt would ruminate in her stomach for many days.

"You couldn't have said it better. There's nothing else left there for me. I'm just glad the boys got to meet her."

The thought of attending the funeral with Mama Jo's actual family was intimidating for Annie. She had said her goodbyes, she had spent the time she needed, and now it was time to move on. That was the first night in many months that Annie slept peacefully, knowing that her angels were watching over her.

Without skipping a beat, the next morning Annie woke up and headed to the Hall with a smile on her face and her chin held up high.

Throughout the service, Annie played so many memories of Mama Jo through her mind. She thought about all the wisdom she had shared and all the grace she had shown. Mama Jo didn't live a life much easier than Annie. Being a person of color wasn't easy. Their skin tones were different, but Annie and Mama Jo understood each other, more than anyone else ever understood Annie. They had been through so much together that there was no comparison.

Mama Jo was right, she thought. *Me just being me and moving forward is winning every day. I might not be the smartest, or the most beautiful, and I may be a shitty mom at times, but I have the strength to move forward every single day.*

"Dear God, please clean my heart. Allow me to be healed from my past. Amen."

1973
TWENTY-SIX YEARS OLD

*T*he cotton felt imperfect between her fingers: the rawness of the plant and the remnants of dirt and grass embedded between its fine layers. Beads of sweat dripped down Annie's young tan face and landed gently on top of the cotton she'd piled into her wicker basket. She giggled to herself, overhearing the conversations of Gerry and Ruth. Two crazy sons of bitches.

A red plastic toy accidentally hit Annie a few millimeters below her left eye. Before she could realize what was happening, she held her hand against her face, stood up from the living-room sofa, and made eye contact with Paul, who had the fear of death across his face.

"Mamita, I'm sorry. I'm sorry. It was an accident. Are you okay?" Paul's loud and confident voice carried a long way for a young boy, his eyes wide in grief, scared to have hurt his mother.

"Mi amor, I'm okay. I know it was an accident," Annie said as she sat back down and opened her arms for Paul to come close and embrace his loving and forgiving mother. "You need to be more careful. We don't throw toys in the house like that. Because—"

"Because someone can get hurt," Paul finished the rhythmic mantra they had shared many times before now.

"Exactamente!" Annie said, pleased with her son, who always knew when to apologize and make things right. He had a big soft heart and always wanted to make his mamita proud. "Now go wash up. I'm going to be making dinner soon and you need to be dressed properly by the time your padre gets home."

"Yahoo!" the boy squealed as he ran to his bedroom, making loud car and train noises.

"Paul, quiet, or you're going to wake up your sister and I just put her down to nap a few minutes ago."

He nodded, running on his tiptoes the rest of the way. Annie could hear the two boys talking in the background. She sighed as she stood up again, wiped her hands on her khaki pants, pulled down the hem of her purple blouse, and headed to the kitchen to clean up the counters while the kids were occupied.

She loved her little ones, but the constant cooking and cleaning up after them (and Art) made her feel hollow inside. Sure, she was tired, but being tired as a mom was a different kind of tired compared to working in the fields. Her body wasn't seizing from overheating, her hands weren't always bleeding or feet aching—she just felt like less of herself. No one to talk to and learn from, just her kids.

Annie's mind became less present; she was often away in her own thoughts and dreams. It was obvious that her priorities had shifted to being a mother, and to being a great mother at that, but something was missing. The fact of the matter was: Annie's dreams never dissipated.

Her mind was in constant limbo: challenging herself to spend more time working with a tutor but with literally no time to do so. I mean, three kids are a lot for anyone to handle and now that Greggy was starting kindergarten in August her priorities were to ensure he had everything he needed to be successful. There was this uneasiness about not pursuing something you want more than anything in the world. At some point, the itch that you want to scratch so badly starts to burn and then it slowly becomes numb.

Every day was the same routine, but with that routine came very little appreciation and even less satisfaction. There was no sense of camaraderie. Annie was raising three beautiful children alone most of the time while Art was working non-stop to compensate for Annie being a full-time mom.

It was a long meeting at the Kingdom Hall and the elder had shared the message of providing for the family and allowing the woman of the household to focus on raising a strong family built on the foundation of Jehovah. Art parked the car in the driveway and huffed angrily into the house, slamming the door while Annie unloaded the two boys from the backseat.

Art was a lovely man, but there were times when he was moody. Like a tsunami building momentum, he would only settle down after some time alone. So rather than poke and prod at his rudeness, she went to the kitchen and started making lunch.

Annie was wearing a light-pink knee-length dress and beautiful pearl earrings. It was in the middle of summer and her face looked flushed from carrying the boys and their belongings from the car into the house.

As she washed her hands, she giggled.

"Oh Art, I love you!" she said as she wiped her hands on the cloth towel and walked over to her husband, who was reading the newspaper. "I wonder how long your tie has been crooked like this. Like a little boy!" Her attempt at flirting was greatly ignored.

"Annie, what will people say if I have you working. What will they think of me? That I can't support my family. That's what they'll think. And I'll have none of that. If it's God's will then so be it, you will not be working anymore. And that's final. This is not up for discussion."

"Art, I love working with Guti and the gang. They're my friends—and even though it's part-time, the money is nice. You and I both know that."

"As I said, this is not up for discussion. A woman's place is at home and since you can't have a real job, you will focus on raising our children."

"What do you mean, a real job?" Annie yelled, feeling all the anger pent up over the years finally release. "I work harder than anyone I know. Cooking, cleaning, then going to work to clean more, then come home, wash your clothes, and feed Paul in the middle of the night while you stay sound asleep. I change diapers, I get groceries, I make sure everything is taken care of. I may not be able to read or write, but that sure as hell doesn't make me a fucking idiot. Yes, I'll stay at home, but don't make it sound like it's God's will. This is your will. Your pride."

That afternoon was easily the end of their marriage. The look in Art's eyes as he degraded her intelligence and doubted her abilities would be forever branded in her mind. There were days like today, where she missed working, getting out of the house, and accomplishing things for other people. She enjoyed showing others that she was more than a mom, she was more than a cleaning housewife. Annie started to suffer from one of the worst pains imaginable: loneliness.

The community of women from the Hall didn't understand her past. They'd get together on Wednesday nights, each woman bringing their own dish to share with the group. They'd sit in a circle while the kids played with each other and open up about their struggles and the obstacles that God had been placing in their life.

Some would cry about their childhood bullies, others would explain that they couldn't conceive; there were hard times that these women went through, no doubt. Annie's heart would break as they shared their stories and she appreciated the community she was building. There was just one thing: when it was Annie's turn to share, the women treated her as though she was diseased. How come no one saved you? What kind of father doesn't let his own daughter go to school? Their situations were somewhat relatable, whereas Annie's experiences were so rare and painful that many times the women couldn't even comprehend what she was saying. And the crazy part is that Annie felt she was sharing the "normal" stuff. The sympathy she felt wasn't sympathy at all—people felt sorry for her. They asked if she would let her own kids go to school. Annie's eyes were wide open in shock. "Of course my kids will go to school! I'm not against school." It was merely their inability to understand that pushed Annie further and further away. Was it that everyone kept their secrets so deeply buried, or was it that

Annie truly had no one to relate to, no one to confide in while Art was away at sea?

Hannah used to be that person for Annie. Even though Hannah clearly had no comprehension of Annie's past, the two were close and it was nice to share secrets and stories with another woman. Especially since Mama Jo had passed. But there's something about life that changes when you have kids. And now Annie had three of them. Lunches at Los Deliciosos became fewer and far between. Over time, their lives went different directions; no malice of course, just living two totally distinct lives.

Sofia cried in her bedroom and Annie ran to visit her little one with lots of love and kisses. There was nothing like her daughter's waking-up breath and getting soft kisses all over her face; she loved that time with Sofia more than anything else.

Walking into her daughter's room, the small lamp in the corner continued to play the jingling sounds of "Twinkle Twinkle Little Star." The light-pink walls had a narrow strip of teddy-bear wallpaper in the center, flanked by shelves of Sofia's stuffed animal collection: rabbits, dogs, cats, bears, and dolls. Her favorite was Mr. Ears—Sofia went everywhere with that bunny.

"Hi, mi amorcito! How was your nap?" Annie asked as she walked in to give her little one a shower of post-nap kisses.

Standing up in her crib, her pudgy hands holding the railing, Sofia's hair was wild, one of her pigtails had fallen out, and her eyes were still glossed over and trying to adjust to the light from the hallway. She smiled and bounced on her mattress as Annie stepped closer.

"I love you so much, mi niña linda!" Annie whispered as she held Sofia close to her chest. There was something special about her relationship with her little girl: Sofia filled Annie's heart in so many ways.

As they hugged, a tear slid down Annie's face. Today was Sofia's second birthday.

A trance fell over Annie as she wiped the tear from her face and started moving rapidly, like a bat out of hell.

"Boys, let's go. We're going to the store!" Annie shouted as she grabbed her purse and Sofia's pacifier. "Now!"

"But, Mom, we're in the middle of … " Greggy whined as he came out of his room wearing a cowboy hat and red cowboy boots with an army shirt and little shorts.

"I said now. Get in the car. We're having a party today. Before I change my mind."

"But, Mamita!" Greggy's eyes grew big as he ran to the car holding Paul's hand behind him.

Annie threw her kids in the Cadillac and wore her newly prescribed eyeglasses to ensure her driving was safe with the kids in the car—though her logic was slightly skewed, considering she still didn't have a driver's license. Nonetheless, the kids were in the car and no one said a word all the way to the store.

As they pulled up to Woolco, Annie was a woman on a mission, and today's mission was to celebrate Sofia's birthday. Despite everything the Hall had said about such celebrations displeasing God, Annie wanted a birthday party for her beautiful daughter, and if that meant they were going to hell, then so be it.

Annie threw balloons of every color into her shopping cart. She walked methodically down every aisle with a grimacing, mysterious smile on her face, pushing Sofia in the cart, the boys trailing behind her. Oh, she knew what she was getting herself into, and she thrived in this moment. She'd been through so much shit in her life that throwing her kid a birthday party was not something to be negotiated any longer. Life was worth celebrating; and if Art, and the Hall, felt differently, he could find the door.

"Mija, tell me what you want your cake to be: chocolate, vanilla, strawberry?" Annie said as she looked at Sofia, who was still sporting the single pigtail, the other half of her hair standing straight up.

Sofia's eyes were big and round and beautiful, just like her mother's. "Cake! We get cake!"

"Yes! You get cake because you know why?"

"Because I no hit Greggy?" Sofia said, confused.

"Well, yes, but because it's your birthday. You are two years old and we are going to celebrate you today!"

"I'm not two, I'm one," Sofia whined.

"Nope, not anymore. You just turned two! Now hold up your hand and show me two fingers." Sofia put her tiny, chubby hand in the air and Annie gently curled Sofia's ring finger and pinky, then pressed Sofia's thumb down to meet then. "This is how old you are now."

"Mamita, we are not supposed to celebrate things," Greggy scolded his mother, a worried look across his young, innocent face. "Birthdays are for the devil, mamita. We cannot do this. I don't want to get in trouble."

"Greggy, I promise you I will protect you forever. Do you want a party too? We can have one for you next week, my mijito. I promise you, life is too short for us to be scared of everything. We have to live!"

Annie seemed somewhat crazy to her young children. They were rule-followers and their mother was breaking one of the biggest rules of all time: falling into the ways of the world. The cart was filled with snacks, hotdogs, cake, ice cream, streamers, gifts: everything needed for a wonderful party.

As the white Cadillac pulled into Chapala Drive, Annie's heart sank. Art had been standing outside; he'd arrived home early from his fishing trip.

"Shit, shit, shit," Annie said out loud as she slowed down her approach to the house.

"Okay, kids, help me get the groceries inside," she said, staying calm and giving Art his usual welcome-home kiss.

Art walked into the house smelling like sweat and the sea. He threw his luggage down on the sofa and walked immediately to the shower. You could feel his irritation as the excited kids ran up to love their daddy, who had been out of the house for nearly ten days straight.

Annie ran to the phone and made a few calls, inviting Hannah, Guti, and some of her other former coworkers to a party that would start that evening at five o'clock sharp. Sofia's party quickly turned into a birthday party for all the kids. They were always conceived during the fishing offseason and, well, that's how you get three babies in July.

Walking into the living room and kitchen, Art realized the counters were covered in bags of decorations. His vision became impaired and he started to feel dizzy.

"What kind of nonsense are you bringing into this home?" He gritted between his teeth as he slammed his fist down on the counter. "Holidays, birthdays, and celebrations of this world are a sin, Annie. I don't know why that is so difficult for you to get through your head. Please go to the bedroom and ask for forgiveness while I watch the kids. Get those worldly thoughts out of your mind, now."

"No," Annie said as she crossed her arms and stuck out her

hip. "I'm not going to pray for forgiveness. We never have any fun around here and everything that we want to do upsets you and it isn't fair anymore. I won't have our children living in a home where everything they want to do—watch cartoons, sing, laugh, trick-or-treat—is all evil. It's ridiculous."

"I don't know who I fell in love with. But it isn't this devil of a woman."

"Art, enough is enough. I feel suffocated in this house. I feel suffocated not working, not living. Just going through the motions."

"Not again with the job shit, Annie. No. We are done with this conversation."

"Papi, it's my birthday," Sofia shouted as she came to hug her papa.

"And, Dad, we can have birthdays soon too. Mamita said so!" Greggy chimed in.

Annie was sweating but knew she was going to keep her stance. "That's right. People are going to be here around five, so be sure to go to your room and clean up! I've got a lot to get done."

"Annie, what the hell is going on? I am not having a party in *my house*!" Art shouted with shock and anger.

Annie knew this wouldn't go over well, but she was in too deep to stop. She had already given up her freedom to work, her time to study had been taken away; now the only thing she had left was to celebrate her family, and even that was being taken away. But not anymore. Not now.

The only people who showed up to this last-minute birthday party were Hannah and her fiancé, Kenneth Goldberg, a CPA. Art didn't attend, but it didn't matter. They had a wonderful party—the only party the kids would experience until they left the Hall as adults. Annie paid a sacrifice in her marriage that day: one that she never regretted but one she always wished would have turned out differently. She knew she was disobeying everything their family believed in. Confusing the kids, making them cry as Art burned their decorations post-party.

Annie was lying in the hot bedroom. Sweat covered her body as she sat up quietly not to wake Art. Tiptoeing to the kitchen, she grabbed a small clear glass and filled it to the top with cool water. As her lips pressed against it, she immediately felt the relief tingle down her throat and into her belly.

There were so many things wrong with the life she was living, and it was eating her from the inside out. She missed working, she missed feeling like she had purpose and people to be around. Being a mother was wonderful, but as the kids grew older she knew she needed to find work and needed to take a stand for the life she wanted for herself.

In late August, Greg started kindergarten while Paul went to preschool for half-days. There was something so special about this time. Every day she would wake the boys up and get them ready for school, make them a tortilla with beans, and pack a small meal in their lunch sacks. Sometimes she'd look at them and remember the dream she had walking down County Road 34.

If I had known then what I know now, I would have left a lot sooner. But I wouldn't change what I went through for the world. Because it put me here, with these beautiful, crazy kids.

"Mamita, what does this mean?" Greggy sat at the kitchen table one afternoon with a packet of papers in front of him. The top page showed eight large clocks, each displaying a different time. The task was straightforward: write the description of the time.

"Oh mijito, you know I don't know how to read or write. This is why it's very important that you get to school early and ask your teacher. I'll take you first thing in the morning," Annie said as Greggy sat there puzzled.

It was true, the Garza boys were always the first ones in their class, making sure they got the extra help they needed for their homework to be completed. Not a day went by where they weren't the first ones there and the last ones to leave. Annie made sure not to tout her inabilities, but she always made it very clear that it was the teacher's responsibility to teach and when you came home it was family time, when you contributed to the family with chores or fun or both.

The next morning before sunrise, Annie sat at the kitchen table and drank her black cup of steaming hot coffee. She had poured Art one too. The aroma filled the house.

"You know, a good pot of coffee always gets me out of bed early, Annie."

"Art, we need to talk."

"What's going on?"

"I am going back to work. I've reached out to a few places and I've gotten an offer as a housekeeper for The Beach Motel. It'll be during the day, so I won't miss anything with the boys. And Linda from the Hall said she'd help with Sofia when you're away at work. Art, I won't take no for an answer."

"Annie, you have so much potential. Why are you refusing to live the life I'm giving you and go back to cleaning toilets? What is it with you that you're just so damn stubborn?"

"Sometimes I feel like you barely know me," Annie said to Art, then stood up from the table and walked away with a heavy heart.

1978
THIRTY-TWO YEARS OLD

The old Cadillac popped the curb and parked on the sidewalk of Garriga Elementary School. Still running hot, Annie grabbed her small purse and puffed inside the school. Her bright-red face matched her work uniform, her hairnet still covering her abundantly wild and frizzy curls.

She pulled on the large metal handle of the entryway door and marched right by little Ms. Etheridge, the school secretary, and straight into the principal's office, where Paul was sitting with tears streaming down his cheeks. Annie's heart broke, but she never changed the stern look on her face.

"Mr. Sanchez, can you tell me what's going on. I got here as fast as I could," Annie demanded, staring at the young principal, who appeared more scared than Paul.

"Mrs. Garza, please lower your voice and take a seat. We're all doing our best under these circumstances," Principal Sanchez said with a small tremor in his voice. His Spanish accent was strong, and his shoulders looked tense beneath his light-blue button-down shirt and navy tie.

"What I want to know is why my son is here crying hysterically, nadie debería hacer llorar a mi hijo. You mentioned on the phone that another boy called him stupid—where is that student?" scrambled Annie. Her anger had her mouth moving in and out of English and Spanish—better known as Spanglish. She was trying hard to keep her head on straight.

"Mrs. Garza, I called you in today because Paul is struggling in most of his classes. He and I have talked about it and we think it's in his best interest to be held back next year, allowing him some time to get more confident with his reading," Principal Sanchez said, his light-brown eyes dispirited. He quickly dabbed his forehead with a tissue to blot the sweat forming on his bumpy forehead.

"Que lastima," Annie said angrily between her teeth as she brought her face right up to Mr. Sanchez's. She could smell his cologne and hear his breathing speed up. Her heart was pounding and all she wanted to do was cry for little Paul. She wanted to hug him, but now wasn't the time. Now was the time to protect him and give her son everything she never had. "You're telling me that another asshole kid calls Paul dumb and stupid in front of everyone, and instead of *him* being punished you're *agreeing* with him? What kind of school is this?" She threw her hands up in the air and dropped her purse into the empty seat next to Paul.

"Paul, can you please step out for a second?" Mr. Sanchez requested softly.

The boy nodded and stood up slowly. Annie scanned over his every inch to ensure there was no physical evidence of abuse, taking in his Dallas Cowboys T-shirt with a tiny mustard stain and his faded blue jeans. He picked up his book bag and, with his shoulders hunched forward, walked outside the office into the lobby area with Ms. Etheridge. He sat quietly on the itchy gray chair and listened to the muffled sounds from behind the large wooden door.

"Okay, continue," Annie demanded after the door was shut. Her arms were crossed tight, her foot tapping furiously.

"Mrs. Garza, we know Paul gets dropped off at school early every day for tutoring, and that he does a great job with directions and wants to get better. We think he should repeat the fourth grade so that he doesn't become frustrated. He's a July kid so he'll go from being the youngest in his class to the oldest, which will be good for him. We want him to do well, we want him to feel like he can succeed rather than barely pass. Give him another year and what he's learning now will be a breeze, I can assure you of that."

A high-piercing sound overwhelmed Annie's ears and her vision became slightly blurred. She was in shock and disbelief. Her face felt numb and her legs started to tremble. This was her fault; it was her fault that her son was struggling just as she had for years and years.

"No. We will keep him in summer school and he will move on to the next grade with all his friends. You are a disgrace." A single tear slid down her hot red face. Annie replayed all the times she'd met with her kids' teachers to explain that she couldn't help them with their homework. She had to relive her own pain over and over and continue to feel responsible for this moment. If only she had the ability to tutor them on her own, they wouldn't be in this position. If only she could have read the directions to them, or helped them understand the assignment better, or double-checked their work, but it was too late to change the past. This was where they were.

"Mrs. Garza, I respect that, but if you change your mind and if Paul has any interest in repeating the fourth grade, please let us know. I know it wasn't easy coming here today and having to leave work for this, but I'm glad you did," Mr. Sanchez said gracefully as Annie headed out of the small office.

She stepped into the reception area and gave her hurting boy a big loving smile. His eyes were swollen and his smile was slightly crooked. He needed his mama and she was right there for him.

"Mamita, what happened? Did you figure it out? Am I repeating the fourth grade?" Paul asked, his voice low and husky from all the crying.

"Don't worry about it, mijo. We got it all taken care of," Annie said. The two of them held hands as they walked to the car, which was still idling, parked on the curb. Paul shook his head in amusement and gave his mother a side eye.

"Mamita, I can't believe you parked like this. They could have given you a ticket."

The two of them laughed as Annie put on her big thick eyeglasses and they skidded out of the parking lot, heading straight to Dairy Queen for Paul's favorite: a dipped cone.

The sounds of Paul crunching the ice cream cone between his teeth filled the interior of the Cadillac. When the two of them got home, he threw his bag on his bedroom floor and fell asleep on his bed, emotionally drained from the painful experience and his hurting heart.

Annie knew that Paul was slow to open up, but that in time he would. He was soft like his daddy and enjoyed sharing his thoughts and feelings.

A few hours later, just as Annie had predicted, he came out and hugged his mother from behind as she was washing dishes.

"Mamita, do you think I'm dumb?" Paul opened up as he held her tight.

Annie took her soapy hands out of the sink and gently squeezed her son's big cheeks. "Mijito, you are *perfect*! And you always do your homework and you give everything your best. That is being

247

not only smart but also hardworking." As the soap dripped off her hands, they shared a deep moment together, staring eye to eye.

"But everyone laughs at me when we read out loud, and I hate it because it makes me more nervous, and then I keep messing up more, and then the teacher has to help me and she doesn't have to help anyone else," Paul said, his breathing starting to speed up. He was reliving the moments of embarrassment and it was difficult to articulate his pain.

"Paul, why haven't you told me this before?" Annie asked as she dried her hands on a dish towel. "Why didn't you tell me this was hard for you? We could have gotten you more help, more time at school."

"I don't know," Paul sighed, staring at the floor. "I didn't want you to be mad at me or think I wasn't trying. I try all the time."

"Paul, sit down and let me talk to you about something very private to me. Something very few people know." They sat at the dining table as Annie prepared to pour her heart out and connect with her hurting son on a deeper level than ever before.

"You know that I never had the opportunity to go to school, right?" Annie started, staring into Paul's eyes. He nodded in agreement. "I want you to know that you don't need to be perfect in school, all you need to do is give it your best. Because there are people in this world who could only dream of the opportunities you have. To learn, to fail, to try again and again. You are not dumb, you are not stupid. No matter what anyone says, you are smart. And as long as you never quit trying to be better than you were the day before, that is all I will ever ask for and all I could ever hope for you. I know what it's like for people to think I'm dumb because I can't do certain things, because I can't read or write. I see the way they look at me and sometimes the way they talk to me. But you are none of those things, Paul. Do you understand me?"

Paul's heart broke for his mother as his perception shifted completely. He realized he was smart and that it was okay to ask for help. He got up and hugged his mom again while she sat at the table.

"So," Annie said as she took another look at her handsome young boy. "We will make sure that you continue to get the help you need in reading. If you need to repeat the fourth grade to feel good about it, then that's fine. But I want you to know, if you repeat the grade or not, you are nothing close to dumb. If anything, I am so proud of you for continuing to try every day."

Annie picked up extra evening shifts to pay for Paul's reading specialist three days a week. It was an expensive investment that helped his confidence skyrocket. She was working as a janitor on the weekends to ensure that her kids had all the resources they needed to be successful. Money was tight, but it was so worth it when Paul received the most improved reader award during the fifth-grade graduation that next school year.

1987
FORTY-ONE YEARS OLD

Annie looked at herself in the mirror as she smoothed out the wrinkles of her silver dress. She secured the backs of her pearl earrings and puckered her orange-tinted lips. This was the first time in ages that she and Art were going to have a romantic evening out together. It was long overdue.

She moved closer to her reflection to inspect the wrinkles that now made their mark on her soft face. She looked a little older than she remembered and a little more tired than she had before. Her hands were calloused, her cheeks had less elasticity than in her twenties. She wanted to feel beautiful again.

"You look amazing, mi amor," Art said as he walked into the bathroom and kissed her gently on the neck. "Are you ready?"

Annie smiled and nodded as she grabbed her purse and waved goodbye to Sofia, who was lying comfortably on the living-room floor with her best friend, Katy, watching TV. Annie walked confidently to the car, wondering what the special occasion was for this evening out on the town.

Art pulled into a restaurant that overlooked the beach. He dashed around the car to open Annie's door and held out his left arm for her. The two of them strolled arm in arm as they were greeted by the young host. Smooth piano music was playing in the background as they were seated at a lovely booth with a bouquet of red roses and baby's breath nestled into a vase. The roses were so fancy that Annie didn't realize at first that they were for her.

"Art, these must have been so expensive. What is all this for?" she asked as he looked back and forth from the flowers to her expression, yearning for her satisfaction.

"Well, Annie, it's been a long time since we've had time alone and I wanted you to feel special. So, they're for you, enjoy them!"

"You always know how to spoil me." She pulled the large vase closer, inhaled deeply, and closed her eyes as she took in the sweet aroma. Instantly the image of Mama Jo popped into her mind: how she had loved tending to her rose garden. "They're beautiful, muchos gracias."

Art had officially retired from shrimping to spend more time at home with the family. He spent most of his time working in the seafood department at the local grocery store. Money was tight, but having Art home every evening had been nice. It had been months since they had enjoyed an evening out. The two of them sat quietly at the table as Art perused the menu. Annie knew she wanted a big steak, and certainly they'd have that at a fancy place like this.

"Welcome to Romero's Steak House & Oyster Bar, what can I get you both started with today?" The tall waiter was old and stern, wearing all black.

Art requested two waters with no ice and asked for more time before they ordered their meals. Annie could see that he was sweating profusely, but as he got older and heavier that had become more normal. Except this time seemed different. Her senses were heightened to his motif.

"Art, what is all this about? We haven't done this in years, and out of the blue you take me to the nicest restaurant in town, we probably can't even afford it, and you're sweating all over. What is going on?"

"You don't think I can just do something nice for you? Our relationship has been suffering, Annie. And I'm trying to fix it, and here you are just attacking me." He shook his head in disappointment.

"Forgive me. You're right, I was being ungrateful, you're right. I'm sorry," she said as she placed the napkin on her lap. Her guard was down, and she felt guilty for being so abrasive. "It's just been so long, so I figured that something was up."

"No, nothing. I'm just treating my wife to a beautiful dinner that she deserves."

Over dinner, the two of them enjoyed steaks, shrimp, and sparkling water with lime. They shared a chocolate mousse, and the butterflies were filling Annie's soul. Ever since Hannah had moved away, it had felt like ages since she had connected with another adult. Then Greg and Paul had moved out to live on their own in Port Isabel and Sofia was busy being a teenager. Annie was lonely, and this was the connection that she had needed, that she had craved. The love from her husband was something she had missed more than anything she could have ever communicated.

After dinner, they walked hand in hand through the parking lot and onto the beach to watch the sunset over the amber-blue sky. The sound of seagulls tickled their ears, and the smell of the ocean filled their lungs. Annie leaned in and kissed Art passionately, loving him more than she had in ages.

What happened to us? she thought. Maybe it was because she no longer attended Kingdom Hall? Maybe it had been difficult to see beyond their kids' needs. Maybe it was because they had become different people over the years, focusing on their family and putting their own needs last.

So many factors played a role in the disintegration of their marriage. Now that the kids were older, maybe it was time for Art and Annie to rekindle the love they once had, start fresh. Maybe he could spend more time at home while she would get to go back to school. But the fact that that thought even crossed her mind again felt uncomfortable. She instantly got frustrated at herself and had to regain her focus back to the moment: the two of them on the beach.

That evening, they made love and lay in bed talking for hours, like they had many years before. They laughed at how they'd both changed, both in their desires and in their own physical appearances. They cried thinking of the stories they had told each other and the pain they hadn't resolved.

The morning sun welcomed the both of them as they continued talking in bed, now for nearly seven hours straight.

"Annie, I need to tell you something," Art said calmly as he played with her curly hair.

"Okay," she said, her eyes closed, listening to his heartbeat and breath.

"I got a job offer to move to Austin as a manager at a new grocery store. We need to be out of here within the next week so we have time to find a new place. I have put the house on the market and we should start getting bids soon."

"Why didn't you tell me sooner?" Annie asked calmly.

"I knew you'd think that's why I did the dinner and all the nice stuff for you this evening. But the truth is, we both know we needed an evening like this. I didn't want to ruin it with my news."

"You made me think you wanted to work on us when the reality is you took me out to dinner so we could celebrate *you* and your job. When was the last time you asked me about my job? About my life? Huh? Everything is always about you … "

"I'm sorry you see it that way, Annie. You have until next week to decide if you and Sofia want to come with me. I can understand if you choose that staying here is better for you both." Art and Annie laid there silently in each other's arms. She had nothing left to say to him.

Later that morning, Annie got out of bed and called the only other person she knew to call: Hannah. Their lives had ventured into different directions. Her best friend now lived about an hour away and they didn't hang out much. But Annie always knew that Hannah had great advice.

"Hannah?"

"Annie, what's going on, it's seven-thirty in the morning?" she said, sounding concerned.

"Art wants us to move, next week."

"Okay. Where to, hunny?"

"Austin."

"No shit. With all those hippie-dippies? Good luck!" Hannah sarcastically rolled her eyes, and Annie could hear her moan as if she was getting up out of bed.

"Yeah, I don't know what to do. If I stay here, I'll be on my own. Sofia is basically doing her own thing now that she's sixteen and driving. But if I go, then, well, I have to start all over again. I like it here. I have two great jobs where they trust me and I work hard and make good money. In Austin, there's just so much unknown. So much that Sofia and I would have to start over with."

"Well, Annie, you're not someone to coward against the unknown. Do you want to go with Art? Do you want to continue your relationship with him? Y'all have been so up and down over the past couple years."

"You're right, Hannah." Annie's head hung low. It wasn't Austin that she was scared of; she was scared of staying married to a man she felt she no longer knew—a man who had grown so far apart from her spiritually, emotionally, and physically. What was left of their relationship were three beautiful children and wonderful memories, but that didn't mean they needed to stay together, did it?

"Think it over, hun. I can come into town for lunch sometime if you want to talk about it more, but don't run away from new experiences. You're better than that. Plus, Sofia is a strong woman like her mother. She'll make new friends in no time."

"Hannah."

"Yes, Annie?"

"Thank you for always being honest with me. I know I can count on you."

"Of course, that's what friends are for."

Annie thought it over that morning, playing out the different scenarios in her head. If she stayed, what would that mean for Sofia's junior year in high school? Yes, she was independent, but she knew Sofia wouldn't take the news lightly. If she went, that would mean seeing a new part of Texas and that adventure could be fun.

Throughout the rest of the week, Annie started to pack up their belongings. However, it was evident to both her and Art that she hadn't decided what she was going to do. Time was ticking before they would need to accept the offers made on their family home. She felt it was unfair for her to just have to pick up her life within a few days' notice and move to a new place. She felt that Art had disregarded her life and her jobs—he wasn't the only one contributing to their household income, as much as he'd wished he was.

This was a difficult situation for Annie to consider: one life was with Art in a new town meeting new people, while the other was here at home, just her and Sofia. She started talking to Mama Jo as she had many years before, asking for guidance—between Mama Jo and Amá, the two of them would certainly send some good advice down from God.

The thoughts were overwhelming, and she knew she needed some fresh air to think it all over. Annie headed out for a walk to the corner store. She stared at the For Sale sign on her lawn and a thought popped into her head, a feeling that was both comforting and exciting. What if she moved to Austin on her own accord? Sure, it was Art's original idea, but it would be good for the kids. Although their parents were going to have different lives from each other, at least they lived in the same city to come visit. She knew that she and Art would be fooling no one by staying together. That was that. Her decision was made. She beelined it back to the house to talk to Art.

"I've decided what I'm going to do," Annie said as she walked through the front door, out of breath.

"Okay, what's that?" Art asked. He was packing kitchen items into a cardboard box.

"I'm moving to Austin with Sofia," she said, with emphasis on the *I'm*.

"Claro!"

"No, I'm moving on my own. To get my own place near you to make it easier for the boys to visit," she said in an abrupt tone.

"That's a good idea," he said as he started to tape up the box and label it with black marker.

"Really?" Annie asked, confused. She was hoping just a little that he would have been disappointed, but she also felt relieved.

"Yes, really. Whatever will make you happy, Annie. You haven't been happy in a while, and that's important to me. Honestly."

There was a sincerity in his voice that let Annie know he just wanted what was best for her. The two of them hugged for a moment, then cried together, and packed up their home for the last time. Austin was going to be their start of something new.

Driving through downtown Austin for the first time was one of the most surreal moments Annie had ever experienced. As she sat in the passenger seat, she kept her eyes focused on the scenery around her: the deep green lake, the buildings, that giant stadium in the middle of the city. It was all so immaculate and breathtaking.

"That's The University of Texas at Austin," Art said as he drove them through downtown. "This is a great school, the best in the country. Only the smartest students go here. Sofia, maybe even you could go here after next year."

Sofia was about to be a junior in high school and a move like this wasn't sitting well with her. She had no time to say goodbye to her friends; however, her bestie, Katy, would come visit shortly after they had settled in. Though she was torn about leaving the only place she called home, Sofia always had a sense of adventure that made this new journey only mildly tolerable.

Annie's jaw dropped in amazement as they drove by the stadium. It would be a dream come true to attend a school like that. *I wonder what the people are like?* she thought as she imagined befriending some of the students she saw walking around, with their big brains and unique fashion sense. *How lucky they must be.*

Art pulled up to a big brown-and-green apartment complex just a few miles away from the UT campus. If you went outside in the evenings, you could hear the drumline practicing for the big games. On the first floor, Art unloaded his belongings; three doors down, Annie and Sofia unloaded their things as well.

They were still in close quarters, but it was a good start for all of them to adjust to their new lifestyle. It was what was best for everyone.

Over the next few months, Annie and Sofia bonded closer than Annie ever imagined they would. Both Paul and Greg even came down a few weekends to help their parents get adjusted and enjoy what Austin had to offer. It was the summer of 1987 and Austin was young, vibrant, and full of opportunities. Art was enjoying his new job and felt relief knowing that not only his daughter but his beautiful friend and love of his life was close by.

1993
FORTY-SEVEN YEARS OLD

"Mrs. Garza, why do you think you'd be a good fit for the Leander Independent School District?" Mr. Santiago asked in a low husky voice. He sat with a large notepad in front of him on the table, nervously clicking his pen. He had bushy brown eyebrows and transition eyeglasses that looked a bit too dark for the setting. A little underdressed for the interview, he sat comfortably in well-worn blue jeans complemented by a navy collared shirt with the district's logo embroidered on the left-hand side.

"It would be a dream of mine to work in this district with such smart students. I've heard nothing but great things about the faculty. Some people think they know what hard work is, but I can assure you, you will never have to worry about me showing up late or not finishing my work."

"That is great to hear. We've had difficulties in the past with employee punctuality. Working in a school, there are no excuses for tardiness. The kids, teachers, and even the parents expect the school to look and feel a certain way. You'd be a large part of that. Is that something you think you can handle?"

"Without a doubt! I have three kids of my own, and they're grown now, but I've been able to build great relationships with them and my grandchildren too. Working here will give me something to look forward to and give me purpose in life. I want to be here, more than you will ever know."

"Great! Seems like you're more than qualified to work here. We will finish your background check next week and then I'll be in touch."

"Thank you, Mr. Santiago! I'm very excited about this opportunity." Annie stood up and smoothed out her long skirt before extending her right hand for a formal thank you and goodbye.

Walking to the parking lot, the joy just radiated from her face. She had knocked the interview out of the park, scoring a job she'd been eyeing for many years—to be part of a great school district, surrounded by brilliant minds. She would soon be the newest school janitor.

"Mom, how was it?" Sofia asked, sitting in the driver's seat of her Toyota. "Tell me everything!" She could sense it would be good news and couldn't wait to hear all the nitty-gritty details of her mom's interview.

"Oh, it went well. Real well," Annie said, trying to be modest as she got into the passenger seat. She looked at Sofia, always so pretty: she was wearing a bright polka-dot dress and had her permed dark-brown hair in a high ponytail to accentuate the volume. Her twinkling brown eyes full of excitement. The two were incredibly close and had decided to be roommates until Annie felt confident enough to live on her own in the small town of Leander, just northwest of Austin.

"And …?" Sofia urged.

"He said that once I pass the background check—then I'm in! I'm in!"

The two women bounced up and down in the car's tiny seats, screaming loud and proud.

"That is so exciting! I am so proud of you, Mom. Now, we need you to get your license so you can go to work on your own."

"One thing at a time, okay. Let's do one thing at a time."

"I know, I know. I'm just saying. I can help you study so that you're able to pass the driving test. I want you to be able to be free how you want to be. And driving, especially here in the country, is the only way you're going to feel that way."

"You're right! I'll think about it. But for now, let's celebrate. At Sonic. Drinks on me!"

Through many jobs at fast-food restaurants and hotels, Annie had always been looking for something that paid a little extra and had more consistent hours. Sofia had finally landed her mom this wonderful interview with a school district that had great reviews. Now Annie would be able to afford her own car in no time at all!

PART IV
AUSTIN, TEXAS

1997

The moment I thought would never arrive was finally here. My family and I had been preparing over the past couple of months: buying new outfits, practicing my manners, and stuffing my first backpack with all the necessities. I was particularly excited about the variety of snacks in the pantry I had to choose from—fruit rollups and crackers with cheese dip were on the top of the list.

On the night before my first day of school, I strutted all my new outfits down the center of the living room as the crowd went wild for my twirls and hair flips. My ears went deaf from my mother's applause, and after much debate I finally chose the perfect first-day-of-school outfit. I went into my purple bedroom and bent my knees on the soft beige carpet. Item by item I organized my belongings on the right side of my bed: a dark-blue denim dress, a brand-new pair of Dr. Martens fisherman sandals, and my hunter-green JanSport backpack.

At exactly 6:15 a.m. the next day, my alarm finally went off. Like a bouncy ball, I got out of bed, ran to the bathroom to brush my teeth, ran back to my bedroom, threw on my outfit, and was ready for school by 6:18 a.m. Looking back, I probably could have spent more time brushing my hair and my teeth, but don't worry, my hygiene has significantly improved over the years. I sat on my unmade bed, waiting to accomplish the next milestone. My stomach grumbled gently, reminding me to eat breakfast.

Trying not to trip over my own feet (the sandals were taking some getting used to), I walked slowly down the stairs, choking the handrail as I made my way toward the kitchen. Upstairs you could hear the rumblings of my dad getting my little brother dressed and ready for daycare.

"Wow, someone looks beautiful for their first day of school," my mom said as she poured herself a cup of coffee.

"Stop it!" I whined. I was not in the mood for any mushy-gushy crap. "You told me I had to get up without a fuss or you'd take me to school in my pajamas. And that would be embarrassing."

"That's right. I would have dropped you off in your pajamas. But I'm so proud of you for getting up right when you were supposed to. Are you hungry?"

"Yes, can I have some cereal, please?"

"Yes?"

"Yes, ma'am."

"That's right. Don't forget your manners. Did you already brush your teeth and wash your face?"

"Yes, ma'am," I said begrudgingly. "I'm not a baby. I did that already."

"No need to get snarky, young lady. I am just asking you a simple question. After you eat your cereal, you need to brush your teeth again."

"Yes, ma'am."

I shuffled over to the kitchen table and grabbed the box of cereal to look at the pictures on the back while I ate my breakfast. Little critters started to fill my stomach and my hands began to sweat a bit as I realized what I was in for the rest of the day.

"Mom?" I asked nervously.

"What's wrong?"

"What if I don't make any friends? And what if the teacher doesn't like me?"

"Oh, everyone is going to like you. It's okay to be nervous, but you're so much fun, and you're sweet and funny. You're going to make lots of friends. Now finish up, grab your things, we've got to get going soon."

Using the bowl's built-in straw, I slurped the rest of my cereal milk as slowly as possible, to delay the inevitable. I brushed my teeth for the second time that morning, grabbed my backpack filled to the brim with school supplies, and headed downstairs to wait for the official "We're leaving!" announcement from my mother.

I didn't say a word the entire car ride to school. My mom and dad both bombarded me with pointers on how to behave, reminding me for the thousandth time to use my manners, not talk while the teacher is talking, and be a good listener. My baby brother was sound asleep in his car seat beside me—just another day for him.

The front of the school reminded me of Disney World. Greeters welcomed families and ushered us to the wall where our assigned classrooms were posted. Little maps were handed out and the principal was meeting with the nervous Nellies who had made their way to their first day of school too.

My teacher's classroom smelled of cinnamon and apples. As soon as I walked in, I was greeted with a warm hug from Ms. Flores. She had long black hair that covered her bottom and was curled at the end. I looked around to get familiar with the room where I would be spending all my time. Bright posters covered the beige walls and portions of the green chalkboard. Other kids like me were posing for pictures, and some were even playing around and laughing.

I walked to the back of the room and placed my belongings

in a cubby, my mom following closely behind as my dad stayed at the classroom door peeking in with my baby brother. Using one of the markers provided, she carefully printed my name in large black letters on the piece of tape outside the cubby so that I could remember which one was mine. Then I went and hung up my lunchbox in my own tiny locker. As I sat at my new desk, next to my new classmates, I waved goodbye to my mom, dad, and brother as they stood right next to me, wiping tears from their eyes.

"Don't cry. I'm fine. Go, I'll be okay." I was nervous but also very excited for what the day had in store. My parents nodded and giggled as they looked at each other, teary-eyed. They both kissed my cheek and walked out of the classroom with my brother.

The day was full of fun surprises. I had never been in a structured environment before and loved how we did everything as a unit. My classmates and I did everything together: we ate snacks together, we napped together, we even played games together. School was awesome!

By the time the last bell rang, I had so many great stories to share with my dad, who was at the very front of the parent pickup line. I ran out of the school and hopped into the backseat of our green minivan. As his classical music played on the stereo, I began spilling out all the details of my eventful first day while he drove us to Sonic to celebrate with a sweet treat.

" … And the kids were awesome. MaryBeth has a pet frog at home, and guess what?" I said.

"What?" my dad replied with a big smile on his face.

"It eats real live mouses," I said with astonishment.

"Mice."

"What?"

"The frog eats mice," my dad corrected me gently.

"Yeah! And then during naptime I lay next to Dino, and we just stared at each other the whole time. We didn't even nap. But every time Ms. Flores would walk by, I'd close my eyes so that I wouldn't get in trouble."

"I am so excited for you, Alice. It sounds like you had a wonderful day."

"I did, Dad. It was the best day ever. I love school and I want to go to school every day!"

"Lucky for you, you get to go to school five days a week," he said with a smirk, hoping my honeymoon phase with education wasn't short-lived.

I sang the whole way home about school while I slurped on my Sonic strawberry milkshake and ate cheese sticks. That evening, when my mom got home from work, I got to repeat the highlights all over again as she gasped with excitement and prodded for all the fun stories and details. I slept like an angel that night and had a much harder time waking up for my second day of school, but I still loved everything about it.

The first couple months of elementary school were a blast. I was challenged by the printing of letters, learning the sound that each letter made, and learning to read and associate words with items. I made a few friends, but I would have much rather hung out with the teachers and learned about their lives and how they grew into such brilliant people. I was fascinated with school and with learning. I wanted to be the smartest person in the class and wanted more homework so that it would keep me busy when I got home from school.

I loved telling my parents every detail about my day: learning to count with the colored blocks and learning how seeds turned into plants with sunlight and water. There was never a dull day, and my parents couldn't have been more proud of me.

"All right, if you are at tables 1, 3, and 5, please head to the front of the classroom door and line up," Ms. Flores requested in a soft yet demanding voice. She always knew how to get her students lined up in the most orderly way possible.

I double-checked my table number and quietly headed to the door. I squeezed my hands in excitement because it was painting day in art and I couldn't wait to get my fingers all messy, with creativity flowing through me. I could just picture the dinosaurs and dragons I would paint with ease. I wore an old dance T-shirt, as per the art teacher's request. In case any paint got on it, I wouldn't get in trouble at home.

A long snake of children walked down the hallway and stopped at the double bathrooms. One by one we were asked to use the restroom prior to making the journey across the school and into Ms. Eubank's art class. I had my hands in my pockets and was staring off into space. I didn't need to use the restroom, I just wanted to get to art class as fast as possible. As I made my way toward the front of the bathroom line, I noticed a familiar shape washing her hands at the sink. *Could it be?*

"Nanny?!" I shouted in confusion and excitement but got hushed very quickly by my peers. She turned around and I saw her bright-green eyes and her big curly hair all pinned back. *It was her!* We made eye contact and I rushed over to give my grandma the tightest hug that my little body could squeeze out.

"Go, go back in line, mija. Don't get in trouble." She was excited to see me, but she was also very shy and protective. She was wearing a gray T-shirt and jeans and looked a little flushed. I didn't care about getting in trouble. I hadn't seen my grandma in months and here she was at my very own school. I grabbed her hands and dragged her in front of my teacher.

"Nanny, this is my teacher, Ms. Flores. Ms. Flores, this is my grandma. She's the best!" The students started getting restless, but Ms. Flores quickly greeted my grandmother and she started moving the line to art class. I wanted to spend every moment I could with my grandma—my mind was no longer focused on art. I had so much to show her, my new backpack, my sweet lunchbox, my favorite green water bottle, and my lucky eraser that I had won from the treasure chest for being a good listener.

However, I had to follow my classmates to art so as I walked to the back of the line I waved goodbye wildly to Nanny. As we made our way to the other side of the school, I started to wonder why she was at my school in the first place: *Was she going to join me for lunch? Was she picking me up early? Was everything okay with Mom and Dad?*

We settled into our seats in the art room and put on giant aprons speckled with dry paint. Ms. Eubank explained the instructions for our assignment and then we were off to get our hands messy in the cold wet globs of delicious paint.

"Hey, Alice," my classmate Kevin asked as he fingered his way through a masterpiece.

"Yeah?" I said, keeping my eyes focused on my artwork.

"Why was your grandma here?"

"I don't know. She probably wanted to see me at school or something."

"That's cool. My grandma died," Kevin said, matter-of-fact.

"Whoa, that's sad. Are you sad?"

"No, she was mean."

"My nanny isn't mean at all. She's the best and makes the best food, and sings the best songs, and she always gets me the best birthday presents. She used to babysit me when I was little."

"She sounds awesome," Kevin said with amazement.

"She is." I smiled a braggadocious smile and continued painting with the utmost concentration of any five-year-old.

Throughout the rest of the day, I could feel my grandma's presence around me: love and warmth. It had made my whole day to see her at school. I prayed it would happen again.

The final bell rang and I walked quickly to the parent pickup line. There was my dad in our bright-green van in front again, waiting for me. I threw my things into the back and flung my body into the seat and buckled up. Before we even began moving, I started talking excitedly.

"Dad, Dad, Dad. Guess what?!"

"What, what, what?" he said, overenthusiastically, as my younger brother cried loudly in his car seat next to me.

"Nanny was at school today! I saw her washing her hands and I ran up and hugged her, but she didn't stay. I had to go to art class. In art class I made a crazy cool painting, but I couldn't bring it home today because it had to dry."

"What an adventure you had today, Alice. And your mother called me and told me Nanny's been transferred. She's going to be working at the middle schools and elementary schools over here."

"NANNY'S A TEACHER?!" My mind couldn't grasp that my grandma was one of those brilliant people I aimed to be exactly like one day.

"Not quite, but she helps make the school beautiful. It's a very important job."

"THAT. IS. AWESOME." I couldn't believe that Nanny was going to be at my very own school *and* she had the job of making it beautiful.

My dad turned the car air conditioning to freezing while he played classical music and waited for my brother and me to fall asleep. It would become his normal routine before taking us home. I dreamed of Nanny taking art class with me, running into her all the time, and having her bring me presents in front of all my friends. They would think I was so cool.

That same week, I felt like I was playing Where's Waldo? every time I entered the school hallways. I would look around feverishly, trying to find Nanny hiding throughout the building: in the bathroom stalls, in the cafeteria, in the teachers' lounge. And at least a few times a week, my wish would come true.

Nanny would be carrying large things and what I thought were probably very important things from one place to the next.

My classmates would say hi to her too, and she became the most popular school worker there was! I loved telling everyone how my grandma was in charge of making the entire school beautiful. It was up to her.

I could feel students envying me. I had the coolest grandma around town. Seeing her in the hallways made kindergarten that much better. And now that she lived close, she'd even join my family for dinner like the old days when she lived with us.

"Nanny, when I grow up, I want to be like you," I told her one evening over a warm bowl of Mexican spaghetti.

"No, no. When you grow up, you are going to be smart. Read all the books and learn as much as you can," she told me, a sternness in her voice.

"Oh, I will," I shouted with glee. "I'll read all the books and be smart like you so I can work in a school. My teacher is the smartest and I told her you were even smarter because you helped make the school beautiful. There are a lot of teachers, but nobody else does what you do, Nanny." I slurped my noodles and smiled my gap-toothed smile.

She stared at her bowl of soup, twirling the spoon. "You're funny," she told me as she got up to wash the dishes and help my mom with my baby brother.

Over Christmas break, I couldn't wait to get back to school and my normal routine. I'd lay in my pajamas and spend my time trying to practice writing my name and all sorts of new words I was adding to my memory bank. Sometimes when I didn't want to do my writing practice, I could hear Nanny's voice in the background: *"You need to study hard so you can be smart. If you're smart, you can do whatever you want in this world."*

I would picture my future as a teacher or a doctor, and I knew that doing well in school was key to making my grandmother proud. For whatever reason, Nanny's approval was the silver lining. She was a woman of few words, but when she was happy her smile was contagious and to receive one of them from her felt unlike anything else in the world.

One of my favorite pastimes was playing school. Obviously, I was the teacher in charge and my baby brother was the student. Sitting cross-legged on the living-room floor, I was surrounded by some of my workbooks. My brother was playing with his stuffed animals and I called for his attention or he would be sent to the scary principal's office. He sat ready to begin his lesson and I opened up a bright-orange-and-pink book with a large tree on the front.

I stood up tall, pushing my invisible glasses up to my eyes so I could properly see all the letters and read to my room of students. Page by page I read until my baby brother fell asleep. He was a good student and only needed to be hushed once or twice. He still didn't know all his manners, but talking while the teacher was talking was unacceptable! As I finished turning the last of the thick pages, my grandma walked in with a big smile on her face.

"Nanny, Nanny, come read with us." I ran up to her, holding an armful of books and giving her my best puppy-dog eyes.

She sat down on the light-brown sofa. She was wearing black pants and a Whitestone Elementary School T-shirt—I could tell by the big Wildcat design on the front. She seemed tired, but her encouraging smile didn't fade. "Okay, mija, go ahead."

"No, Nanny, you're the teacher now. It's your turn to read." I handed her the book and laid my head on her right arm as I snuggled up next to her.

"Alice, you need to read to me. It's important you practice," she said with less impatience in her voice.

So I read her my favorite book and waited for her to help me as I stuttered through the words. It was much easier to read when I was making up the words with my brother; certainly my grandmother wouldn't tolerate that. To my surprise, she didn't help me as I stumbled. She told me to sound it out and work hard to figure it out on my own. As long as I didn't quit, I would be progressing.

1999

My hot face was covered in wetness. Snot dripping out of my nose, tears streaming down my red cheeks, and spit flying everywhere as I cried an ugly, hysterical cry. My heart had been broken.

Just moments before my devastation, I had been sitting on the bench at our oak kitchen table in the downstairs kitchen—my designated spot for finishing homework immediately after school. I took pride in organizing my folders, making sure the corners of my papers lined up evenly, and showing off my electric-green pencil sharpener that went with me everywhere.

Today's assignment was quite difficult. I had missed two questions on my spelling test and my mom had requested that I spend double the time practicing so that I'd get them all right for the next spelling test.

"Nanny!" I screamed toward the upstairs. "Can! You! Please! Come! Here! I! NEED! YOU!"

"What, mija!" Nanny shouted as she came to the banister at the top of the stairs. "What's wrong?!" She was clearly out of breath, worried I was hurt or injured.

"I need help with my spelling quiz. Can you help me?"

"Not right now, I'm folding towels," Nanny said, irritated at my urgent yelling.

"But my mom said I have to do this or I'll be in really big trouble. And last time I … "

"No, you're a big girl now. Figure it out," Nanny said.

"I can't do this by myself. I can't quiz myself, that's why it's a quiz!" I called out, far more snarky than I intended to. I mean, I was a snooty little seven-year-old who wanted to be the best at everything.

"I said no." She turned around and looked at me sternly. I should have taken the hint to quit asking, but I didn't. I continued pressing her, as I knew she would help me if I kept asking.

"But you always tell me to do good in school and if you don't help me, then you want me to do bad!"

Nanny shook her curly head in frustration and walked back into my parents' room to continue the cleaning she always liked to help out with. She looked mad and I knew I had upset her.

Truth was, I was upset too. I marched right upstairs to give my grandmother a piece of my seven-year-old mind. I needed help and she was basically telling me to go fail. She was ensuring that I would just be dumb!

As I walked into my parents' bathroom, the green floor tile was super shiny, looking as though it had just been mopped. Sitting on the floor like a mermaid was my grandmother, who was busy organizing the lotions and soaps in the cabinet under the sink. I tiptoed my way across the drying tiles and tapped on my grandmother's left shoulder.

She ignored me.

I tapped on her shoulder again, as I could feel my patience dissipating.

"Why do you want me to fail my test?" I asked angrily. I knew I had gotten her. I knew that I had shown her that she was being mean and that I wouldn't allow her to let me fail.

"Alice, you have no reason to talk to me that way, young lady," Nanny said sternly as she continued to organize the cabinet.

"I asked you nicely to help me study and you won't. When someone asks for help and says please, you're supposed to help them. You're mean," I said in an ugly voice.

"You need to practice on your own. Have your brother help you," she said.

"My brother is in kindergarten—he can't even read yet! How is he supposed to help me?"

"Well, I can't read either."

"Yes, you can!" I said, disappointed that my own grandmother would lie to my face.

"No, I can't read. I never learned how. Never went to school and I don't know how to read or write. Only thing I know how to do is write my name."

"What do you mean, you never went to school?" I was still shocked by what she had just shared.

"Well, when I was a little girl like you, my dad made me work in a cotton field and I never had the chance to go to school. So I can't read."

"But … " my voice trailed off as I became so sad for my grandmother. How is it that my biggest hero had never gone to school? I started to think about the childhood she had and how she had to go to work like a grown-up even though she was just a kid.

I ran out of my parents' bathroom and locked myself in my bedroom until my parents came home. I wasn't convinced she was telling the truth. Everyone went to school, why would she be any different? My grandmother was the smartest person I knew, and she had just rocked my whole perspective on who she was.

When my mother came home that evening, she woke me up, as I had fallen asleep on my bed holding my teddy bear Mr. Cuddles close to my chest.

"Alice, wake up. We need to talk," she said as she stroked my back gently. "I heard you were disrespectful to your nanny earlier today. What happened? That doesn't sound like you."

I sat up and rubbed my eyes. Instantly, I felt defensive. My grandmother had snitched on me. *Kick me while I'm down, why don't you?*

"Yes, Nanny wanted me to do bad on my spelling test. She wouldn't help me even after I said please, and then she told me she never went to school. Mom, everyone goes to school. She's a grown-up so I got mad because she is lying because she doesn't want to help me."

"I have some sad news to share with you, Alice," my mother said as she pushed my long brown hair behind my ears. "Nanny doesn't know how to read and write, she wasn't lying. She doesn't know how to help you with your spelling words. When I was a kid, she couldn't help me either. I had to go to school super early and my teachers would help me. And when my teachers weren't available, I had Uncle Greggy and Uncle Paul help too. Nanny can't help you with that. It's true."

You may have guessed it, but I was an unusually sympathetic child. My heart was broken for my grandmother. The reality sunk in that not only had I been a little shit, but also that I felt terrible for the life she must have experienced. How do people survive without knowing how to read or write?

"Momma, what do you mean? Why didn't her parents let her go to school?"

"Well, Nanny's mom died when she was a baby and her dad was a mean man who only wanted Nanny to work to get money. He didn't care that she couldn't read. All he cared about was money. So I need you to go apologize to your nanny right now. Tell her you are sorry."

I walked out of my bedroom with my head hanging low. Nanny was making dinner and I whispered softly, barely able to be heard, "I'm sorry I was rude to you, Nanny. I love you."

"It's okay, mija. I love you too," she said as she sprinkled salt into the big pot.

Like a blubbering mess, I continued on, "I'm sorry you can't read. I didn't know, Nanny. I didn't know." I was sad at the words that were leaving my mouth.

"Mija, come sit on the sofa with me. Take a deep breath, don't be so upset. Wipe your face," she said as I made my way to lie on her while she calmed me down.

"I'm sorry," I continued to cry.

"What I want you to learn from this is that everyone's life is different. I didn't go to school, but I am the luckiest woman in the entire world. All you need to do is continue doing your best in school and work hard every day because not everyone is as lucky as you. I've worked really hard so that you as my granddaughter get to live a better life than me. You get to be smarter than I was. Never ever take that for granted."

Those words resonated with me, even as a young and sassy seven-year-old. I realized that very day how incredibly fortunate I was to be able to read a book and spell my name and be in second grade. I was a very lucky girl, and someone as important as my grandmother depended on me to show her how much I loved her by being as smart as I could be and trying my best in everything.

I knew that I wanted to make her proud, whether it be on my next spelling test or math test—I would give it my all. People like my grandmother deserved to know their hard work wasn't going to be for nothing.

That week when I went back to school, I had a new perspective. I asked other students if their grandparents had been to school. I asked my teacher if her grandma could read. I was so interested to find out about a population who had never experienced education before. To my surprise, Nanny was one of very few people who had never attended school. Her childhood and her life became even more fascinating to me. I wanted to know everything about her and her life.

It wasn't until much later in life that I would really understand who Annie Garza was.

2000

To the right of the entryway was a large black caldron filled to the brim with an assortment of candies, from Snickers bars to bubble gum, M&Ms and Red Hots. A silver Sony stereo played a series of Halloween top tracks, including "Monster Mash," to create a creepy atmosphere that would draw in the neighborhood's trick-or-treaters. As the doorbell rang, I sprinted to the front of the house, holding my witch hat so that it wouldn't fall over my eyes. I jammed my hand into the giant caldron and swam it around to pick out the best candies. It was up to me to determine who would get the most candy based on each trick-or-treater's costume and perceived level of effort. I took this task very seriously, as any nine-year-old would.

After passing out the candy, I would give a giant smile, waving goodbye to the neighborhood kids, and run back to my beloved science-fair project: a formicarium filled with the most plump and lively ants you've ever seen. I lay in the living room, belly to the carpet, writing a report on the most interesting creatures on the planet.

Everything about ants intrigued me. It was a few months ago, during the summer, when I watched an entire *National Geographic* special on these fascinating insects. Since then, I had become obsessed with learning about them: from the number of naps they took a day to their incomparable strength. Ants were the most underrated and most underappreciated species on earth and my science-fair project was about to show everyone why.

The neon-yellow poster board had some of my best drawings of an enlarged ant. I used a ruler to map out the different segments of their anatomy: head, thorax, and abdomen. I'd be lying if I said I wasn't proud of my work and excited to share my discoveries with anyone who would listen. I could picture the blue ribbon already; I would win the science fair and share my expertise with the world!

"Shouldn't you be out trick-or-treating?" my nanny asked as she walked into the living room wearing a bright-orange shirt with purple earrings. "Go spend time with your friends and eat candy! You're only young once, and one day you'll wish you would have spent time trick-or-treating rather than working."

"Are you kidding me! Tomorrow is the biggest day in my

entire life and if I want to win the science fair, then I have to make sure my project is absolutely perfect." I kept ranting about the importance of this project while envisioning my next creative move. I picked up a brown Crayola marker to keep refining my work. "Plus, I'm already nine. I don't want to be trick-or-treating with a bunch of babies."

"Mija, you are too mature for your own good. But I'm proud of you and I'm sure your project is going to be wonderful." Nanny sat on the brown leather sofa and watched as I focused on the project at hand, zoning out everything else except for the doorbell—that, of course, was a must-do.

As I finished up the last round of edits on my poster, I headed to the bathroom to practice my presentation skills. Fifty percent of the grade was going to be based on the presentation of my science-fair project. Projection, confidence of the topic, and eye contact were major factors. I wanted to be well prepared before presenting before my entire third-grade class. They'd be harsh critics and I had to give them my best.

I watched my demeanor in the mirror; I practiced lifting my chin as I spoke so that I appeared confident, as my mother taught me to be. I gave myself cues as to when to slow down so that the audience would know that it was their time to laugh. There was something about sharing this presentation that excited me and filled my heart. I wanted—more than trick-or-treating, more than hanging out with friends—to give the Third Grade Science Fair everything I had.

The only thing left was to win. Deep down, I wanted to be out trick-or-treating with the others, but I knew, as my grandmother had always taught me, that education comes first. The rest will fall into place. I practiced in my bathroom mirror until my tongue felt dry. Before heading to bed, I said a prayer and organized my items perfectly next to my bed. My stomach was in knots and my mind started racing. I was uneasy and nervous that all my hard work was about to be judged by my peers.

There was a light knock on my bedroom door. "Alice, are you doing okay?" Nanny asked in the middle of the night, long after the last trick-or-treaters had gone home. She opened my door and looked in on me.

"Yes, I'm fine," I replied, agitated at the world.

"I heard some crying in here and something told me to check on you. Did you hear the crying too? Was it the neighbor, maybe?"

A flood of emotions overcame me. "I, I, I can't do it. I can't go into my class with this stupid poster and these stupid ants." I was trembling in my light-pink pajamas as I sat up in discomfort.

"Whoa, come here, mija. What's going on?" Nanny stretched her arms out to hold me tightly against her warm chest. I was drowning in fear, imagining the worst: my project wouldn't be good enough and everyone would laugh me out of school.

"What if my project doesn't win?" I looked up at my grandmother as I wiped my tears.

"If your project doesn't win, who cares? Did you enjoy learning about ants?"

"Yeah, I did. But if I don't win, then it doesn't matter."

"No, no, that's not true at all," she said as she used her hankie to clean my face. "You can't let what you have be impacted by what others think. If you think ants are awesome, what anyone else thinks should never change that. You are so very brave and smart, mija, and when I was little I would have never dreamed of doing something like this. You pick your chin up and give the best presentation you can."

I continued to wipe my eyes. "Can you and Mommy come watch me present?"

"I promise. We'll be there." Nanny lay next to me in my twin trundle bed. She rubbed my back until my nerves calmed and I fell asleep.

The next day at school, the hallways were decorated with colorful paintings that celebrated the 100th day of school. Bright construction paper glittered with an assortment of creative ways to display 100, including 100 artfully arranged beans glued to paper and 100 googly eyes stuck on mini-monsters.

Small bodies covered Mrs. Gerlinger's classroom floor, all sitting criss-cross applesauce. Each student was squirming with excitement to present their project. Proud parents with large camcorders stood shoulder to shoulder in the back of the class, waiting for their star's turn to shine. I kept looking over to make sure my mom and Nanny would see me present.

"We are so excited that everyone has joined us today," Mrs. Gerlinger said at the front of the room. She was wearing a knee-length khaki skirt and a denim button-down. She was in her early twenties, but you could feel the students tensing up as she spoke. She had earned their undivided attention and respect. "The Third Grade Science Fair is a wonderful time for students to demonstrate their critical thinking and quantitative skills. All students' projects will be presented today in the order of the number that they pulled from the hat. Students, please remember your number! Before we get started, I want to remind everyone that we clap after every single presentation. It can be nerve-wracking speaking to a big group of people, but don't worry, we are all your biggest supporters. And last but not least, absolutely no talking during another student's presentation. If I catch you talking, you will automatically get ten points taken off your final score. Does everyone understand?"

"Yes, Mrs. Gerlinger," the class responded in unison, and the parents looked at one another, impressed by her ability to control the room.

"All righty then, first up we have Gavin!"

Gavin was a geeky little fellow. He had dirty blond curls, big gold glasses, and wore his socks up to his mid-calf. He rolled a cart over that had three large jars with bones in them. The presentation focused on the elements that impact and expedite bone decay. He'd collected the bones from the local butcher and was gleaming that his hypothesis had matched his conclusion. Gavin's presentation was spectacular and certainly he'd be a future valedictorian.

There was an audible gasp at how impressive his findings were. You could tell that in less than five minutes, many of the adults in the room had learned more from Gavin's presentation than they had ever anticipated learning from a third-grade science fair. How immaculate his young mind was, and what a bright future he had ahead of him.

Compared to Gavin's presentation, the next couple of students were sub-par. One student, obviously the class clown, focused on different farts and how our bodies produce gas. Another student shared her findings on the creation and history of volcanoes. Her 3D figure—a fully functioning volcano that foamed up in eruption—clearly was made by her mom, who clapped extra loud as her father whistled annoyingly at the end.

"Alice, you're up next!" Mrs. Gerlinger called. Suddenly I felt like I was about to vomit, but I couldn't let any of that show. I had worked so hard for this moment, and I wanted it to be everything I'd practiced and more.

I stood before the class wearing an antennae headband that

bobbed around as I set up my ant display. Staring at my mom and Nanny, I took a deep breath to try to reduce the sour taste building up in my mouth. This was my most treasured work and it was time for me to present it to a room full of my friends and smiling adults. I paused for what felt like hours and stared at the ant farm, trying to remember my first line. I glanced back at my grandma, who gave me a powerful nod and pierced her eyes into me. I could feel her encouragement.

"Ants are awesome." A roomful of giggles welcomed me, calming my nerves. I was slowly getting into my element. "No, seriously. Ants are some of the strongest creatures in the *entire* world. They're some of the smallest bugs, but did you know that ants can lift up to one hundred times their own body weight? That would be like me, or you, or you"—I pointed dramatically at different classmates—"lifting one thousand pounds." I flexed my biceps with a gritty smile. I could feel my passion permeating through my voice and body language.

"Here, I have a small colony of ants." I grabbed my plastic ant farm to show it to the class. "They've been my roommates for the past few weeks, but don't tell my mom." I added a dramatic wink, and another wave of giggles complimented my theatrics. "These ants work non-stop to make sure their nest is set up for the queen to lay thousands of eggs every day!"

I continued holding up the formicarium, pointing to the

different lines that weaved through the glass. "Ants take several hundred naps a day, mini-naps of course. Each nap is around five minutes long, so that they're always working and getting things done."

My mind went blank. I couldn't remember my next line. My heart was beating in my ears, my hands were shaking, and I knew that it was about to go really bad. I started to panic. Instead of freezing, I decided to improvise. I started marching at the front of the class, trying my best to emulate a tiny but mighty ant.

"Ants march around, working all day and night to contribute to building their colony."

I scanned the room, trying to find some cue to help me remember what I was supposed to talk about next. I could feel my face turn bright red. And when I thought this moment would end, it didn't, so I just kept on going.

"Actually," I said as I marched in place, "people and ants have a lot in common. For example, my grandma is *exactly* like a marching ant." I pointed to the back of the room and Nanny shot me a mortified look. "Yeah, she is always working for her family and barely even sleeps. Just like these ants, Nanny does everything she can to make sure her family's home is always neat and tidy. She works all the time, cleaning and cooking. Ants also are willing to do anything for their families, just like my grandma."

In that moment, all Nanny's insecurities had been swept away.

She felt a wave of warmth rush through her veins. She realized that I had never judged her for what she couldn't do or what she saw as her own inabilities. It was during that presentation that Nanny realized I saw her for all the contributions she made to our family. It had been ages since she'd felt so valued, and having that kind of validation felt like a message from God. *A marching ant*—Nanny liked the sound of that.

A smile crept across my teacher's face. I had to keep going. *Remember my lines, remember my lines.* "We should all want to be like ants—contributing to a colony ... and—" *That's what it was: colonies! I am finally back on track.*

"Ants create these amazing colonies so that the queen can lay several thousand eggs a day. There's always a queen, she's the leader of the entire colony. And together they create more little ants that help keep the colony alive and strong. Last but certainly not least, ants are helpers to one another and to the environment. They do what is called aerating the soil, which is a fancy way of saying they help plants get oxygen and water. Like I said at the beginning, ants are awesome!"

I took a big bow of relief in front of the class. I had ended my presentation slightly abruptly, but I garnered a large applause from everyone as I showed off my family of ants. A curtain of embarrassment came over me as I recalled the different subjects I had forgotten to go over. I skipped the entire part about the ant's body and the different types of ways they eat and forage for food.

The rest of the presentations were a blur, but I had gotten a smile from my teacher and honestly, I was glad it was finally over. Once everyone was finished, we took a class photo next to our projects and enjoyed an ice cream sundae party to celebrate our hard work and efforts.

While I was adding sprinkles to my Styrofoam bowl of ice cream, I could hear muffled conversations going on with my mom and Nanny. "Your granddaughter brought tears to my eyes. It's so clear how much she loves you," said one of the other older ladies.

I could see Nanny's face blushing as she bashfully downplayed the compliment. I prayed and hoped she wouldn't be mad at me. I felt a light hug from behind me.

"Alice, that was so sweet of you to say all those things about me," Nanny said as she and my mom hugged me goodbye. I had chocolate ice cream on my face and was relieved that my improv skills had been well received.

When my dad picked me up from school a few hours later, I was exhausted.

"So, how'd the rest of your day go?" he asked with suspicion in his eyes.

"It was great. Mom and Nanny came and saw me this morning! Gavin took home first place. And then I don't remember who got second or third." I was staring at my family of ants, not even phased that I hadn't placed in the top three.

"That's wonderful! I'm sorry I couldn't be there this morning, I had a meeting, but Mom and Nanny said you did great. Forgot a couple of your lines, but you made up for it with style?"

"Yes, I totally forgot about colonies! I couldn't believe it. But everyone seemed to love my project. Carrie and Evan said that mine was the coolest.

"Well, that's wonderful! And how are you feeling about it?"

"I thought it was so fun that I don't really care now if I didn't win."

"That makes me happy for you then. I'm so proud of you. I heard you made Nanny cry?"

"I did?"

"Yeah, Mom said that you said some very kind words in front of your class. Nanny didn't know how to respond but was so honored."

"Yeah, well. When I think about it, Nanny is the strongest person I know. You know? After everything she's gone through, she just keeps on going."

"You're absolutely right about that one, girl," Dad said with a smile in his eyes. "Your grandmother is one tough woman. You can learn a lot from her. Take advantage of it! Not everyone is as lucky as you to have a grandmother that incredible."

I woke up in shock because of all the yelling and commotion. I slowly opened my bedroom door to the bright light in the back of the house toward the playroom. Moving quietly and listening intently, I followed my mother's voice.

"Mom, it was just a dream. You're okay, you're okay," I could hear her saying soothingly as I heard loud crying.

I walked into the messy playroom through the splatter of Legos and toy cars toward my grandmother's place at the back of the house: an attached garage converted into two rooms. I peeked through the cracked-open door to see my mom and Nanny sitting on the bed together.

It was an image burned in my memory: my grandmother was crying uncontrollably. I felt my eyes grow bigger as I took in the scene. She was wearing a long white nightgown shirt with a gray cat on the front, her purple fuzzy socks covering her small feet. My mom was holding her close like a child, brushing her sweaty hair back as she cried and let out the sorrows of her soul.

Saddened, I walked into the room to console my grandmother. Whatever was happening must be painful. I didn't understand it, but I kissed Nanny, told her I loved her, then headed back out to the living room, where my dad and brother sat quietly.

"Daddy, what happened to Nanny?" I asked, clutching Mr.

Cuddles, my ponytail running wild on my head.

"Nanny suffers from nightmares. She has trouble sleeping, and sometimes those nightmares make it hard for her to know when she's asleep or when she's awake."

"Oh my gosh, Dad! That's scary."

"It is very scary. Your grandmother has lived a hard life, and she never likes anyone to know about it. So this is very private to her. I need you to go back to sleep with your brother while your mother and I take care of Nanny, okay?"

"Okay?"

"Okay?" my dad said in disbelief.

"Okay, sir." I added the *sir* so he'd know that I knew why he'd repeated my statement.

That evening I prayed for Nanny and for all her nightmares to go away. As I paid more attention, I realized that these were not the first nightmares Nanny had had, nor would they be the last. Whatever she was dreaming about was scary enough to make the strongest woman alive weak in the knees.

2004

The middle-school cafeteria smelled sour, and it was so loud you could hardly hear yourself think. I remember sitting near the exit doors so that I'd make it to my next class on time and not get trampled by all the racing bodies. I was a quiet kid. I sat during lunch and would watch different people interact with one another. Observing people is something I've always been fascinated by.

As I ate my steak fingers and mashed potatoes, I heard rambunctious kids playing to the far left of me. Two boys were having a milk fight, where they each opened a small carton of chocolate milk, stuffed as much food as they could into it, and then banged their fist on top of their carton so the contents would splatter everywhere.

My eyes zeroed in on their little game. These idiots were my age, yet they acted like babies, making a mess like that. *They're disgusting*, I thought. But then it went from bad to worse.

The bell rang and those two boys left their mess all over the cafeteria table, running out the door as fast as they could to their next class. I was outraged.

As the cafeteria slowly emptied, I stood there contemplating what to do: help clean up or make it to class on time? I kept going back and forth, I couldn't make a decision. Finally, I set my books down on the long gray cafeteria table to clean up. As I looked up, I caught the eye of a small figure across the cafeteria. She had her hair tied back and her custodian shirt was far too big.

Milk cartons, napkins, and utensils were scattered all over the cafeteria, and there was my beautiful grandmother picking up every little piece with a big smile on her face.

I waved and smiled at her, while inside I was boiling over with anger. I went to greet her properly. She spent time between the middle school and the elementary school, so seeing her was always a nice surprise.

"Nanny, I'm going to help you clean this up," I told her kindly as my mind flashed back to the milk cartons stuffed with nuggets.

"No, mija, go to class," she demanded. "This is my job."

I was so angry. I felt frustrated that my peers could just make a mess and assume some old janitor was going to pick it up. Not on my watch, they wouldn't. Those buttholes.

My face went numb and I refused to leave the cafeteria. Looking around, I felt so sad that this is how people lived. I knew that being twenty minutes late to Ms. Duncan's history class would get me in trouble, but I also recognized that helping clean up this mess was the right thing to do.

As I picked up the trash, I wanted to write a letter to everyone, letting them know that it's our responsibility to clean up our own mess, not to make more of a mess for someone else to clean up. That's not grown-up; that's immature and rude and inconsiderate.

After throwing away the disgusting "art" left all over the cafeteria, my perception completely changed. My beautiful grandmother wasn't someone in the background; she was a real person who didn't deserve to be a slave to the incompetency and ignorance of seventh-grade boys and girls. For my entire walk to Ms. Duncan's class, I didn't know how to release my anger. It just continued to boil up through my hands, my feet; I was sweating profusely and my head was pounding.

As I walked into class, I wasn't prepared to explain myself for being incredibly late. All eyes were on me—not the kind of attention I needed for my level of emotional instability.

"Well, do you have a note for being so late?" Ms. Duncan asked firmly in front of everyone—and rightfully so.

"I was cleaning the cafeteria because"—the panic in my voice started to rise, as I knew I was about to be in a lot of trouble—

"because these other students had a milk fight and didn't clean it up, and the janitor has to clean it up and it isn't fair." My anger and disappointment burst forth in the tears starting to stream down my face. The entire class stared at me having a mental breakdown. Ms. Duncan placed her right arm over my shoulder and ushered me out of the classroom.

"Alice, what's going on? You're in hysterics right now." She looked me in the eyes and guided my breathing. Ms. Duncan was a tall woman, close to six feet, yet her voice and presence was so gentle and kind. She knew that I was a good student and that this behavior was outside my norm.

"One time we took a quiz on what we wanted to be when we grew up. And when *janitor* was listed as one of the options, everyone in the room laughed," I went on, referring to an incident that had happened months earlier in computer science class.

"Okay?"

"And my grandma is a janitor here and she cleans up the mess that everyone else makes. And no one else cares that their mess is cleaned up by someone else." I felt protective of my grandmother because the students I went to school with didn't know her life story and the hard work she'd put in day in and day out just to come this far.

"I know, Alice. Students can be callous at this age," Ms. Duncan said as she grazed her hands across my back. "Take a minute out here, and when you're ready, come back in."

After a moment I wiped my tears and went back to sit in class, where I promised myself I'd never be the kind of person who expects other people to clean up my mess. I knew that my grandmother would rather I focus on my studies than on her, but I couldn't help it. She was my everything, and I felt like no one appreciated her like she deserved to be appreciated.

"All right, Mom, I'm home!" my mother shouted as she walked through the front door wearing a dark suit and carrying loads of groceries. "I've got your cards, let's get started!"

I ran outside to the car to help unload the rest of the groceries and organize the pantry. I loved organizing all our supplies perfectly.

When I walked inside, my mom was already sitting at the oak kitchen table with notecards and markers. Nanny was sitting across from her with a cynical look on her face. I listened intensely as I pretended not to, putting the groceries away and making trips back and forth from the car to the kitchen.

"Mom, we will make the cards and someone will ask you the same questions on the test. You have to do this. We can't have you drive illegally, it's not okay."

"What are y'all talking about?" I asked, being my nosy pre-teen self.

"Nanny's finally going to test to get her driver's license!" my mom said excitedly, trying to convince my grandmother that this was great news.

"No, I'm not," Nanny said in a matter-of-fact tone.

"Yes, you are, and you're going to do great! We're going to help you memorize the pictures, Mom. It'll be good for you," my mom continued.

"Nanny, that's so cool!" I said loudly as I poked around in the refrigerator for new snacks to try before dinner.

My mom spent the next several hours prepping notecards for Nanny. She drew and colored stop signs, yield signs, and all sorts of other traffic symbols I wasn't too familiar with. On the back of the cards she wrote out descriptions that I was to review with Nanny every day after school until she'd memorized all 120 cards.

Nanny was a very shy student. I think it was because she was embarrassed that I had to read the cards to her while she repeated them to me. I'd show her the sign and she'd often find a way to make a joke.

"That means go!" she'd say, laughing.

"Nanny, you know that's a stop sign," I'd say as I rolled my eyes. Nanny had been driving illegally for years and felt that this test was a waste of time and energy.

"Okay, okay, try again," she'd say.

I'd show her a picture of a green traffic light.

"That means stop!" she'd say, making herself laugh again.

"Nanny, you have to take this seriously," I'd scold her gently.

I could tell she was nervous. But when my mother came home, the studying got serious. Nanny would go through the cards with my mom for hours and practice repeating the instructions in both Spanish and English to ensure she understood all the questions.

After about six weeks of preparation, the big day was finally here.

We all piled into my dad's green minivan and headed to the Austin DMV. My dad played loud Spanish music to hype up my grandmother for her test. She was quiet and stared out the window like a little kid not wanting to participate in anything. I prayed for her the entire ride to the DMV; I could only imagine the stress she was feeling. But she wanted to drive freely, and this was the key to do so!

My dad left us in the car with the A/C on while he walked Nanny into the brown-brick building. A few minutes later he came back with an unsure tone to his voice.

"Well, kids, let's send good wishes to Nanny. She's been working hard and this is a very big deal for her," he said as he turned up the AC and played the classical music a little louder, hoping to put us to sleep. (Even though my brother and I were both well over the napping age, he still believed in his heart this was the trick to inducing us to fall asleep.)

I prayed hard, and about an hour later Nanny came back with a big smile on her face.

"Sí, sí! I passed!" she said.

We celebrated and sang the entire way home. This was one of those moments that you'll never forget. She bounced and danced in her seat, screaming like a little kid. Nanny hadn't been able to read or write, yet with the help of my mom and me, she was able to pass her state driver's license exam and was now legally able to drive us around!

Over dinner that evening, Nanny bragged jokingly about her study skills, about how easy the exam was, and how she could take any test and pass it—even if she'd never been to real school.

It was beautiful seeing her light up. You could tell that she had found something within herself that she didn't even think existed. I honestly think this might have been one of her proudest moments.

2008

stood before the National Honor Society and presented a plan to serve our school in a unique and powerful way. I was confident that our commitment to our own staff would create a better environment and build a stronger bond between students and staff. Plus, we needed volunteer hours to stay active as National Honor Society members, so this was the perfect combination.

"We have a group of staff at this school who are rarely recognized," I said as I paced the front of the classroom. "I want to propose an honorary dinner for our janitorial staff." I saw a few puzzled faces look in my direction, but I continued pitching my idea. "What we can do is have a potluck where we all dress up and serve our janitors a nice meal, and then we clean up and honor them for the evening. It's something that can show them just how much we care! We do teacher appreciation, but we never do janitor appreciation. Without janitors, our schools would be a complete mess!"

I smiled and waited for questions from my peers before sitting back down. Fingers crossed they would like my idea, and we could start to honor the staff I felt were so incredibly underappreciated.

In just a few weeks, our plan was coming to fruition. Juniors and seniors at Vista Ridge High School dressed in their nicest outfits to serve our janitorial and cafeteria staff a potluck meal. A few of the staff shed tears, feeling more appreciated than ever before, and it was a small gesture that warmed all our hearts as students. We had the ability to come together and make a positive impact on the people who needed it!

As I walked through the front door of our home, I saw my grandmother organizing the shoe closet at the entryway.

"Nanny!" I shouted as I closed the large oak door. "Tonight was incredible! Guess what we did?"

"Well, hurry up and tell me," she said as she sat on the closet floor looking up at me.

"We had a beautiful dinner for our janitorial and cafeteria staff this evening. Everyone was so grateful and ugh, Nanny, it was just so amazing! And it's all because of you!" I told her with a big smile.

"Because of me?" she asked. "Bullshit!"

"No, I promise. Because you taught me to appreciate everyone. I don't know what our janitorial staff has been through, and I wanted the students in the NHS to see just how special our staff is. We got to know them, hear about their children, and learn about their lives. Nanny, our staff are all wonderful people, and it made me proud to know that you taught me that!"

"Well, good. Now go do your homework," she said as she shooed me away from her busy work.

Later that evening, when I couldn't sleep, I walked through the playroom into Nanny's living space. Her door was slightly ajar so I knocked gently before making my way in. She was lying on top of the bed in her nightgown and I lay down next to her to talk. Earlier that evening, while I was asking so many questions about all the staff who worked at my school, I realized that I knew so little about what made Nanny who she was.

Sure, I knew she had never gone to school. I knew she had never learned to read or write. But I didn't know who she was on the inside. What did she dream about as a kid? What did she want to be when she grew up?

That night, she and I lay side by side as she spilled her heart out to me. It had been a while since someone had asked her about her hopes and dreams. She wanted to tell me every detail, so I started to take notes and write down what she said. After that night, I would lie with her in bed for many months asking her questions, hearing her painful cries, and learning about the life she lived as a child and young adult.

Her stories inspired me so much: to be a better daughter, a better student, a better person. To hear about everything that she'd endured was so powerful to me. I wondered, *If she had stories this deep, what else was the rest of the world facing?*

PART V

2013
SIXTY-SIX YEARS OLD

t was time to get help—but asking for help wasn't one of Annie's strong suits. She was sitting in the living room with a throw pillow squished to her stomach, holding it tight, trying to ease the discomfort. On the coffee table to her left was a rainbow of medications: antacids, Pepto-Bismol, acetaminophen, and black coffee. The pain in her stomach had been getting constantly worse, making it harder to eat and keep food down.

Her son-in-law walked into the living room to help her stand. His dark-brown hand pushed on the small of her back while the other hand gently lifted her up. Annie wore soft baby-blue jeans, navy loafers, and a white three-quarter-sleeved shirt. She hated the doctor's but was grateful she didn't have to experience it alone.

The ride to the doctor's office was nearly silent. To try to break the ice, Roy made jokes about how she was being dramatic and overexaggerating her sickness. Annie wasn't having any jokes, though; she wanted to feel better and was willing to do whatever it took to ease the pain. She stared outside the passenger window and took in the passing surroundings. She felt helpless, her hope was disintegrating. Every speed bump and pothole flared the excruciating pain throughout her body.

As she started to remember the only other time she'd thought she was dying, a smile crept over her face.

"Suegra, I see a smile over there. What are you thinking about?" Roy glanced at her. She was always such a hard egg to crack.

"Oh nothing, mijo. I'm thinking of when I was young and I had stomach pains. It's a long story." She rubbed her tummy again and moaned as her hand tried to displace the discomfort.

The green minivan pulled into the front of the doctor's office. Roy got out and walked around the van to help Annie get out of the vehicle with ease. His white visor had been pushed to the right as Annie's arm made its way around his broad shoulder. Thankfully, he was short, making it easy for him to walk her inside and help her get settled.

"Antonia Garza is here for her appointment," Roy said and ran back to park the van. The administrative assistant was an older white woman with long, curly white hair and gray-blue eyes. Her wrinkles demonstrated her commitment to smoking and her inability to smile.

"Mrs. Garza, please come collect this clipboard so you can fill out the information."

Annie ignored her. This feeling had happened so many times before that she was numb to it all.

"Excuse me, Mrs. Garza, please come here to fill out this form." Her long pink nails tapped the clipboard, demanding attention and urgency. Again, Annie ignored her and looked down at her stomach, wishing this woman would shut up.

Luckily, Roy walked in just as the admin assistant started to get more flustered and uneasy. "Look, lady, she feels like shit. Give her a break. I'll take these forms and fill them out for her. Learn to have some grace. You work at a doctor's office, for crying out loud." Roy grabbed the clipboard and a pen that was decorated to look like a giant flower.

He sat next to Annie and filled out the paperwork as she continued to stare into space. The chairs were so cold and uncomfortable, they confirmed exactly why she hated the doctor's office. Annie didn't bother trying to share her information with Roy; there wasn't anything on that form he didn't already know, and in less than five minutes it was all complete.

"Here you go, ma'am." Roy snarkily dropped off the clipboard at the front and went to sit by Annie to distract her from the pain.

A short while later, the doctor called Annie into the

examination room and Roy stayed behind. Sitting in a white gown on top of the exam table, Annie felt incredibly vulnerable. The nurse had explained that they would do a full-body exam to make sure everything was considered for the proper treatment. Annie's hands sat in her lap, her uneasy fingers fidgeting with one another.

Three knocks announced the entrance of a Hispanic physician in a long white coat with black hair that fell to her mid-back. She was accompanied by a much younger nurse with wildly permed brassy-blond hair.

"Mrs. Garza, I hear you aren't feeling well lately. Haven't been eating, experiencing stomach pain, is that correct?" the physician said as she reviewed Annie's chart.

"Si," Annie said quietly. "I feel sick all the time. I can't eat, I can't sleep, it hurts to do anything."

"I see, and how long have these symptoms been going on?" The nurse was hurriedly taking notes as Dr. Ramirez continued to ask questions and respond in fluent Spanish to ensure Annie's comfort.

"A little over a year," Annie said, staring at the doctor's short black heels.

"Wow, okay. Well, I'm glad you're here then. I'm going to do a full-body physical and then we'll see what's got you down in the dumps, okay?" Dr. Ramirez had a beautiful smile and a warmth about her that made Annie feel a little more at ease.

"Okay," Annie replied, just wishing this was already over.

Dr. Ramirez placed her hands over Annie's body, gently looking at every major part. She started at the head and noticed the large scar on Annie's skull.

"Mrs. Garza, when did you have brain surgery?"

"Huh?" Annie asked in confusion.

"The large scar here looks as though you've had a major surgery on your head. Can you tell me when this was?"

Annie's already weak body coiled in shame. "No, I never had surgery."

"Okay. Well, you have a five- to six-inch scar on your head. Are you aware of that?"

"No."

Dr. Ramirez made eye contact with the nurse to indicate that this wasn't normal. How does a woman have a scar this large on her head and not remember?

"You have severe scarring on your arms as well. Was there a traumatic event that you can tell me about?"

"No."

"It looks as though you had long cuts on your arms that didn't heal properly. The skin is very tight here at the elbow, indicating that this healed without a doctor's intervention."

Annie nodded at the observation. And as memories started to creep into her mind—the ashtray breaking on her head, the beer bottles cutting her arms, and the cigarettes burning her stomach—she felt so vulnerable sitting there, being looked at like some sort of circus freak. The rest of the appointment was completely black. She didn't remember what else happened.

"All right, Mrs. Garza. You're all set. I'm going to consult with some other physicians and see if we can find any additional medical records for your brain surgery and then we'll discuss next steps for finding a solution to your pain. Go ahead and get dressed and I'll be back shortly."

The nurse helped Annie get down from the exam table and left her on her own to change into her clothes. Before Annie slipped on her little loafers, she looked at her feet and was relieved that the doctor didn't mention her missing toe. Just another thing to be aware of. She was constantly protecting someone who had been so awful to her. It didn't make much sense, but that's the way it was.

Some minutes later, Dr. Ramirez walked in, requesting that Annie get some tests done on her stomach and bowels. She had felt a mass during the examination and wanted Annie to go straight to the office next door for an emergency CT scan.

Several days elapsed before Dr. Ramirez called to share the grim results. She used a lot of fancy terminology, but one thing was for certain: the colon cancer had spread all over. On the plus side, Annie would be given a plethora of medications to help her sleep and relax her body to be in far less pain.

Over the next couple of weeks, Annie was busy going from one appointment to the next. Fortunately, Roy worked odd hours and was able to help Annie get the medical attention she needed. It was hard to keep track of where she was being driven to. All she wanted to do was miss as little work as possible, so that she could continue life as she knew it—working at the school with her favorite teachers and students!

Sometimes it was difficult for Annie to understand what was going on with her own body. All she knew is that she had to continue fighting—not just for herself but for all her grandkids, who looked up to her so much.

Annie's health deteriorated steadily, and it was her family's goal to make her as comfortable and loved as possible in the short time she had left. She continued to live with her daughter and her family in their newly rented home. She'd wake up before the sun and start her days with a big cup of coffee.

Per usual, she'd start cleaning the already clean kitchen, and make herself relax by organizing towels, cabinets, and shelves. You could see the comfort in her demeanor as she meticulously worked in the mornings, though her pace was much slower than it had ever been. If you didn't know she'd been diagnosed with stage 4 colon cancer, you probably wouldn't be able to tell. Annie, true to her stubborn self, refused to stay still. It was almost as if she didn't know how. It didn't bother anyone, and that's all she'd ever known:

work, work, move, move, move, move. That was her way of life. Except now, she didn't have a janitorial job to go to every day so she tried to keep her normalcy through cleaning at home.

The house looked like a vanilla-sprinkled cupcake. Colorful eggs were meticulously placed in every crevice of the house exterior; between the rain gutter, under the bushes, below the doorbell. Inside, the oak kitchen table was covered with dips, cheeses, nuts, crackers, fruits, vegetables, and meats. It was almost too artistic to eat. The tall living-room windows let in a glowy natural lighting and brought an airy feeling to this crisp spring day.

The house was filled with laughter, playing, and love. Annie's grandchildren were all excited to reconnect and spend Easter together. The Garza siblings—Greg, Paul, and Sofia—knew how to throw a fantastic party. Their excuse over the years was always the same: "We never celebrated anything as kids, so we have to make up for it now!" And make up for it they did! Everything they coordinated was always over the top and well executed; they had great taste, even on a budget.

Annie wore a three-quarter-sleeved turquoise top with soft-blue jeans and white Keds. Turquoise was her favorite color and she looked lovely that afternoon. Everyone was snapping pictures on their phones, capturing the family reunion.

"Lunch is served!" Roy shouted at the top of his lungs. Cousins and siblings from the backyard came stampeding into the living room.

"Now circle up. We're not savages. We need to pray first," he demanded as the jubilant family stood in the living room all holding hands.

Roy and Sofia's oldest son, RayAnthony, now a young man, cleared his throat loudly as he stepped forward. "I'd like to say some things first."

Instantly, everyone knew where this was headed: a sincere "shout-out" to the beautiful grandma in the room.

"Nanny, we're all here because we're your family and you play such an important role for us. You bring us together when we don't see eye to eye and you're the best grandma we could ever have."

Sniffles spread throughout the room as the reality of the event hit. Yes, it was a wonderful time to celebrate life, but they also realized this was probably going to be their last time together as an entire family before Nanny would visit heaven.

She smiled big, knowing she was sick but not knowing exactly what was wrong with her. Her kids took care of most of the medical talk, and she trusted her kids with her life.

Everyone went around the room, holding back tears, and

sharing their favorite story about their crazy grandmother.

The family enjoyed loud Mexican music and even hit a piñata, with candy flying out of the large bunny and spilling across the concrete floor. It wouldn't have been an amazing celebration without one big happy photograph at the end, a photo they all cherished.

In an effort to give her the best life possible for what the doctors said would be only a few months, Annie's kids would doll her up with makeup, help her get into her finest outfits, and shopping they would go.

Annie never particularly liked shopping, but she did love to find a good deal. Her body was too tired to walk from store to store, but that didn't stop Sofia from taking her mother around town.

Starting at the local Kohl's, Sofia parked the car in a handicap spot, ran inside to get an electronic scooter, and off they went. Annie laughed the entire time in her "old people" scooter while she cut people off, flipping them the bird while doing so.

She and her daughter would die laughing in the aisles as Annie said, "I don't give a shit, I have things to do." She continued being her feisty self, scootering over to the children's section, where she fingered through the deals and found outfits for her younger grandkids.

"Oh, and what about this one?" Annie held up a basketball shirt, imagining either of Sofia's youngest boys,

Andrew or Kristian, wearing it proudly. They were her two most rambunctious grandkids, always running around and playing sports.

"Yes, they'd both love that," Sofia chimed in happily.

"Excuse me." A black woman in her mid-forties kindly tapped Sofia on the shoulder. "Is this Antonia Garza?"

"Yes. Yes, it is. Mom, say hi."

Annie looked up, surprised.

"Mrs. Garza, it's me, Ponchetta. I was a teacher at Running Brushy Middle School. I think about you all the time and, well, here you are."

"Sí, sí. I remember you. Loud teacher with all those kids!"

"I sure was. You know, it's so wonderful seeing you here. I wanted you to know that the school hasn't been the same without you. Many students ask about you, missing your jokes and smile. You made the schools you work at a better place. Mrs. Garza, my sincerest thanks for being you." Ponchetta's eyes welled up as she turned to Sofia. "You are a lucky woman to have her as your mother. She's got love and kindness unlike anyone I've ever met."

Ponchetta went over to hug Annie gently and asked, "Is your health okay, are you doing okay?"

Annie laughed and said, "Bullshit doctors, I'm fine."

"My mother was recently diagnosed with colon cancer, so she'll be home with us for the next couple of months." Sofia's face flushed and she looked to the ground. Ponchetta understood that the diagnosis was grim.

"Well, it must be a God thing, seeing you today, Mrs. Garza." Ponchetta wiped the few tears from her face. "You are a beautiful woman and we're cheering you on to get well soon."

"Gracias. Tell everyone I'll see them soon!"

Shortly after that visit, they left Kohl's to return home. Sofia's heart was torn in two: it was as though Annie didn't want to or couldn't grasp the reality of the situation. It was bittersweet watching Ponchetta thank Annie and truly mean it from the bottom of her heart: to see the difference her mother had made in so many lives but carry the pain of knowing that she couldn't do that much longer.

"You know, I'm not dead yet," Annie said lightly as she slowly got into the car.

"Mom, we know. But what she said was so sweet and kind. You're a good woman, you know that?"

"Yes, yes, yes, now take me to Sonic. I'm hungry and want a green cheese." Annie was now ready for the next part of her day: lunch. For whatever reason, her accent wouldn't allow her to say "grilled cheese"; it always sounded like "green cheese."

"How was the shopping day?" Roy asked as the women, laughing and hollering at each other, made their way inside the house.

"Oh, she's just crazy, I tell you," Sofia said as they walked into the kitchen.

"No, I'm not crazy. I'm just honest." Annie had a serious tone.

"What happened?" Roy asked.

"Mom wanted a *green-cheese* sandwich for lunch. So we headed over to Sonic and when I left, I didn't use my blinker to exit the parking lot and, well, I got pulled over." Sofia started to laugh as she told the story. Roy ping-ponged between looking at his wife and looking at his mother-in-law.

"Okay, did you get a ticket?"

"No, because Mom—" Hard laughs interrupted her sentence and a wheezing overtook Sofia's story. She was crying hysterically as Annie sat at the kitchen table tapping her nails along the oak. "Because Mom—"

"Spit it out already, woman." Roy was getting impatient and felt left out of their hilarious story.

Annie chimed in: "Well, my chest was hurting, and I did think I was having a heart attack. So, I just told the officer, I'm having a heart attack and closed my eyes so he thought I was dead."

Roy's eyes grew ten sizes bigger as Sofia validated the story, nodding her head and still laughing uncontrollably.

"No, you didn't, Suegra. You played dead?" Roy asked.

"I sure did. Green cheese was in my hand and everything. The officer believed me so we left. No ticket."

"Roy, I was in pure shock. I couldn't believe that she'd just said she was dying, but also that the officer didn't question it because, well, Mom's lost half her hair and she's so tiny."

"You can thank me now," Annie said with the utmost confidence.

"No, Mom. You cannot do that again." Sofia caught her breath and started to scold her mother. "We could have gotten in a lot of trouble."

"We're fine. It's not my fault. I couldn't tell if it was my heart or that my stomach was hungry."

"Mom, it totally is your fault."

"What's Nanny's fault?" Andrew came out from the playroom into the living room, where all the commotion was happening.

"Oh nothing, your nanny is just one crazy lady," Annie answered for the rest of them.

"Nanny, can we do ninja time?"

"Sure, mijo. I'll be right there."

Once the laughter in the kitchen had finally simmered down, it was time to get on with making dinner and watching telenovelas.

After a few minutes had passed, Andrew made his way back into the living room. "Come on, Nanny, let's do ninja time now."

Grunting loudly from the pain as she stood up, Annie slowly made her way into the small playroom and sat on the old red sofa that had been nearly destroyed by years of children's imaginations.

"Okay, you're going to be the red ninjas and I'm going to

be the blue ninjas. Got it?" Andrew handed Nanny his favorite stuffed animal as he started to explain the rules of the game. Nanny noticed the little black curls on the top of his head were all wild, and his crooked smile was full of promise.

"I got it. Bam!" Annie threw the plush toy to the other side of the room, indicating that her team had just won. "Now what?"

"No, no, not like that, Nanny. We have to fight each other like ninjas. No weapons." Andrew's disappointment was evident, but he knew that explaining all the rules would be worthwhile for a solid game of ninja.

"All right, all right," Annie complied as he handed her back the toy.

The game went on for a few minutes before Annie coughed. The pain made her moan.

"Nanny, are you sick?"

"No, why?" she lied between her teeth.

"No lying, Nanny. Are you sick?"

"Yes, a little."

"Who is going to take care of you? Your mom and dad?" Andrew asked with deep concern. "Are you going to get taken cared of by your mom and dad like I do?"

The question burned Annie's soul more than the cancer ever would. "No, mijo," she responded adamantly. "I take care of myself." Annie nodded her head, trying to convince herself.

"But everyone has a mommy and daddy. Why doesn't your mommy and daddy take care of you?"

"Because they are dead. You get old and die. It's what happens."

"I don't want to die."

"It's just going to sleep for a long time. It's okay."

Andrew wasn't content with the answers Nanny was providing. He was unsettled; and instead of asking more questions, he headed back to the kitchen to get some fruit snacks. While doing so, Annie got up and slowly made her way to her bedroom for a nap.

A little later, there was a quiet knock on her bedroom door, followed by the door slowly creaking open. "Nanny?" Andrew asked quietly to make sure she didn't sleep too long. "Nanny, want to play ninjas?"

Annie's back was facing the door and her eyes stayed closed, not moving a muscle.

Andrew stepped closer to Nanny to make sure she was, in fact, just asleep. He was relieved to see her breathing and he left, slowly closing the door behind him.

Once the door shut, Annie's eyes flooded with tears. Hearing the words, and saying the words out loud, hurt her more than any diagnosis would.

"God, it's not fair." She prayed out loud and cried as the terrible memories of her abusive father played in her mind and in her heart over and over again.

2014
SIXTY-SEVEN YEARS OLD

The morning had been pure disarray. Two young brats ran up and down the stairs in their underwear, fighting over a shiny blue Hot Wheel and neglecting to change into the formal outfits that were laid out on their bunk beds. A hazy fog of burnt breakfast biscuits rose from the oven, triggering the ear-piercing smoke alarm. Freshly showered, wearing just a towel around his hips, Roy opened the master bedroom door and shouted, "What the hell is going on?" from the upstairs balcony. All the while, Annie sat on the brown leather sofa, drinking her black coffee and humming peacefully.

Weak and cold, her body was numb. And now, like many times before, her mind would wander to a place far more comfortable and enjoyable. She smiled to herself as she slowly sipped the coffee, her dry lips cusping the white mug. The liquid gold filled her mouth, then warmed her body as it flowed through her veins. She licked the bitter taste off her lips.

Art waltzed through the front door of the small white house, loudly announcing his arrival. He wore gray slacks, an undone orange tie, and a white button-down. His dark hair was still damp from his shower; clearly he had been running behind. His hearing had gone, so he yelled constantly, everywhere he went.

"Annie, how are you?" He hugged his loved one gently and continued to yell, not letting her respond. "What's burning?" Art looked around dramatically and caught the eye of Roy, still in his towel, throwing away the burnt biscuits.

"Just the biscuits," Roy commented as he hustled back upstairs to change. "Don't worry, Suegro, we are coming! Just keep Suegra company."

Annie smiled as Art sat down next to her on the sofa, as they had for many years. Though Annie and Art had parted ways as spouses, they had spent the past two decades living separately as best friends. Every week they would enjoy a cup of coffee with fresh homemade tortillas and talk about old friends from Port Isabel. Art always had a way of staying connected with people from back home, and Annie enjoyed his stories and, of course, his company, even though she often rolled her eyes at how loud he had become.

Taking another slow sip of coffee, Annie closed her eyes.

She felt too weak to play hostess and ask how he had been. The chemotherapy had taken everything out of her, except her sense of humor. A woman who never knew how to sit, never knew how to stop working, never knew how to stop fighting, was suddenly limited by her own body. It felt like her mind was being eaten alive from the inside out; she wanted to move and be free but couldn't. Every fiber in her body felt as though it was working against her, while the world continued to spin. The only way her mind could steady was when she enjoyed her cup of coffee.

After about five minutes of silence between them, Art started yelling upstairs, reminding everyone else of the time and the urgency to leave. Annie told herself that despite the chaos happening around her, she was going to enjoy her morning.

Slowly but surely, the family made their way to the green minivan. The two youngest boys had a movie picked out for the drive downtown. As everyone got comfortable for the thirty-mile trip, Roy prepped the front seat of the van with a pillow and blanket and ran back inside to get Annie.

"Are you ready, Suegra? We can't leave without you! You're the star of the show," he said. He had exchanged his towel for a pair of black slacks and a white button-down, cleaning up nicely. Annie smiled softly and leaned into Roy as he carried her to the van.

Weighing only about eighty-five pounds, she was easy to move around. She had always been a petite woman, and now she was that and even less, wearing a beanie to keep her head warm in late spring. As Roy carried her outside, the bright May sun felt wonderful on Annie's face. She sat in the front seat, comfortable, and stared out the window as the green minivan made its way to downtown Austin.

Per usual, the congestion on I-35 was a bitch. Sitting in bumper-to-bumper traffic, Roy decided to play some classical music to soften the atmosphere. It was as if everyone in the van was so excited that they didn't know how to process the emotion. Instead of playing it cool, the whole family decided to panic and worry and exude stress, even when the reality was that the stress was over. It was time to celebrate. They'd still arrive in plenty of time to get great seats for the graduation ceremony.

As the van finally made its exit for MLK, Annie stared over her right shoulder in amazement. The incredible stadium filled her eyes and a smile warmed her numb and weak body.

My granddaughter is graduating from college today. A dream come true, she told herself as she closed her eyes, taking in the moment. Annie was looking forward to this day, feeling as though a piece of her was achieving the impossible.

This is the school Annie had dreamed of attending. She remembered the eagerness within her heart, the desire she had to learn. The inability to remember the sounds that the letters made and how they worked together to create beautiful stories.

She thought about her lessons with Mr. … *Who cares what his name is?* She replayed his slow voice and remembered that other loco lady teacher. All the memories flooded Annie's mind and she started laughing out loud—almost a cackle—as if she couldn't control herself.

"Mom, what happened? What's so funny?" Sofia asked from the second row of the van.

"One summer, your papi paid for me to have a tutor. I used up nearly thirty notebooks of yellow lined paper practicing my ABC's."

"What are you talking about?"

"Señor Joffrey, he was a nice man. I wish he could have been my teacher forever, but he probably died playing cat puzzles." The laughing turned hysterical, the kind of laugh where you can't breathe and you continue to try to explain yourself but no one else knows what's going on. Her laugh was contagious, and everyone else in the van started laughing too. Annie took in a big exhale to relax her body, wiping away her happy tears.

Just when it got quiet again, Annie's laugh started right back up—this time with another memory of the good ol' days. Uncontrollable laughter followed by a big smile and lots of tears.

"I told Papi on our first date I wanted to be a writer. And that's the day we got married. Can you believe that? And people thought I was the dummy! He believed me—a writer! Man, am I funny or what?"

"Believe me, mija," Art addressed their daughter, Sofia, then gradually got louder, yelling over the second row to ensure Annie could hear him in the front seat. "Your mother was a sneaky one. She did fool me, but I'm a smarter man now."

"Dad, okay, we hear you," Sofia said sharply as Annie continued to laugh at herself. Art loosened his tie for the fifth time, sweating away.

Roy took a hard-right turn on MLK and then a hard left toward the Frank Erwin Center, where all the graduates and their families crowded the streets. Cops and firetrucks lined the road, controlling traffic. Like a parking guru, Roy spotted an empty space up the street and parallel-parked beautifully. The emotions in the van were rising: what a day to celebrate!

Thousands of people gathered at the entrances, getting their bags checked by security and walking through metal detectors to ensure no weapons entered the arena.

Wearing a small black dress with a red blazer and a big smile, Annie held her hands up sarcastically as Roy wheeled her through security.

"How harmful can I be, I'm in a wheelchair," she mouthed off to the guards. Roy apologized quietly to the security staff, saying she was feeling a little loopy on her medications that day.

"Suegra, what's gotten into you? You're going to get us kicked out if you talk back to the wrong person."

"I'm not scared of nobody," she said confidently. You could tell this event had gotten to her head and she was the most excited of them all.

Sitting there among the crowd, Annie blended in with all the other proud parents, grandparents, and friends. She had a perfect seat to spot her granddaughter across that decorated stage. The graduates walked in to the reverberating chords of "Pomp and Circumstance." Annie's hands trembled with overwhelming joy.

Standing at the front of the stage was a tall, thin white man wearing an even whiter Navy uniform. His tone was demanding, his presence confident. As he addressed the graduates, a few words pierced Annie's heart:

"That great paragon of analytical rigor, Ask.Com, says that the average American will meet 10,000 people in their lifetime. That's a lot of folks. But, if every one of you changed the lives of just 10 people—and each one of those folks changed the lives of another 10 people—just 10—then in five generations—125 years—the class of 2014 will have changed the lives of 800 million people." Admiral McRaven carried on, but Annie held on to these words as she replayed her life:

That feeling the first time she picked the most cotton, kicking Grumpy Gerry's ass. And all the times she heard her amá's whispers of love and encouragement through heartbroken prayers.

Hannah's kindness in filling out Annie's first job application. Art's unending love to provide Annie with the best life he could. Mr. Jones's efforts to give Annie the best education he knew how with the resources he had available. Annie's beautiful children, who inspired her to constantly work her hardest. Annie's deadbeat father, who motivated Annie to be better than him every single day. That bastard Mr. Brown, who showed Annie the importance of self-worth and never settling for anything. And now this: from picking cotton to being here watching her granddaughter graduate college. Annie was overwhelmed with joy and how through all the odds, she had, indeed, achieved her dreams. She felt that through her suffering, through her sacrifices, she had finally achieved the dream of a beautiful family, one full of love and joy, unstoppable brilliance and dedication.

As her granddaughter walked across the convocation stage, Annie used every ounce of energy to stand and clap. Roy kept an eye on her so that she wouldn't just tip over. The family hugged and cried tears of joy as Alice made her way across that stage, smiling big and bright.

This moment wasn't just for Alice—this was for the generations before her and for the generations thereafter.

Annie was bundled up in blankets, staying warm and comfortable in Alice's old bedroom. It was evident that Annie had given the graduation ceremony her all, and she hadn't much strength left.

"Nanny," Alice whispered as she walked through the bedroom door holding her cap and gown. "Thank you so much for coming today." Alice wiggled herself next to her grandmother and they lay there together silently.

"I love you so much, and I'm so grateful for everything you've done for me."

"I love you, mija," Annie muttered as she exhaled painfully.

Alice kissed her grandmother's wrinkly skin and looked into her beautiful green eyes. "Nanny, everything I do is for you. I'm so lucky to have you as my grandma."

"That means so much to me. Now, remember one thing, mija. When you're smart and when you work hard, no one can take that away from you. Never forget that."

"I won't, Nanny." Alice laid her head next to Annie's and played a beautiful Spanish song from her phone to take her back to the past. To a time where she wasn't in pain. They say music is the best therapy for the soul, and Alice was willing to do anything she could to help her grandmother escape this current suffering.

The song played as they lay next to each other silently. Annie closed her eyes and pictured the walk down County Road 34.

EPILOGUE

After nine months of suffering from colon cancer, Antonia Garza, my beloved grandmother (Nanny), died on September 9, 2014. Though she was never able to read, this book is dedicated to fulfilling her dream of writing a book.

I feel so blessed to have had someone as strong as Nanny lead my family. As a grandmother, she taught us by example. How hard work and dedication can lead to a life that you're proud of. I can honestly say that woman never sat down for more than five minutes at a time; she was always busy cleaning and serving others to make sure we were more comfortable than she ever was.

Throughout my youth, Nanny worked as a janitor at my elementary and middle school. Every time I saw her, she'd have a brilliant smile on her face, and I'd run up and hug her as tight as I could. I remember as a young middle-schooler being so proud of her. All the teachers loved her charisma and the little treats she'd leave on the teachers' desks as a reminder to keep up the great work. At times, I got defensive and protective of Nanny. I wanted to make sure the other students at school realized how hard she worked. There's something really unique about growing up with someone who has a servant's heart to the degree of Antonia Garza.

She was proud of the hard work she could contribute to keeping our schools as beautiful as possible. Whether it was scrubbing toilets or vacuuming the offices, she did it all and never complained. Nanny was the first one in the building and generally the last to leave. I can only hope my contribution to the world is an ounce as influential as the mark she's made on me—not only on me but on our entire family and those she worked for and worked with.

Oftentimes our family thinks about our grandfather's commitment to Nanny's education and what went wrong. Based on our family's genetic makeup, we believe Nanny suffered from dyslexia, like many of her kids and grandchildren do today. Though we are incredibly grateful for today's advancement to serving those with learning disabilities, Nanny didn't have the resources and her teachers didn't have the tools available to effectively teach her how to overcome her learning disability.

"An education is something that should never be taken for granted. Go, mija, learn and take in as much as you can. Read every book that's ever been written. Write down everything you see and experience. Because you are smart, you can accomplish anything you put your mind to. No one can take your education away, just remember that, and remember me."—Antonia Garza

Little does she know, education wasn't the key to my success. She was.

Nanny, thank you for the wisest words ever spoken to me.
I miss you dearly and I am so grateful for you
and the legacy you've left with your family.

I love you forever,

Allyson Chapa

9 781087 959016